Australian
Composition in
the Twentieth
Century

Australian Composition in the Twentieth Century

Edited by
Frank Callaway and
David Tunley

Melbourne
Oxford University Press
Oxford Wellington New York
1978

OXFORD UNIVERSITY PRESS
OXFORD LONDON GLASGOW
NEW YORK TORONTO MELBOURNE WELLINGTON
IBADAN NAIROBI DAR ES SALAAM CAPE TOWN
KUALA LUMPUR SINGAPORE JAKARTA HONG KONG TOKYO
DELHI BOMBAY CALCUTTA MADRAS KARACHI

NATIONAL LIBRARY OF AUSTRALIA CATALOGUING IN
PUBLICATION DATA

Australian composition in the twentieth century.

    Index.
    Bibliography.
    ISBN 0 19 550522 0.

    1. Composers, Australian—Addresses, essays,
    lectures.   2. Music, Australian—Addresses,
    essays, lectures.   I. Callaway, Frank, ed.
    II. Tunley, David Evatt, joint ed.

780.994

The publication of this book has been assisted by
the Music Board of the Australia Council.

Filmset in Monophoto Times New Roman
by Asco Trade Typesetting Limited, Hong Kong
Printed by Bright Sun Printing Press Company Limited
Designed by Vicki Hamilton

Contents

Musical Examples

Preface

This symposium is primarily about the music of selected composers who were either born in Australia or who have come to live here. Detailed biographical information has largely been omitted except as it impinges upon works under discussion or upon a composer's musical outlook. The result is a series of separate studies each based upon either a broad examination of a composer's output or close analysis of a few characteristic works, the choice of approach being left entirely to the discretion of each contributor. It will be seen that the first-mentioned approach is most evident in those chapters dealing with earlier composers of this century; the more detailed and rigorous analyses are largely associated with works written in recent years. This is not surprising, for the highly structured nature of much contemporary music makes it more than usually susceptible to analytical study. But it does raise the problem that certain chapters in the book may be less accessible than others to the general reader; yet to modify the penetrating analyses provided by some contributors would do less than justice to the composers.

The emergence of many gifted composers in recent years posed an unenviable problem in selecting those who were to be given a chapter devoted to their own music, limitations of space alone precluding a number of other composers whose works deserve close study. While the strength of the symposium treatment of a subject lies in its utilizing the specialist knowledge of individual contributors, it courts the danger of leaving the threads untied. An opening essay therefore provides a backdrop against which the separate studies can be projected. The final chapter aims to complete the broad picture of Australian music by reviewing the work of many other composers who have contributed to its repertoire. In this way the more obvious weaknesses of a symposium approach have, it is hoped, been lessened.

In making the select lists of works the traditional subdivisions into opera, orchestral, etc. (chronological order within each subdivision) have been favoured, although there are a number of minor variants. In one case there is a complete alphabetical listing, and in several others complete chronological tables. Generally, works have not been identified as published or unpublished.

We believe that the use of both the symposium and analytical approaches in this book mark it as another stage in the study of Australian music (outside periodical literature), complementing others which have appeared on the same subject. The inclusion of many musical examples (some from manuscript sources) will, it is hoped, help the reader to come closer to matters of style in contemporary Australian music. Readers not conversant with the technical processes of contemporary music described by some of the contributors to this symposium are referred to such publications as *The New Dictionary of Music* by Arthur Jacobs (Penguin) or *Dictionary of Music* by Theodore Karp (Dell Publishing Co. Inc. 1973). A list of general references on Australian music will be found at the end of the volume; those referring to a single composer are included in the relevant chapter.

In preparing the book for publication the editors wish to acknowledge the assistance of Rachel Lowe-Dugmore of the Department of Music, the University of Western Australia. Except where they are facsimiles from composers' own scores, and for the excerpts from Alfred Hill's Viola Sonata (Figs 2–6), the music examples were drawn by Denis Pendergrast.

David Tunley
Frank Callaway

Australian Composition in the Twentieth Century

A Background

David Tunley

It has been said that the natural evolution of a transplanted culture tends to come to a standstill in its new environment. If this is true the achievements of many of the composers included in this symposium clearly represent a new phase in Australian composition which in recent years has displayed a vigorous growth. Yet few would deny that music-making (in its widest sense) in Australia was modelled, long after frontier ways had given place to a more urban sophistication, upon traditions inherited from Britain, more especially from Late Victorian England. They were to harden more firmly in Australia than in England where musical styles, under the impetus of composers like Vaughan Williams and Holst, were able to push past the restraining forces of Victorian fashions fairly early in the century. In Australia it took much longer.

The one man who might have loosened their hold here sooner was virtually an expatriate; moreover, on his visits back to Australia Grainger the Visionary was overshadowed by Grainger the Fashionable Pianist, and still further by Grainger the Eccentric whose colourful idiosyncrasies so baffled and amused his public as to prevent his extraordinarily original ideas from being taken very seriously. It is only now being realized that his aesthetic viewpoint (persuasively summed up in his lectures 'Music—A Commonsense View of All Types') lies close to much of today's musical thought. In striking contrast to the music of another early radical, the American Charles Ives (1874–1954), Grainger's far-sighted concepts when realized in his own music often result, to modern ears, in a period ring because of the musical idiom in which he chose to write. Yet it is precisely because his compositions were so accessible in their day that the ideas underlying the most original of them might have quickly stimulated the emergence of a school of Australian composition striking new paths appropriate to a young country. That they did not is perhaps just further confirmation of the theory about transplanted cultures, cited by Curt Sachs and others, that while things develop in the mother country, natural evolution tends to come to a halt in foreign environments.[1]

This is not to say that late nineteenth-century styles were practised for endless decades in Australia to the exclusion of more modern ones (except perhaps in *academia*), but that the attitudes of those days prevailed in our society for an inordinately long time. These have been wittily summed up by Bernard Shaw:

Englishmen take their business and their politics very differently from their art. Art in England is regarded as a huge confectionery department, where sweets are made for the eye and ear just as they are made for the palate in the ordinary 'tuck shop'. There is a general notion that painting tastes better before dinner and music after it; but neither is supposed to be in the least nutritious. Too great a regard for them is held to be the mark of a weak character, or, in cases like those of Ruskin and Morris, a derangement due to genius.[2]

If to attitudes inherited by our transplanted culture are wedded those derived from a frontier society, it is small wonder that for a long time our concert programmes were marked by a rigid conservatism and that our composers struggled to find their voice and to have it heard. To appreciate the achievement of Australian composition during the twentieth century we need to understand something of its environment. As this brief essay will show, it is an environment that has undergone a radical change.

Musical life in the early years of the present century had been immeasurably strengthened by the establishment of three institutions during the closing decade of the previous one. They were Melbourne University Conservatorium, the Albert Street Conservatorium, Melbourne (later known as the Melba), and the Elder Conservatorium within the University of Adelaide. It would seem that few musical developments in Australia before the 1890s had more than temporary influence, although the popularity of choral societies and the many successful tours of visiting opera companies during the second half of the nineteenth century were hopeful signs for the future.[3] But the appearance of the institutions mentioned above[4] (to which was added the State Conservatorium in Sydney in 1915) opened up new opportunities for professional training and provided permanent facilities for the propagation of music, each becoming a focal point of activity and attracting to them men of the calibre of Marshall Hall, Fritz Hart, Henri Verbrugghen and Alfred Hill, all of whom can unhesitatingly be described as the Founding Fathers of Australian music. That the influence of these men went far beyond mere pedagogy can be seen in the striking example of Marshall Hall who established regular orchestral concerts in Melbourne (as Verbrugghen was to do in Sydney). His University Orchestra, later taken over by Bernard Heinze, played a crucial role in Melbourne's musical life until as late as 1940 when the University handed over the organization of these concerts to the Australian Broadcasting Commission.[5]

With the exception of commercial operatic performances, it was largely around these institutions that serious professional musical life revolved. With their establishment modern musical Australia may be reckoned to have commenced and it is no mere coincidence that the work of the first composer dealt with in this symposium (Alfred Hill) was centred for many years on the Conservatorium in Sydney. It is a matter of speculation only whether or not some of the causes of musical conservatism in Australia can be traced to the institutional climate prevailing early in the century.

From 1932 the hitherto limited outlets for Australian composition were vastly increased with the creation of the Australian Broadcasting Commission, the impact of which, through its varied roles as broadcaster and entrepreneur and through its eventual establishment of orchestras in all capital cities, could hardly be overestimated, although it should be remembered that only in recent years has the A.B.C. lent positive and sustained support to serious Australian composition beyond the five per cent 'local content' demanded of its broadcasts by law. For this latter need a seemingly endless flow of impressionistic piano miniatures and outback vocal ballads (which listeners might have been forgiven for imagining was the sum total of the native repertoire) provided a useful stockpile of Australiana; but until fairly recently there were few instances of extended orchestral works by local composers presented at prestige A.B.C. concerts. Two such events are worth recalling, for the music sounded a note of modernity which took their audiences by surprise: Antill's *Corroboree* (1946) and Hanson's Trumpet Concerto (1947), the performance of both works owing much to the personal encouragement of Eugene Goossens, then Resident Conductor of the Sydney Symphony Orchestra. That these works also revealed a sureness of touch might have been expected since the composers had a considerable output of works behind them; in the case of Antill a formidable number of compositions written over a period of twenty years, most of them unperformed except for his film scores. If Hanson's Trumpet Concerto achieved success less spectacular than Antill's well-known piece its performance nevertheless firmly established the composer's reputation, and his works can be seen as a link between the present contemporary school and the 'middle' generation of composers: Sutherland, Hughes, Antill, Douglas, Le Gallienne, all of whom sought direct communication with their audience through a musical language, often personal and subtle, yet readily acceptable to ears familiar with the music of Holst, Walton, Hindemith, Bartók and Stravinsky. The decade of the sixties, however, saw the emergence of a repertoire coming from a group of composers who were to give a totally new complexion to Australian music. So critical is this decade in the development of Australia's musical life that it is necessary to examine it more closely.[6] Amongst other things this period was notable for a growing awareness of music from the European avant-garde. As if to make up for lost time, organizations devoted to the propagation of contemporary music sprang up around the country, foremost of these perhaps being the Sydney branch of the International Society for Contemporary Music which, although established in Australia as early as the thirties, did not become a potent force until some twenty years later when it became associated with the Department of Music at Sydney University through its President, Professor Donald Peart.

The broadcasts of Richard Meale, then recently returned from Europe, also brought the sounds of experimental music to many ears. A significant role was played by the universities through seminars and workshops and the appointment of forward-looking composers to their staffs. It was in this atmosphere that the composers who were to give the characteristic voice to Australian music of the sixties emerged as a powerful influence: Meale, Sculthorpe, Butterley, Werder, Dreyfus, Sitsky, Brumby, a group later to be joined by two composers working abroad, Banks and Humble, as well as by younger composers like Cugley and Conyngham, both of whom had studied with some of those just mentioned. As in the case of Antill and Hanson, some of these men had already written a considerable number of works (Werder being a notable example); yet for the most part, the sixties stimulated and witnessed the appearance of their best-known music. And what is more, this music began to be featured increasingly in concerts at home as well as heard by audiences abroad, as for example, during the overseas tour of the Sydney Symphony Orchestra in 1965, which included in its programmes (in addition to *Corroboree*) Meale's *Homage to García Lorca*, Sculthorpe's *Sun Music I*,

Werder's Chorale Prelude for Strings, as well as the Violin Concerto by the London-based Malcolm Williamson. Further international hearings during the sixties were gained through the inclusion of works from this group of composers at meetings of the International Rostrum of Composers (a UNESCO activity organized for broadcasters who meet annually in Paris to assess, by means of recorded performances, contemporary works submitted by each member with a view to obtaining broadcast material from throughout the world). The award of the 1966 Italia Prize (a competition also in the field of broadcasting) to Nigel Butterley's *In the Head the Fire* was another instance of new-found international recognition accorded to Australian composers. At home, première performances of significant new Australian works became a fairly regular feature of the Sydney Proms, while an extensive project to record Australian compositions, old and new, was commenced by the Australian Broadcasting Commission. Thus the Commission has filled a role of capital importance in stimulating recent developments and it is hoped that its efforts will not diminish, despite the resignation of John Hopkins, its Federal Director since 1963, an acknowledged champion of the contemporary Australian composer.

A further reflection of increased support during this decade can be seen in the growing number of major commissions offered to Australian composers, a practice so sporadic before the sixties as to be virtually negligible. In 1961 three major works were commissioned (from Hughes and Antill); by the end of 1970 some eighty-five commissioned works had appeared, seven of them operas.[7] Most commissions emanated from the universities, A.B.C., Musica Viva, Australasian Performing Right Association (APRA) and the Australian Opera, but towards the end of the decade financial support through commissions and other means was to come from a quarter that had been curiously neglectful of composers, namely the Federal Government, first through its Advisory Board, Commonwealth Assistance to Australian Composers, and later through the Australian Council for the Arts (now known as the Australia Council).

Up to this time the only regular financial support available had been through a scheme which came to be known as the Music Foundation, operated by the Australasian Performing Right Association,[8] providing subsidies towards recordings, publication of scores and the duplicating of orchestral parts. By the middle of the fifties awards had been given to eighty composers, while the scores of sixteen major works had been published through the scheme. Such assistance was greatly strengthened with the creation in 1967 of the Advisory Board, Commonwealth Assistance to Australian Composers, although the funds for its first year of operation ($10,000) now seem pitifully small in comparison with later budgets. One of the Board's first projects was an anthology entitled *Musical Composition in Australia* comprising a catalogue of the works of forty-six selected composers, an historical survey (available in three languages) and a selection of commercially available records and scores, all contained in a handsomely designed box destined for distribution to embassies and various institutions and individuals in different parts of the world and at home. In the period 1970–71, the Board's budget having been increased to $60,000, a number of fellowships were created enabling deserving composers to devote themselves fully to the completion of commissioned works; while scholarships were also provided to encourage young composers to pursue further studies in composition at seminars and workshops. In 1973 the work so ably begun by the Advisory Board was entirely taken over by the Australian Council for the Arts, inaugurating yet a new phase in government patronage.

Some idea of the financial support recently enjoyed by Australian composers can be gained by noting that in the twelve-month period 1974–75 the Australian Council provided up to seventy-five per cent of commission fees paid to some forty composers, has made it possible for the author of a work to attend its première performance (in one case sending him to Europe), and has in the same twelve-month period granted generous fellowships to nineteen composers for the purposes of composition, travel, research or further study. Under the Council's administration financial assistance initiated by the earlier Advisory Board has been considerably increased towards publishing, copying and recording, towards seminars and the general propagation of Australian music.[9]

Thus after a period of virtual neglect the Australian composer has entered an era of patronage that would seem to rival the princely courts of the past. Perhaps it is no mere coincidence that it came at a time when Australia was experiencing an unprecedented level of prosperity and displaying an ebullient spirit of national awareness and independence. Does this mean that as a result we might also expect to see the growth of a 'national school' of Australian composition?

From Grainger's *Australian Up-country Song* to Sculthorpe's *Sun Music* and *Irkanda* series, the appearance of works with Australian-inspired titles has lifted the hopes of those who await the creation of a truly national style. Yet, as so often pointed out, the source of materials from which sprang the great national movements in music (like those in Bohemia and Russia during the late nineteenth century, and in England and Hungary during the early years of our own) namely, a strong and distinctive folk-music, is largely missing in Australia, while the use of Aboriginal music poses problems which many of the younger Australian composers would nowadays regard as being ethical as much as technical.

Yet who can overlook the case of Sibelius who has evoked for countless people the spirit of Finland in music that seems to owe little to folk-culture? Does the answer lie in that by creating so distinctly personal a style it was the composer who gave the national complexion to his country's music rather than the other way round? Which is not to deny that he was also the product of his environment. For many Australians the music of Peter Sculthorpe suggests the continent's 'spaciousness and terrifying sameness' (to quote from Michael Hannan's essay on the composer). Yet does his powerfully individual style, in which heroic and dynamic European gestures have been largely replaced by subtle and static musical elements from Asian cultures, hold the seeds of a genuine national idiom? Only the future can answer this.

As for the past, our composers have not been noted for their interest in distilling or transforming into terms of fine art what folk-music we may possess, and as far as the use of indigenous material is concerned, perhaps it is significant that the composer of *Corroboree* wrote no sequel and that few composers (Douglas and Penberthy apart) have pursued its possibilities very far. What Australian element has been present in our music lies, rather, in programmatic association, itself a powerful element but not one that by its presence alone should persuade us that a distinctively Australian style has been found.

For the present moment the work of the younger generation of composers here is mostly stamped with that mark of cosmopolitanism which is such a strong feature of today's music in sophisticated societies throughout the world. As Gerald Abraham puts it:

> Just as technological man becomes more and more international, our cities get more and more alike and one cosmonaut is pretty much like another, the most advanced music usually appears to have no national characteristics. I say 'appears' because we are too close to it to hear it in perspective. Future historians may indeed detect traces of national tradition in the aleatoric music of the 1960s in France or Germany or Russia. We cannot.[10]

Moreover, national movements are essentially 'popular' movements, and the present upsurge of Australian composition coincides with a time when, regrettably, the gap between the forward-looking composer and the average audience is still wide. Perhaps all that we should expect is that, no matter what their style, serious Australian works should carry the marks of craftsmanship and imagination; in any case, this is the first consideration.

Notes

1. Curt Sachs, *The Rise of Music in the Ancient World, East and West* (New York and London, 1943), p. 105.
2. George Bernard Shaw, *Music in London 1890–1894*, 3 vols (London, 1932), ii, p. 147.
3. Details of the 19th century background may be found in Roger Covell, *Australia's Music: Themes of a New Society* (Melbourne, 1967); see also Andrew McCredie, *Musical Composition in Australia* (Advisory Board, Commonwealth Assistance to Australian Composers, Canberra, 1969).
4. For an account of the establishment of these institutions see Doreen Bridges, 'Some Historical Backgrounds to Australian Music Education—(1) Foundations', *The Australian Journal of Music Education* No. 12, April 1972. Also Ernest Scott, *A History of the University of Melbourne* (Melbourne, 1936).
5. See Doreen Bridges, 'Sir Bernard Heinze—in interview', *Australian Journal of Music Education* No. 12, April 1973.
6. For a more detailed discussion of this period see the writer's 'A Decade of Musical Composition in Australia: 1960–1970', *Studies in Music* No. 5 (University of Western Australia Press), 1971.
7. A list of these commissioned works is given in the article referred to in the previous note.
8. See John Sturman, 'The Role of the Australasian Performing Right Association', *APRA Journal* No. 5, July 1971.
9. This information was made available to the writer by courtesy of the Australia Council.
10. Gerald Abraham, *The Tradition of Western Music* (Oxford University Press, 1974), p. 61.

Alfred Hill
(1870—1960)

Andrew D. McCredie

Until the last decades of the nineteenth century any serious musical composition as had been achieved in Australia had been by the virtuosi and conductors in the employment of commercial theatrical managements.[1] It was at this moment that a first generation of professionally trained Australian composers, the beneficiaries of the musical training offered by the still newly-established Europe-wide network of royal, state or municipal conservatories, could emerge.[2] With this first generation of composers, born in and around 1870, the Australian musician could share a common heritage of cosmopolitan Central European, French and Italian styles already stimulating the slowly emergent creative traditions on the two American continents through such figures as John Knowles Paine (1839–1919), Edward MacDowell (1861–1908), in the United States, Itibere da Cunha (1848–1913), Leopoldo Miguez (1850–1900) in Brazil, and the brothers Arturo (1862–1938) and Paolo (1866–1914) Berutti in Argentina. Many of these North and South Americans received their musical training at the Royal Conservatory of Music at Leipzig, the same institution which was to serve as a Mecca for many young Australian aspiring performers and composers, of whom the most prominent were Alfred Hill (1870–1960), Ernest Truman (1870–1948) and Ernest Hutcheson (1871–1951). In common with their American counterparts these three absorbed the traditions of the tempered directorship of Carl Reinecke (1824–1910), at a time when the young Richard Strauss, Gustav Mahler and adherents of the Munich and Frankfurt schools were already acknowledged forces in German musical life. Hill, Truman and Hutcheson all won early recognition for their creative abilities, Hutcheson almost certainly becoming the first Australian-born composer to have a piano concerto performed by the Berlin Philharmonic Orchestra (1898). But whereas Hill and Truman were to return to Australia to assume important functions in the musical life of Sydney (the former as composer-conductor-violinist-pedagogue and foundation professor of harmony and composition at the New South Wales State Conservatorium, the latter as freelance composer and Sydney Municipal Organist) Hutcheson pursued a lively career in North America, culminating in his election to the Presidency of the Juilliard School of Music in New York.

Alfred Francis Hill, born 16 November 1870, obtained his earliest musical ex-
pertise as violinist and cornet player in the numerous small orchestras then accompanying itinerant commercial theatricals in Australia and New Zealand.[3] Gaining
admission to the Royal Leipzig Conservatory in 1887, Hill's principal teachers
included the composer, theorist, organist and later Reger exponent Gustav Schreck
(composition), the violinist-conductor Hans Sitt and the musicologist Oscar Paul,
whose interests in music ethnography may well have kindled Hill's later interest
in New Zealand Maori and Australian Aboriginal music cultures. The Leipzig
sojourn culminating in the award of the much-coveted Helbig Prize, as well as
experience as an *Aushilfe* in the Gewandhausorchester, also saw publication of
some of Hill's earliest manuscripts such as the 'Scotch' Sonata, a set of keyboard
miniatures '*Aus meinem Skizzenbuch*' and various vocal settings. These early works,
together with the Prelude and Fugue for string trio, display a proficiency and authority in handling conservative German idioms in the Mendelssohn tradition,
while the 'Scotch' Sonata became the first of many works to be imbued by the composer's enthusiasm for Celtic musical folk-lore.

Returning to New Zealand in 1892, Hill settled first in Wellington, where his
cantata *The New Jerusalem*, acclaimed by local critics for its novelties in harmony
and instrumentation recalling the first act Prelude to *Lohengrin* and the *Good Friday
Spell* in *Parsifal*, introduced his earliest music dramatic essays. From 1897 to 1902
Hill's activities were focused on Sydney as conductor of the Liedertafel and several
orchestral societies. From 1902 to 1910 Hill again centred his activities on New
Zealand, as conductor of operatic tours for various commercial managements and
as director of the Christchurch International Exhibition Orchestra 1906–07. In 1910
he returned permanently to Australia, settling in Sydney, becoming Principal of the
Austral Orchestral College, a founder and professor of the New South Wales State
Conservatorium of Music (1916–34), and a regular conductor of the New South
Wales State and Conservatorium orchestras. For his services to music Hill received
the King George VI Coronation Medal in 1937, and was elected as Officer and
Commander to the Orders of the British Empire and of St Michael and St George.[4]

Retrospectively Hill's production appears to fall into three clearly defined phases,
each characterized by the predominance of one or other major musical work form.
The first phase (1892–1923) was focused on the production and performance of
dramatic works, from the cantata *The New Jerusalem* (1892) to *The Ship of Heaven*
(1923). The second phase (1924–40) emphasized chamber music and concertos, in
particular the string quartets of which no less than ten were written between 1934
and 1938. In the third phase (1941–60) the composer undertook revisions of twelve
earlier chamber works reproducing them as symphonies. Involving negligible formal
and thematic emendations, these revisions usually amounted to no more than
reinstrumentations, and illustrate that utilitarianism and facility which enabled Hill
to produce a variety of works through adaptation. (Even several sonatas for violin
and piano permitted alternative combinations such as flute, oboe, clarinet, viola
and violoncello with piano.)

The first phase of Hill's creativity accounted for no less than fourteen music
dramatic works, three cantatas or legends and an ode for the opening of the Christchurch International Exhibition in 1906 (specifying a Berliozian combination of
soloists, chorus, orchestra and military band), and ten operas. In the same period
he was also active as operatic conductor, composer of incidental theatre music

(for G.B. Shaw's *The Devil's Disciple*, for example, in 1913), and under a Maori pseudonym, Arapeta Hira, as author of three one-act plays for the Sydney Repertory Theatre (1914). A contribution of some historical importance was Hill's championship of the aesthetic ideal seeking to create an Australian tradition of operatic composition, imbued by other manifestations of a nascent cultural nationalism in the graphic arts (Heidelberg School of painters), literature and the polemics of the Sydney *Bulletin*. These ambitions crystallized in the formation of the short-lived Australian Opera League, which presented a series of Australian operas in Sydney and Melbourne in 1914, in which Hill's *Giovanni* and Fritz Hart's *Pierrette* were performed. Surprisingly, neither opera was on an Australian theme.

Today Hill's music-theatrical works appear to be easily classifiable either according to formal operatic typology or through their choice of literary materials. Of the ten operas, *The Whipping Boy*, *Lady Dolly*, *Tapu*, *A Moorish Maid*, *Don Quixote de la Mancha*, *The Rajah of Shivapore* and *The Ship of Heaven* represent the comic opera genre with set pieces interspersed with spoken dialogue, while *Teora*, *Giovanni* and *Auster* are through-composed pieces making some employment of leitmotiv devices.[5]

The libretti of the operas and dramatic cantatas appear to be divisible into four groups based on the geographical setting of their literary materials:

1   **Conventional European subjects:**
    The Whipping Boy lib. Arthur Adams (1893 Wellington excerpts 1896);
    Lady Dolly lib. Marjorie Browne (1898, Sydney, 1900); *Don Quixote de la Mancha* lib. William B. Beattie (lib. dated 23 September 1904);
    Giovanni, the Sculptor lib. Harriet Callan (1913, Sydney, 1914).

2   **Exotic Afro or Oriental settings** (in a medley operetta style):
    A Moorish Maid or, *Queen of the Riffs* lib. J. Youlan Birch (1905, Auckland, New Zealand, 1906);
    The Rajah of Shivapore lib. David Souter (1914, Sydney, 1914).

3   **Works employing Maori lore and mythology:**
    Tawhaki lib. A. Dommett (1895);
    Hinemoa lib. A. Adams (1902, New Zealand 1903);
    Tapu, or *The Tale of a Maori Pah* lib. A. Adams (1902 New Zealand 1903);
    Teora, or *The Weird Flute* lib. Hill (1913, Sydney, 1928).

4   **Australian literary materials:**
    Auster lib. after poem of Emily Congeau (1922, Sydney 1922, Scenic 1935);
    The Ship of Heaven lib. Hugh McCrae (1923, Sydney, 1923).

Whereas the first three European settings were number operas with spoken dialogue, a style combining English light opera, French *Opéra Comique* and German *Singspiel*, the fourth of this series, *Giovanni*, sought new methods of dramatic expression and musical characterization, based, as in the Maori chamber opera *Teora* (1912–13) on the possibilities of the Wagnerian leitmotiv system—an interest no doubt reawakened by the German repertories of the visiting companies of the time. In a programme annotation for the Australian League Production in 1914, Harriet Callan and Hill described the work as: 'somewhat in the nature of an allegory', its purpose being to show 'how, in pursuit of fame, a man may pass by the greater treasures of life which perhaps lie close at hand'. The centre of the suggested allegory is the young sculptor Giovanni who, betrayed by the lures of material and professional ambition, finds opportune redemption through acceptance of the virtues of loyalty and simplicity. The characters of the opera, intended as archetypes, are represented through a series of recurrent signature and leading motives which are heard in sequence, alternation or conflict as the plot unfolds. For dramatic continuity and tension, thematic organization and musical characterization *Giovanni* is perhaps Hill's most ambitious and accomplished score for the theatre.

While the exotic settings, *A Moorish Maid* and *The Rajah of Shivapore*, both adhere to the traditions of comic opera and *Singspiel*, the other operas using Maori mythology or Australian literary settings exhibit a wider range of techniques. Of the Maori mythological settings *Tawhaki* was a cantata for the concert room; *Hinemoa*, a spectacular scenico-choral pageant similar to S. Coleridge-Taylor's *Hiawatha*; *Tapu*, a comic opera with spoken dialogue; *Teora*, a through-composed chamber opera with judicious use of character and reminiscence motives. A manuscript scenario in Hill's own hand indicated that *Teora* was originally stimulated by a Traveller's Tale printed in *Household Words* and called the 'New Zealand "Magic Flute"'.

The operas using Australian literary materials are allegorical and symbolic in character. In its choice and execution of its subject *Auster* was at least in part the continuation of a tradition of the semi-patriotic masque, favoured in such nineteenth-century works as Charles E. Horsley's *The South Sea Sisters* (1866), and in the twentieth century by works like Henry Tate's *The Dreams of Diaz* (1917). The central figure of Emily Congeau's libretto is Auster (archetype for Australia), daughter of Oceana, who begged the fates to make her daughter mortal. Instead, Auster was made ruler of a mythical continent inhabited only by her attendant Camoola and a group of sages, elves and demons. As Auster matures she is bestirred by yearnings for mortal love, which, according to the sage Gnomus, will only be assuaged by the arrival of foreign suitors. These include a marauding seaman, a Spanish grandee and a young English adventurer to whom Auster betroths herself. The emergence of this mortal love occupies the first two acts of the opera, permitting an alternative conclusion suggested by the composer. The third act, a series of apparitions for the future, a pageant of Australian historical episodes from 1788 to 1918, seems, by comparison, superfluous. The first two acts include some of Hill's most dramatic writing. In common with *Giovanni*, considerable employment is made of recurrent and situation motives for Auster, Gnomus, Camoola and the demons, and for aspects of the mythological world they inhabit. Unfortunately Hill's musical accomplishment is handicapped through the dramatic weaknesses and tendentious attempts at poetic expression by the librettist.

The setting of Hugh McCrae's *The Ship of Heaven* reverts to the style of the earlier light operas, with twenty-seven musical numbers interspersed by spoken dialogue. Hill's score, despite much deft theatrical invention, does not recapture sufficiently the poetic surrealism and irony of McCrae's verses.

With *The Ship of Heaven* (1923) Hill concluded his series of operas and other music dramatic compositions. Thereafter his interest focused on the production of intrumental forms, in particular the string quartet and the concerto, all of which were to be completed before 1940.[6] In 1932 Hill also composed a major choral work, the Mass in E flat for chorus and organ. In addition to the major forms, he produced numerous short lyric pieces, miniature tone poems for orchestra and other instrumental ensembles. Of the seventeen numbered string quartets, the first five were written before 1920, one in 1927 and the remaining eleven between November 1934 and March 1938.

The first six string quartets carry programmatic titles or subtitles for each of their movements or thematic sections. Of these the second quartet in G minor, subtitled 'Maori Legend' is based on a literary programme from the Maori Legend 'Rata's Cave', and draws on the same sources of Polynesian mythology already used for the operas.[7]

All quartets except the Eleventh adhere to a classical four-movement lineage, usually favouring sonata forms for their first movements, sonata or rondo or their hybrids for the finales. Moreover, the classical heritage is further emphasized in that many of the first movements (in all ten) are preceded by slow introductions, some of them containing materials to reappear in cyclic references in later movements. The most advanced employment of such cyclic devices will be found in the Tenth Quartet (in E minor-major) in which the thematic materials of all four movements are obtained from variants of a four-note theme:

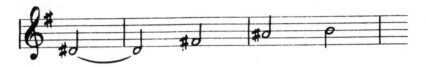

Fig. 1 The four-note theme of the Tenth Quartet

Himself a much practised chamber musician, Hill's part writing is characterized by its idiomatic assurance and easy execution. In common with the concertos, sonatas and symphonies, the string quartets draw on three main melodic and motivic sources: what he regarded as Maori musical folk-lore, folk-melody of Scottish and Irish origins, and the pliable instrumental motivic styles of German origins.

In addition to the string quartets are several extended chamber works, some of a divertimento character, such as *Life*, Serenade for flute and strings (quartet or orchestra) and Septet in E flat for flute, oboe, two clarinets, two bassoons and horn. The interesting philosophico-programmatic work *Life*, for piano, string quartet and (in the finale) eight vocal soloists, was written in 1912 when the use of voices in conjunction with a chamber ensemble was still novel, despite essays by Schoenberg, Ravel and Stravinsky and a general discussion of the technique in *The Musical Times*. Hill's avowed intention, expressed in a programme annotation was 'to evolve a scheme whereby the singers, instead of singing words, will sing notes or syllables or produce chords and intervals like an instrumentalist does' and 'to have them seated with members of the quartet and let their voices blend with the instruments instead of, as now, make the voices a separate part which detracts rather than completes what should be a perfect whole'. This varied use of eight vocal soloists is, however, restricted to the finale. Two further notable features of this work will be seen in the use of cyclic and programmatic elements. An example of the first is the opening phrase of the work's slow introduction, referred to in later movements, and used in the main '*Gloria in excelsis Deo*' theme for the finale. The programmatic intentions of the work are expressed in the titles or subtitles of the movement, and in the numerous literary inscriptions incorporated into the original manuscript which seek to explain the philosophic or poetic intent of the particular thematic, harmonic and textural changes. As in other programmatic chamber works, Hill remained loyal to the traditional closed forms of sonata, rondo and scherzo or their hybrids.

Though drawing on similar idiomatic sources to the string quartets, the series of piano trios and sonatas for varying combinations are works of more modest intention and execution.

The virtuoso element in the flute serenade also explains its classification with Hill's concertos, a series inaugurated by a period piece *Air Varié* for violin and orchestra dated '8th December 1906, Christchurch, New Zealand'. The five surviving concertos for trumpet (or cornet), horn, violin, piano and viola, mainly originating from the years 1932–40, observe accepted classical traditions. Thus, except for the four movements (three of them programmatically titled) of the piano concerto, the structure of the other concertos adopts a three-movement form, favouring sonata-type first movements, usually ternary slow movements and sonata or rondo types for finales.

The best known of Hill's concerted works is the Viola Concerto (1940). In common with the violin concerto, the soloist is offered an exceptionally grateful part, emphasizing both the lyrical and virtuoso personality of the instrument. The first movement in A minor adheres to the conventional sonata procedures, with a second subject in the relative major. The primary thematic substance of the first movement is introduced jointly by soloist and orchestra as follows:

Fig. 2 From the first movement of the Viola Concerto (music by courtesy Southern Music Co. Pty Ltd, Sydney)

The second subject ([4]), pervaded by descending undulating movement, is introduced by the soloist after a two-measure pedal point followed by a *rallentando*. The development of each subject is one of ornamentation and rhythmic activation.

The Andantino, a more extended version of the lyrical miniature with a more animated middle section, a form often favoured by Hill as independent pieces or as slow movements in his string quartets, derives its material almost entirely from the opening phrase for the soloist, which is later transferred to solo woodwind instruments against which the soloist provides gentle counterpoints.

Fig. 3 The introduction of the second subject, from the Viola Concerto

Fig. 4 Development

Fig. 5 From the Andantino, Viola Concerto

The concluding Decisivo is an *allegro alla polacca* well implanted in the tradition of the popular nineteenth-century violin concerto of the Wieniawski tradition.
But whereas many nineteenth century minor masters were content to resolve into simplistic displays of virtuosity, Hill's score had added piquancies in subtle turns of modulation and the frequent attractive sections of imitation between soloist and orchestra.

The remainder of Hill's orchestral production falls into three categories representing concert overtures—Overture in C major (1933), *Overture of Welcome* (1949) —the programme pieces from the *Maori Rhapsody* to the short miniatures, and the thirteen symphonies, of which twelve will be seen from the following table to be adaptations of earlier chamber music compositions.

Fig. 6 From the Decisivo, Viola Concerto

Title of Work	Year of Comp./1st Perf.	Suggested Chronology no.	Alternative Versions/ Earlier Sources
Maori Symphony	1896	1	Score of one movt only. Parts available for second and third movts. Also titled *Te Rauparaha* (Symph. Poem)
Life Symphony for orchestra and chorus	1941	2	'Life' Quintet in E flat for piano, string quartet and 8 solo voices (1912)
Australia Symphony in B minor	1951	3	Three movts from String Quartet no. 14 in B minor (1937), Scherzo and Trio in 5/4 time from Film Score on Arnhem Land

Symphony in C minor 'Pursuit of Happiness'	1955	4	String Quartet no. 4 in C minor (*c.* 1914) 'Pursuit of Happiness'
Symphony in A minor 'Carnival'	1955	5	String Quartet no. 3 in A minor 'Carnival' 1912
Symphony in B flat 'Celtic'	1956	6	String Quartet no. 16 in B flat 'Celtic Quartet for Strings' (1938)
Symphony in E	1956	7	String Quartet in E (1935)
Symphony in A for strings 'The Mind of Man'	1957	8	String Quartet no. 8 in A (1934)
Symphony in E for strings 'Melodious'	1958	9	String Quartet no. 12 in E (1936)
Symphony in C for 'Beethoven Orchestra'	1958	10	String Quartet no. 17 in C (1938)
Symphony in E flat 'The Four Nations' for strings	MS. undated	11	String Quartet no. 5 in E flat 'The Allies'—dedicated to Henri Verbrugghen (1920)
Symphony in E flat	MS.	12	String Quartet no. 13 in E flat (1936)
Symphony in A minor for strings	MS. undated	13	String Quartet no. 9 in A minor (1935)

The statistics of Hill's production of miniatures suggest a creativity as prolific as in the operatic, choral, symphonic, concerted and major chamber music forms. A preliminary hand-count of published and printed titles in the Alfred Hill Collection held by the Federal Music Library of the Australian Broadcasting Commission in Sydney accounted for forty-six miniatures for small orchestra, a further thirty-five for string ensemble groups, sixty keyboard pieces and seventy-three vocal settings. Consistent with his generation, Hill's initial training equipped him with such an assured technical facility that his speed of composition would have frequently defied rigorous self-criticism. In this regard, the popular parallels sought between Hill and the short-lived American composer, Edward MacDowell, would seem a dangerous oversimplification, especially since the latter's training and ideals were an adaptation of those of the German *Neudeutsche Schule* of Liszt, Raff and Cornelius. Hill, for his part, adopted the more conservative and professional stance of Leipzig romanticism, thereafter adapting his enthusiasms for Celtic, Maori and even Australian Aboriginal musical folk-lore to meet its traditions and requirements. In as much as this signified an alternative to the traditions of imported Victoriana, and that his music established hitherto unattained standards in technical accomplishment and professionalism, Hill can be regarded as an innovator. This in itself set an historically significant advance in Australian musical composition at the start of the twentieth century.

Notes

1. J.M. Thomson, 'The Role of the Pioneer Composer. Some Reflections on Alfred Hill', *Studies in Music*, IV (University of Western Australia Press, Perth, 1970) 55; Elizabeth Wood, '1840–1865. Precedents and Problems for Australian Opera Composers', *Quadrant* no. 83, xvii, 3 (1973) p. 33f.
2. Roger Covell, *Australia's Music: Themes of a New Society* (Melbourne, 1967), p. 24.
3. Andrew D. McCredie, 'Alfred Hill (1870–1960). Some Backgrounds and Perspectives for an Historical Edition', *Miscellanea Musicologica* III (Adelaide, 1968), pp. 181–257.
4. The main sources of documentation on Alfred Hill are the Alfred Hill Papers, a series of uncatalogued folios, containing Hill's diploma certificates from Leipzig, letters of appointment to the New South Wales Conservatorium of Music, letters of appointment as King George VI Coronation Medallist, and as O.B.E. and C.M.G. In addition, there is much valuable official and unofficial correspondence (including contracts and letters to conductors), press cuttings and photographic illustrations. The Alfred Hill Papers are in the keeping of the Mitchell Library, Library of New South Wales, Sydney.
5. All Hill's operas, with the exception of the manuscript score of 'Lady Dolly' held in the Alfred Hill Papers, by Mitchell Library, Sydney, are in the keeping of the Library of New South Wales.
6. The main source location for the instrumental and orchestral manuscripts of Alfred Hill is the Federal Music Library, Australian Broadcasting Commission, Sydney. Hill's juvenilia, including student work and assignments in harmony and composition, are kept in the Alfred Hill Papers.
7. The presence of a literary or philosophic programme ('Carnival' (Third), 'Pursuit of Happiness' (Fourth) Quartets, or 'Life' for string quartet, piano and eight vocal soloists), whether continuous or episodic, was not, however, exclusive at that period to the works of Alfred Hill, since Ernest Truman had already adopted a continuous literary programme for his adventurous, cyclically conceived, and rhythmically ingenious (a Scherzo in 5/8 time) quartet 'The Australian Seasons', written for performances by the Austral String Quartet in Sydney in 1912.

Select Catalogue of Works

Music Dramatic Works

(A) OPERAS

The Whipping Boy opera in three acts (A. Adams) 1895
Lady Dolly romantic comic opera in two acts (M. Browne) 1898, Sydney, 1900
Tapu or the Tale of a Maori Pah opera in two acts (A.H. Adams and J.C. Williamson) 1902, N.Z. 1904
Don Quixote de la Mancha comic opera in two acts (W. Beattie) 1904

A Moorish Maid or Queen of the Riffs comic opera in two acts (John Youlin Birch) 1905, N.Z. 1905
Teora a romantic tragic opera in one act for five voices and orchestra (own libretto) 1913, Sydney, 1929
Giovanni a romantic comic opera in three short acts (H. Callan) 1913, Sydney, Melbourne, 1914
The Rajah of Shivapore a comic opera of the East. Two acts. (D. Souter) 1914, Sydney, 1917
Auster a romantic opera in three acts (Emily Congeau) 1919, Sydney, 1922
The Ship of Heaven a musical fantasy in two acts (Hugh McCrae) 1923, Sydney, 1932

(B) PAGEANTS, CANTATAS, OCCASIONAL WORKS, LITURGICAL SETTINGS

The New Jerusalem cantata for soloists, chorus and orchestra (1892)
Tawahaki Maori cantata for soloists, chorus and orchestra (A. Dommett) (1895)
Hinemoa Maori pageant (A. Adams) (1896)
Exhibition Cantata for soloists, chorus, military band and orchestra (1906)
Mass in E flat for four-part chorus and organ (1931)

(C) MISCELLANEOUS ENTR' ACTES AND INCIDENTAL MUSIC FOR THREATRE, FILM AND BROADCASTING

Music for Orchestra

(i) 13 Symphonies (several undated), 12 of them being adaptations of earlier chamber music compositions (see Table on pp. 14–15)
(ii) Overture in C major (1933), *Overture of Welcome* (1949)
(iii) *Maori Rhapsody* in three scenes (rev. 1915)
(iv) About 50 poems, miniatures and lyric pieces for varying small orchestral combinations yet to be investigated
(v) Concertos for trumpet (*c.* 1925), piano (*c.* 1936), horn [undated, MS. score lost], violin (1932), viola (1940). Also *Air Varié* for violin and orchestra (1906)
(vi) 35 miniatures for string orchestra

Chamber Music

(i) Septet for 1 fl 1 ob 2 cl 2 bn 1 hn (*c.* 1949)
(ii) *Serenada* for fl and str qu (or str orchestra) (undated)
(iii) 'Life' Quintet for pf, str and eight solo voices (1912)
(iv) 17 String Quartets: no. 1 in B flat (Breitkopf & Härtel Leipzig 1913); no. 2 in G minor (Breitkopf & Härtel Leipzig 1913); no. 3 in A minor 'Carnival' (1912); no. 4 in C minor (1914); no. 5 in E flat 'The Allies' (1920); no. 6 in G (1920); no. 7 in A (1934); no. 8 in A (1934); no. 9 in A minor (1935); no. 10 in E (1935); no. 11 in D minor (1935); no. 12 in E (1936); no. 13 in E flat (1936); no. 14 in B minor (1937); no. 15 in A minor (1937); no. 16 in B flat (1938); no. 17 in C (1938)
(v) Prelude and Fugue for string trio (1890)
(vi) Five Trios for v v (va or vc) and pf
(vii) Five Sonatas for v or other instrument and pf
(viii) Numerous miniatures for varying combinations

of strings or strings and piano (some re-orchestrated as orchestral miniatures); cf. Music for Orchestra (iv).

Keyboard Music
At least 60 titles in A.B.C. music collection.

Vocal Music
Some 73 registered titles in A.B.C. music collection

Hill's prodigious production of miniatures included frequent adaptations of one work for several varying combinations. The extent of such adaptations within Hill's total oeuvre will only be established after an extended study of his many miniatures.

Discography

(*NRY*—Not released yet; *ABR*—Australian Broadcasting Rights)

Symphony no. 2 in E flat ('The Joy of Life') [36'30"]. Genty Stevens (soprano), Norma Hunter (contralto), Malcolm Potter (tenor), Alan McKie (baritone), Alfred Hill Estate. 3 Mar. 1971.
Festival disc SFC 800/18
Symphony no. 3 in B minor ('Australia') [28'36"]. West Australian Symphony Orchestra (Thomas Mayer, conductor). A.H.E. 16 May 1969.
ABC recording RRCS/377
Symphony no. 3 in B minor ('Australia') [25'00"]. Sydney Symphony Orchestra (Henry Krips, conductor). A.H.E. 16 Dec. 1959.
HMV disc OALP/7524
Symphony no. 4 in C minor ('The Pursuit of Happiness') [19'55"]. West Australian Symphony Orchestra (Verdon Williams, conductor). A.H.E. 27 Jan. 1971.   *ABC tape*
Symphony no. 6 in B flat ('The Celtic') [22'30"]. South Australian Symphony Orchestra (Patrick Thomas, conductor). A.H.E. 16 Sept. 1969.   *ABC tape*
Symphony no. 8 in A ('The Mind of Man') [25'20"]. Strings of the West Australian Symphony Orchestra (Tibor Paul, conductor). A.H.E.
ABC tape (NRY)
Symphony no. 9 in E ('Melodious') [21'35"]. Strings of the West Australian Symphony Orchestra (Georg Tintner, conductor). A.H.E. 12 Dec. 1970.
ABC tape
Symphony no. 10 in A minor [21'38"]. Strings of the West Australian Symphony Orchestra (Tibor Paul, conductor). A.H.E.   *ABC tape*
Symphony no. 12 in E flat (24'00"]. West Australian Symphony Orchestra (Georg Tintner, conductor). A.H.E. 19 Jan. 1971.   *ABC tape*
Trumpet Concerto (1915) [19'25"]. Donald Johnson (trumpet), West Australian Symphony Orchestra (Thomas Mayer, conductor). A.H.E. 4 Oct. 1969.
HMV disc OASD/7556
Violin Concerto (1932) [23'01"]. Alwyn Elliott (violin), Sydney Symphony Orchestra (Joseph Post, conductor). A.H.E. 18 Dec. 1969.
HMV disc OASD/7556

Viola Concerto (1940) [24'40"]. Robert Pikler (viola), Sydney Symphony Orchestra (Sir Bernard Heinze, conductor). A.H.E. 19 Oct. 1967.
RCA disc SL/16372
Viola Concerto (1940) [24'18"]. Robert Pikler (viola), Sydney Symphony Orchestra (Henry Krips, conductor). A.H.E. 16 Dec. 1959.
HMV disc OALP/7524
Piano Concerto (1940) [23'56"]. David Bollard (piano), West Australian Symphony Orchestra (Georg Tintner, conductor). A.H.E. Feb. 1972.
Festival disc SFC 800/26
Green Water. Alistair Duncan (narrator), Sydney Symphony Orchestra (Sir Eugene Goossens, conductor).   *HMV disc OALP/7511*
Linthorpe (1947) [7'53"]. Sydney Symphony Orchestra (Sir Bernard Heinze, conductor). Southern Music. 8 Aug. 1967.   *World Record Club disc S/2495*
Linthorpe (1947) [8'30"]. Victorian Symphony Orchestra (Clive Douglas, conductor). 1959.
ABC recording PRX/4783
The Moon's Gold Horn (1951)—5'15"; *The Call of a Bird*—9'55"; *Waiata Poi*—2'22". Sydney Symphony Orchestra (Sir Bernard Heinze, conductor). 8 Aug. 1967.   *ABC recording RRCS/137*
The Sea [5'54"]. Sydney Symphony Orchestra (Joseph Post, conductor). A.H.E. 16 Jan. 1969.
ABC recording RRCS/377
Serenade for flute and strings [4'59"]. Owen Fisenden (flute), Strings of the West Australian Symphony Orchestra. A.H.E. 4 Oct. 1969.
HMV disc OASD/7556
Septet for wind instruments (1950) [20'6"]. Adelaide Wind Quintet: David Cubbin (flute), Jiri Tancibudek (oboe), Gabor Reeves (clarinet), Stanley Fry (horn), Thomas Wightman (bassoon), with Wallace McKinnon (clarinet), Norman Lewis (bassoon). A.H.E. 12 Sept. 1969.
ABC recording RRCS/378
Salon Pieces for string quartet. Side 1: (i) 'Maori Love Song' (*Erere Taku Poi*)—2'11"; (ii) 'Waltz Carina' —2'33"; (iii) 'Dusk'—4'16"; (iv) 'The Policeman's Whistle's—3'00"; (v) 'Simplicity'—2'55"; (vi) 'An Old Ruin'—2'59". Side 2: (i) 'A Fragment'—2'46"; (ii) 'Her Passing'—3'29"; (iii) 'Prelude to Hinemoa' —2'49"; (iv) 'Two Gaelic Sketches: My Lover Wounded, Willie's Auld Trews'—4'25"; (v) 'Glorious Wellington,—2'26"; (vi) 'Roderick Dhu (The Clanalpine Chief)'—2'11". *ABC recording RRC/56*
Side 1: (i) First Prelude—2'11"; (ii) Second Prelude —2'00"; (iii) Third Prelude—2'00"; (iv) Fourth Prelude—2'09"; (v) 'Why?'—2'42"; (vi) 'Valse'— 1'19"; (vii) 'Haka of the Tuwharetoa Tribe'—0'43". Side 2: (i) 'A Bit o' Scotch'—1'51"; (ii) Music— 2'19"; (iii) 'In the Style of Byzantine Music'—2'04"; (iv) 'Waes Me for Charlie'—2'25"; (v) 'An Old Time Dance'—2'18"; (vi) 'Black Baby'—2'27".
ABC recording RRC/57
Austral String Quartet: Donald Hazlewood, Ronald Ryder (violins), Ronald Cragg (viola), Gregory Elmaloglou (cello). A.H.E. July 1967.
String Quartet no. 2 in C minor ('Maori') [23'02"]. Austral String Quartet: Alwyn Elliott, Ronald

Ryder (violins), Ronald Cragg (viola), Gregory
Elmaloglou (cello). Chappell.
Festival disc FL/30802, Universal Record Club No. 586
String Quartet no. 7 in A [20'50"]. Elder String Quartet:
Beryl Kimber, Lloyd Davies (violins), Harold Fair-
hurst (viola), James Whitehead (cello).
           ABC recording PRX/4954 (ABR only)
String Quartet no. 11 in D minor [18'00"]. Elder String
Quartet: Beryl Kimber, Lloyd Davies (violins),
Harold Fairhurst (viola), James Whitehead (cello).
           ABC recording PRS/4954 (ABR only)
Romance—4'56"; *Waltz Caprice*—2'03"; 'Scottish
Scenery' from *Scotch Sonata*—5'56". Sam Bor
(violin), Jessíca Dix (piano). 1957.
           ABC recording 2XS–455/1 (ABR only)
Mass in E flat 31'56". Dean Patterson (baritone),
James Thiele (organ). Adelaide Singers (Patrick
Thomas, conductor). 18 Sept. 1969.
                    ABC recording RRCS/379
Mopoke 3'40". Rosalind Keene (soprano), Henri Penn
(piano).   *ABC recording O/N40525* (ABR only)
A Little Town I Love—3'04"; *Serenade*—3'00"; *Like
a Lone Bird Calling*—3'57". Robert Gard (tenor),
John Champ (piano). Chappell.
           ABC recording O/N40525 (ABR only)

Percy Grainger

(1882—1961)

John Hopkins

For many years Percy Grainger's fame as a composer rested largely on a number of very popular short works which could be played by almost every size of instrumental ensemble imaginable. This 'availability' was the result of Grainger's concept of 'elastic scoring', a concept producing works different from those having an original (or definitive) form from which may stem a variety of arrangements for different combinations. Grainger's highly ingenious handling of smaller works in this way has, I believe, been frequently misunderstood and could also be a contributory factor to the general lack of recognition of his few large-scale works.

'Elastic scoring' was just one of many theories of all kinds occupying the mind of this remarkable man. In a note to conductors he explained that it grew naturally out of two roots:

1. That my music tells its story mainly by means of intervals and the liveliness of the part writing, rather than by means of tone-colour, and it is therefore well fitted to be played by almost any small, large or medium sized combination of instruments, provided a proper balance of tone is kept.
2. That I wish to play my part in the radical experimentation with orchestral and chamber music blends that seem bound to happen as a result of the ever wider spreading democratising of all forms of music.[1]

He said democratic polyphony was his Australian ideal of a many-voiced texture in which all or most of the tone-strands enjoy equal prominence and importance.

Bearing in mind the stress placed on tone-colour by so many of his contemporaries it is not surprising that one of his friends said he was 'bunged up with theories'.

There is no doubt that the boundless energy of the man himself is conveyed in the vigorous and purposeful movement of parts so that a simple melody such as the *Londonderry Air* takes on interesting and expressive melodic lines in all parts in his version *The Irish Tune from County Derry*. The same effective horizontal liveliness in part writing may be found in works like *Country Gardens, Handel in the Strand, Molly on the Shore* as well as the large-scale works such as *The Warriors, To a Nordic Princess* and *Tribute to Foster*. Listening to Grainger's own piano recordings one recognizes the importance he placed on contrapuntal shape.[2]

Bearing in mind Grainger's statement that tone-colour is of lesser importance than the liveliness of the parts, the rich lustre of his scoring may seem somewhat contradictory. This scoring has to be seen against a complex background. Firstly, Grainger had from his early days a wide knowledge of music of post romantic composers (*Hill Song No. 1* revised version) shows his awareness of the techniques of Schoenberg). Secondly, he had close friendships with many English composers several years his senior, and their influence is evident in his harmonic structure and orchestration. (Several quieter sections in *The Warriors* show a close affinity to Delius, to whom the work was dedicated.) Third, and most important, was the great desire Grainger had to redesign the structure of the symphony orchestra. He disagreed with a balance in the strings which gave superiority to violins against violas and cellos, and a perusal of his scores reveals the even spread of interest through all string sections. His interest and experience in military bands, dating back to a brief period of service in the United States Army band in 1917, developed a love of reed instruments, especially saxophones which form a separate 'S.A.T.B.' instrumental group in some of his works, for example, *The Power of Rome and the Christian Heart*. Further emphasis on reeds is given in this work by the extensive use of organ, and no doubt Grainger had in mind the special reed qualities of American concert organs. The frequent use of harmonium and/or organ further indicates his fascination with such sounds, an exceptionally striking example being found in the original version of *Hill Song No. 1*, scored for two flutes, six oboes, six English horns, six bassoons and double bassoon. In an unpublished typescript in the archives of the Percy Grainger Library Society at White Plains, New York, Grainger wrote:

> I was in love with the double reeds (oboe, English horn etc.) as the wildest and fiercest of musical tone-types. In 1900 I had heard a very harsh-toned rustic oboe (piffero) in Italy, some extremely nasal Egyptian double reeds at the Paris Exhibition, and bagpipes in the Scottish Highlands. I wished to weave these snarling, nasal sounds (which I had heard only in a single line melody) into a polyphonic texture as complex as Bach's.

Grainger's interest in the use of keyboard instruments within an orchestra extends well beyond that of any other composer. Even in a short work like *Handel in the Strand* the composer recommended using at least four pianos for 'good tonal balance', adding that 'as many as twenty pianos may be used to good effect'. The most effective use of pianos in his large-scale orchestral works occurs in *The Warriors*, where three (or nine!) grand pianos are used in extensive solo passages and to augment the large percussion section. The writing could best be described as athletic, and great skill and dexterity are required to do full justice to the parts. In addition to normal keyboard performance the pianists are required to play inside the pianos with marimba sticks. While nothing unusual today, such a direction at the time (it was completed about 1919) was extraordinary. *The Warriors* is an excellent example of Grainger's use of 'tuneful percussion' instruments, his interest in which can be traced back to first hearing the sound of an Indonesian gamelan orchestra (at the Paris Exposition of 1900). This same experience, it will be recalled, inspired Debussy to write 'Pagodes' in *Estampes*, and in 1928 Grainger arranged this piece for 'gamelan-like' tuned orchestral percussion and keyboard instruments, using nineteen or more players.

Grainger was most indignant about those who neglected the wide range of percussion instruments available. In 1929 he wrote:

And what are we to think of the lack of vision, lack of innate musicality shown by 'highbrow' composers and conductors in their neglect of the exquisite 'tuneful percussion' instruments invented and perfected in America and elsewhere during the last 30 or 40 years—metal and wooden marimba, staff bells, vibraphones, nabimbas, dulcitone etc. Yet these same 'classicists'—who probably consider these mellow and delicate toned instruments too 'low brow' to be admitted into the holy precincts of the symphony orchestra—endure without protest the ever-lasting thumping of kettle-drums (which with brutal monotony wipes out all chord-clearness) in the Haydn-Mozart-Beethoven orchestrations. The truth is that most 'highbrows' are much more 'low brow' than they themselves suspect!

In this connection it is interesting to note that it's only the most harsh-toned tuneful percussion instruments (glockenspiel, xylophone, tubular chimes) that have found a place in the symphony orchestra thus far. Can it be that the symphony orchestra prizes stridence of tone only in such instruments? If not, why has no place been found for the mellow toned metal marimba (the continuation downwards of the glockenspiel) and the gentle toned wooden marimba (the continuation downwards of the xylophone)? Perhaps because their quality of tone is too refined to be heard amidst the harsh jumble of the symphony orchestra? If so, it is high time that we revised our symphony orchestration in the direction of a delicacy and refinement that can accommodate the subtler creations of modern instrument-building geniuses such as Deagan and others. To use, orchestrally, a glockenspiel without a metal marimba, a xylophone without a wooden marimba, is just as absurd and incomplete as it would be to use piccolo without flute, violins without lower strings, the two top octaves of the piano without lower octaves. Let us get rid of this barbarism as soon as we can!

Young people love such colourful, easy to play instruments as staff bells, marimbas, dulcitone etc. Let us use such tuneful-percussion enthusiasts 'with both hands': Every orchestra should sport at least 20 such players; 2 on 1 glockenspiel, 4 on 1 metal marimba, 2 on 1 xylophone, 4 on 1 wooden marimba, 4 or more on 1 staff bells, 2 on 1 tubular chimes, 1 on celesta, 1 on dulcitone. (If the metal and wooden marimbas could be used in twos, threes, fours or fives it would be still better.)[3]

The Warriors is also of special interest because of the special nature of the work. Though Grainger was certain of what he wanted to achieve he must have felt slightly nervous about the effect if the work fell into the hands of inexperienced or unsympathetic conductors who might misconstrue his intentions.

At the point in the score where six off-stage brass players perform at a totally different speed from the rest of the orchestra, Grainger writes that 'should the 1st conductor, for any reasons whatsoever, dislike the effect produced, the entire music behind the platform may be left out'.[4]

Grainger wrote *The Warriors* between 1913 and 1919, and though Charles Ives in his Fourth Symphony was undertaking similar experiments at the same time, it is unlikely that his work was known to Grainger. Certainly the random playing off-stage of the march theme by six brass instruments against the slow-moving orchestral parts with its rich harmonies must have shocked many ears at the time.

The bass oboe theme from *The Warriors* was used by Grainger in one of the more unusual 'Room-Music Titbits' called *The Lonely Desert-man sees the Tents of the Happy Tribes*. Here the melody is sung by a tenor voice accompanied by shimmering chords on two marimbas using up to fifteen players. Altogether fourteen chords are randomly played against the free melodic line with magical effect. The Danish Folk Music setting *Under En Bro* (Under a Bridge) contains a similar section of random percussion and it is interesting to note that both these works were finished in the late 1940s when Grainger's interest in 'free music' experimentation was growing.

The Lonely Desert-man has other interesting features and it is a good example of Grainger's use of wordless syllables—tam pam pa ra di da etc. As these vowel sounds are in Italian, great richness and sonority results. This device was used in extended form in the composer's *Marching Song of Democracy*. Grainger also used voices like instruments with great intensity and feeling in the *Colonial Song*.

The link of *The Lonely Desert-man* with *Tribute to Foster* is also worth noting. The music used for the distant happy tribes in both works is played in the distance (off-stage) and in the case of the tail-piece in *Tribute to Foster* at a totally different tempo from the main part of the work. Still farther away is the clatter of the railroad track on the rim of a side drum in yet a third tempo.

Tribute to Foster, written in 1914, was, like so many other works, a gift to his mother Rose, who undoubtedly played a very dominant part in Grainger's life prior to his marriage to Ella Ström in 1928. The blending of the Australian and American scenes is explained by Grainger in his own programme note:

> One of my earliest musical impressions is that of my mother singing me to sleep with Stephen C. Foster's entrancing ditty *Camptown Races* (or 'Doodah').
> In my *Tribute to Foster* (which is scored for five single voices, mixed chorus, musical glasses, solo piano and orchestra) I have wanted to give musical expression to this American genius—one of the most tender, touching and subtle melodists and poets of all time; a mystic dreamer no less than a whimsical humorist.

Grainger continued that he meant that the tail-piece referred to earlier would symbolize 'the fading away of those untutored forms of Negro folk-music from which we all think that Foster drew inspiration for his "art-songs"'.[5]

Tribute to Foster has special effects similar to those found in *The Warriors*, giving amazing tonal perspective at the conclusion of the work. Also of interest are the tuned musical glasses played by members of the chorus and the bowed metal marimba, played by members of the string section who are given specific instructions on how the violin, cello or double bass bow should be drawn at right angles across the marimba bar. The music for the latter group is printed in the orchestral string parts, and an instrument now held in the Grainger Museum, University of Melbourne, retains marks clearly showing how it was prepared for use in this work. On this instrument the individual bars, with reasonators attached, can be easily removed and distributed among the nominated string players.

Whilst *Tribute to Foster* is Grainger's most extended and sophisticated arrangement of folk-music, there are many very beautiful settings of a shorter and less complex nature. Grainger's interest in folk-music was stimulated by his discovery of some folk-song settings of Edvard Grieg around 1904, leading to the virtual relinquishment of his concert career as a pianist the next year in order to devote his time to work with Vaughan Williams, Cecil Sharp and others in collecting, studying and publishing English folk-songs. The results of his labours were reflected in the fifty or so works published in the 'British Folk Music Settings'. He also made settings of folk-songs from Ireland, Scotland, Denmark and the Faeroe Islands, and used Polynesian material in such pieces as *Random Round*. Where possible he collected the materials himself which meant studying the language of the country. At other times he took material from available recordings. An example of this method is *sekar gadung* for Javanese ensemble (based on Slendro scale), which as stated on the manuscript score, was 'roughly noted down from a gramophone record (Musik des Orients No. 9—Odeon—01936) by Norman Voelcker and Percy Grainger' for soprano and baritone solo, piccolo, xylophone, wooden marimba, high and low metal marimba and staff bells. The purely instrumental settings such as those in the *Danish Folk Song Suite* are models of inventiveness and good taste. Above all he aimed to preserve the song-like character of the music.

In 1934 Grainger gave a series of twelve lectures for the Australian Broadcasting Commission. The opening paragraph of the first lecture contains a statement of his belief in a universal attitude to music.

> It seems to me that a commonsense view of music is to approach all the world's available music with an open mind, just as we approach the world's literature or painting or philosophy. It seems to me that we should be willing, even eager, to hear everything we can of all kinds of music, from whatever quarter and whatever era, in order that we may find out from experience whether or not it carries any spiritual message for us as individuals.[6]

Grainger was thinking of European art music written between 1700 and 1900 and today it is still true to say that the main concentration of listening falls into a period of about two hundred years of Western European music.

These twelve lectures have much relevance in showing Grainger's breadth of interest in the whole world of music around him, a breadth even more remarkable when one recalls the severe limitations in radio and recording which prevailed at that time. The last lecture is entitled 'The Goal of Musical Progress' in which he claimed

> that music must progress technically until it is able to tally the irregularities and complexity of nature ... [and] ... the filling up of gapped scales, increasing discordance of what we consider 'harmony', the irregularisation of rhythm, the breaking up of artificial musical forms (Fugue form, sonata forms etc.) the increasing use of sliding intervals—all moving in the direction of free music.

Grainger considered that his work on 'free music' was his only truly valuable and original contribution to music. By 'free music' he meant essentially gliding tones and beatless, irregular rhythms. He said his first thoughts about 'free music' came to him around 1892.

> Personally I have heard free music in my head since I was a boy of 11 or 12 in Auburn, Melbourne. It is my only important contribution to music—my impression is that this world of tonal freedom was suggested to me by wave-movements in the sea that I first observed as a young child at Brighton, Victoria and Albert Park, Melbourne.[7]

From his early youth he was sketching ideas for multistrand polyphony and one can find links between several of the works written in the first two decades of the century and the experiments which occupied his thoughts and energies in the fifties. Those sections of *The Warriors* which, because of the many rhythmic complexities, need two and three conductors could be compared with Grainger's extension of the normal use of player piano rolls to produce music of greater rhythmic complexity than one pianist could possibly perform. His *Random Round* 'tone wrought around 1912–1915 in Holland and tried out in England not very hopefulfillingly soon after'[8] is another example of his efforts to break the strict rhythmical bonds of Western European music. Lack of knowledge and skill of improvisation and aleatoric music so hampered early performances of this work that Grainger ultimately felt the need to write it down in more conventional terms, though this obviously placed the work in shackles and removed the very freedom he wanted to achieve.

Writing in 1915 Grainger said:

It will be seen that a fairly large range of personal choice was allowed to everyone taking part, and the effectiveness of the whole thing would depend primarily on the natural sense for contrasts of form, color and dynamics displayed by the various performers, and their judgement in entering and leaving the general ensemble at suitable moments.

Thus one player, by intruding carelessly and noisily at a moment when all the rest were playing softly, would wreck that particular effect, though, on the other hand, such an act, if undertaken intentionally in order to provide dynamic variety, might be very welcome. Last summer in London some fifteen of us experimented with the Random Round and the results obtained were very instructive to me personally. Several of those taking part quickly developed the power of merging themselves into the artistic whole, and whereas at the outset the monotonous babel produced somewhat 'resembled a Dog's Home, Battersea' (as a leading critic once described Albéniz' marvellous and touching piece *Jerez* when I introduced it to London audiences some years ago), after a little practice together the whole thing took on form, color and clarity and sounded harmonious enough, though a frequent swash of passing discords was noticeable also. I look forward to some day presenting to English and American audiences a performance of this blend of modern harmonic tendencies with experiences drawn from the improvised polyphony of primitive music, although of course my piece represents only the veriest beginnings of what may ultimately be evolved in the realms of concerted improvisation.[9]

The melodic aspects of Grainger's free music were concerned with achieving gliding sounds and the main realization of his ideas came through his association with a New York physicist Burnett Cross who, though not a musician, was sympathetic to Grainger's ideas. Together they designed and built various types of machines on the roller principle. Prior to this in 1935 Grainger had, for the first time, an example of his free music 'performed on man-played instruments conducted by Percy Code' whose performance Grainger complimented as most skilful and sympathetic, but added that 'Free Music demands a non-human performance and should pass direct from the imagination of the composer to the ear of the listener by way of delicately controlled musical machines.'[10] His search for a suitable machine included the uses of Theremins,[11] as well as composing directly on to piano rolls which were then used on the first free music apparatus devised with Burnett Cross. This apparatus consisted of a silenced keyboard, the notes of which were attached to three melanettes (early keyboard electronic instruments), which were tuned so that between them each tone could be split into six equal parts. Thus an effect of gliding was possible. Burnett Cross and Grainger also worked on the Butterfly piano which was a normal piano with each note tuned 1/6th apart.

Grainger and Cross developed the piano roll method to what was called the 'Estey reed tone tool' consisting of perforated brown paper thirty-six inches wide, passing over the edge of a giant mouth organ, the reeds of which were tuned in quarter tones. Though this machine allowed Grainger to use gliding chords, there were many difficulties due particularly to suction and consequent tearing of the brown paper. Grainger and Cross then moved in the direction of a 'composing' rather than 'performing' machine using graphic notation. Eight oscillators were used to obtain a pitch range as wide as that of the piano. This free music machine permitted complete freedom of voices and led to their final invention which was, in their terms, 'electronic' though not in the sense we use the word today. During the latter years of his experimentation with Burnett Cross, Grainger was aware of the electronic music developments at Columbia University, New York, but he chose to follow his own path towards free music which was linked to his own musical conviction rather than to scientific discovery. Viewed today, Grainger's struggles in this field, when seen against the latest electronic music developments, might be compared to man's earliest attempts to fly and the latest supersonic aircraft.[12]

The extremely wide spread of Grainger's musical interest, his arduous performing schedule as a concert pianist and his many other activities fully occupied his middle later life. Though he made many new versions of early works, his really outstanding creative imagination was at its height during the first two decades of this century. *Lincolnshire Posy*, written during the busy years of the 1930s is a singular exception and shows immense creative imagination. Essentially he was a romantic; his was the rhapsodic approach to musical structure, averse to 'architectural' formal procedures since he believed that music is experienced not as a series of isolated moments but as a gradual unfolding. He said 'I view the repetition of themes as a redundancy— as if the speaker should continually repeat himself'.[13] This was the philosophy of his life and the source of its strength and weaknesses.

Notes

1. 'To Conductors and to those training, or in charge of amateur, and chamber bodies'. Foreword to Grainger's 'Jutish Melody', *Danish Suite* (London, Schott's, 1929).
2. Alertness to the shape of these horizontal patterns is of fundamental importance when performing Grainger's music, so frequently heard with this consideration missing. It is also important for string players to interpret Grainger's phrasing and articulation with great care and an understanding of the style of string playing prevalent at the time the works were written. Broadly speaking there was much more 'off the string' playing in the middle and lower part of the bow than there is today. This should be kept in mind in fast moving pieces such as the *English Dance*, *Mock Morris*, *Handel in the Strand*, etc.
3. Foreword, *op. cit.*
4. Composer's note on full score of *The Warriors*.
5. Composer's note on piano score of *Tribute to Foster*.
6. Percy Grainger, *Music—A Commonsense View of All Types* (Australian Broadcasting Commission, Sydney, 1934) being a synopsis of lectures delivered for the Commission in December that year.
7. Contained in a Statement (dated December 1938) by Grainger in an exhibit case at the Grainger Museum, University of Melbourne.
8. Note on MS. score of *Random Round* in composer's hand.
9. Percy Grainger, 'The Impress of Personality in Unwritten Music', *The Musical Quarterly*, i, 3, 1915.
10. Statement, *op. cit.*
11. An instrument to provide gliding sounds invented by Professor Leon Theremin (inventor of acoustical instruments).
12. For a further account of these experiments see Ivor C. Dorum, 'Grainger's "Free Music"', *Studies in Music* (University of Western Australia Press) No. 2, 1968.
13. Contained in an unpublished typescript concerning *Hill Song No. 1* in the archives of the Percy Grainger Library Society, White Plains, New York, compiled by Percy Aldridge Grainger in September, 1949.

Select Bibliography

Bird, John. *Percy Grainger*. Elek, London, 1976.
Slattery, Thomas C. *Percy Grainger—The Inveterate Innovator*. Instrumentalist Co., Evanston, Illinois, 1974.

List of Works

For a full list of works see: *A Complete Catalogue of the Works of Percy Grainger*, edited, catalogued, and with a foreword, afterword and explanatory notes by Teresa Balough. Music Monograph 2, University of Western Australia Department of Music, 1975.

Discography

Youthful Suite (1899–1945) [24'22"]. (i) 'Northern March'—4'48"; (ii) 'Rustic Dance—3'47"; (iii) 'Norse Dirge'—8'30"; (iv) 'Eastern Intermezzo'—1'50"; (v) 'English Waltz'—4'07". Sydney Symphony Orchestra (John Hopkins, conductor). Schott. Dec. 1966.   *World Record Club disc S/4433*

The Danish Folk Song Suite [8'15"]. Two movements only: (i) 'The Power of Love'—3'20"; (ii) 'Lord Peter's Stable Boy'—2'50". Melbourne Symphony Orchestra (John Hopkins, conductor). Schirmer. 29 Sept. 1967.   *ABC recording RRCS/131*

The Danish Folk Song Suite. Percy Grainger (piano; duo-art piano roll).   *Vanguard disc VRS/1072*

My Robin is to the Greenwood [5'55"]. Sydney Symphony Orchestra (John Hopkins, conductor). Schott. Dec. 1966.   *World Record Club disc S/4433*

My Robin is to the Greenwood Gone [5'32"]. English Chamber orchestra (Benjamin Britten, conductor).   *Decca disc SXLA/6410*

My Robin is to the Greenwood Gone. Eastman Rochester Pops Orchestra (Frederick Fennell, conductor).   *Mercury disc CDS/1495*

Mock Morris (1910) [3'10"]. Sydney Symphony Orchestra (John Hopkins, conductor). Schott. Dec. 1966   *World Record Club disc S/4433*

Mock Morris (1910) [3'25"]. Australian Youth Orchestra (John Hopkins, conductor). Schott. 13 July 1970.   *HMV disc SOELP/9721*

Mock Morris (1910). Philharmonia Orchestra (George Weldon, conductor).   *World Record Club disc PE/736*

Mock Morris (1910). Stokowski's Symphony Orchestra (Leopold Stokowski, conductor).   *RCA-Victor disc LM/1238*

Mock Morris (1910). Eastman Rochester Pops Orchestra (Frederick Fennell, conductor).   *Mercury disc CDS/1495*

Irish Tune from County Derry (1902–11) [3'20"]. Sydney Symphony Orchestra (John Hopkins, conductor). Schott. Dec. 1966.   *World Record Club disc S/4433*

Irish Tune from County Derry (1902–11) [3'38"]. Australian Youth Orchestra (John Hopkins, conductor). Schott. 13 July 1970.   *HMV disc SOELP/9721*

Irish Tune from County Derry (1902–11). Stokowski's Symphony Orchestra (Leopold Stokowski, conductor).   *RCA-Victor disc LM/1238*

Irish Tune from County Derry (1902–11). Eastman Rochester Pops Orchestra (Frederick Fennell, conductor).   *Mercury disc CDS/1495*

Irish Tune from County Derry (1902–11) [3'31"]. Percy Grainger (piano; duo-art piano roll).   *Everest disc X-913*

Handel in the Strand (1912) [4'14"]. Sydney Symphony Orchestra (Joseph Post, conductor). Schott.   *ABC recording PRS/1653*

Handel in the Strand (1912) [4'12"]. Sydney Symphony Orchestra (John Hopkins, conductor). Schott. 27 July 1971.   *World Record Club disc S/5257*

Handel in the Strand (1912). Percy Grainger (piano). Strings of Stokowski's Symphony Orchestra (Leopold Stokowski, conductor).   *RCA-Victor disc LM/1238*

Handel in the Strand (1912). Eastman Rochester Pops Orchestra (Frederick Fennell, conductor).
Mercury disc CDS/495
Handel in the Strand (1912) [4'02"]. Cyril Smith and Phyllis Sellick (pianos). 1966. *HMV disc CLP/3563*
Colonial Song (1911–12) [6'36"]. Joan Dargavel (soprano), Lance Stirling (tenor), Melbourne Symphony Orchestra (John Hopkins, conductor). Schott. 29 Sept. 1967. *ABC recording RRCS/131*
Colonial Song (1911–12) [6'30"]. Pearl Berridge (soprano), David Parker (tenor), Sydney Symphony Orchestra (John Hopkins, conductor). Schott. Feb. 1972. *World Record Club disc S/5257*
Colonial Song (1911–12) [5'23"]. Percy Grainger (piano; duo-art piano roll). *Everest disc X-913*
Colonial Song (1911–12). Eastman Rochester Pops Orchestra (Frederick Fennell, conductor)
Mercury disc CDS/495
Molly on the Shore [3'20"]. Sydney Symphony Orchestra (Joseph Post, conductor). Schott.
ABC recording PRS/1653
Molly on the Shore. Stokowski's Symphony Orchestra (Leopold Stokowski, conductor).
RCA-Victor disc LM/1238
Molly on the Shore. Eastman Rochester Pops Orchestra (Frederick Fennell, conductor).
Mercury disc CDS/1495
Molly on the Shore. Percy Grainger (piano; duo-art piano roll). *Everest disc X-913*
Shallow Brown [4'35"]. Brian Hansford (baritone), male voices of the Kenneth Taylor Singers, Melbourne Symphony Orchestra (John Hopkins, conductor). Schott, 29 Sept. 1967. *ABC recording RRCS/131*
Shallow Brown [5'31"]. John Shirley-Quirk (baritone), male voices of the Ambrosian Singers, English Chamber Orchestra (Benjamin Britten, conductor).
Decca disc SXLA/6410
Shallow Brown [4'30"]. Christopher Field (baritone), male voices of the Oriana Singers, Sydney Symphony Orchestra (John Hopkins, conductor). Schirmer. 22 Feb. 1971. *World Record Club disc S/5257*
Spoon River (1920–29) [4'10"]. Melbourne Symphony Orchestra (John Hopkins, conductor). Schirmer.
ABC recording RRCS/131
Spoon River (1920–29) [2'10"]. Percy Grainger (piano; duo-art piano roll). *Everest disc X-913*
Spoon River (1920–29). Eastman Rochester Pops Orchestra (Frederick Fennell, conductor).
Mercury disc CDS/1495
Green Bushes (1905–06) [8'08"]. Melbourne Symphony Orchestra (John Hopkins, conductor). Schott, 29 Sept. 1967. *ABC recording RRCS/131*
Green Bushes (1905–06) [8'13"]. Melbourne Symphony Orchestra (John Hopkins, conductor).
HMV disc OASD/7554
Shepherd's Hey (1908–13) [2'12"]. English Chamber Orchestra (Benjamin Britten, conductor).
Decca disc SXLA/6410
Shepherd's Hey (1908–13). New Symphony Orchestra (Anthony Collins, conductor).
W & G disc ACL/108
Shepherd's Hey (1908–13). Stokowski's Symphony Orchestra (Leopold Stokowski, conductor).
RCA-Victor disc LM/1238

Shepherd's Hey (1908–13). Eastman Rochester Pops Orchestra (Frederick Fennell, conductor).
Mercury disc CDS/1495
Shepherd's Hey (1908–13) [2'03"]. Percy Grainger (piano; duo-art piano roll). *Everest disc X-913*
Hill Song No. 2 (1901–07) [4'49"]. Melbourne Symphony Orchestra (John Hopkins, conductor). Leeds. 29 Sept. 1967. *ABC recording RRCS/131*
Hill Song No. 2 (1901–07) [5'45"]. Eastman Rochester Pops Orchestra (Frederick Fennell, conductor).
Mercury disc MG/90388
The Warriors (1913–16) [18'50"]. Melbourne Symphony Orchestra (John Hopkins, conductor). Schott. 22 Sept. 1967. *ABC recording RRCS/131*
The Immovable Do (1933–39) [5'15"]. Sydney Symphony Orchestra (Joseph Post, conductor). Schirmer. 21 Sept. 1971. *ABC tape*
Children's March: Over the Hills and Far Away [6'33"]. Sydney Symphony Orchestra (John Hopkins, conductor). Schirmer. 16 Aug. 1971.
World Record Club disc S/5257
Children's March: Over the Hills and Far Away. Eastman Rochester Pops Orchestra (Frederick Fennell, conductor). *Mercury disc CDS/1495*
Under en Bro [3'45"]. Lauris Elms (contralto). Ronal Jackson (baritone). Sydney Symphony Orchestra (John Hopkins, conductor) MS. 6 May 1971.
World Record Club disc S/5257
Country Gardens (1908–50) [2'08"]. Sydney Symphony Orchestra (John Hopkins, conductor). Schirmer. 27 July 1971. *World Record Club disc S/5257*
Country Gardens (1908–50) [1'40"]. Percy Grainger (piano; duo-art piano roll). *Everest disc X-913*
Country Gardens (1908–50). Stokowski's Symphony Orchestra (Leopold Stokowski, conductor).
RCA-Victor disc LM/1238
Country Gardens (1908–50). Eastman Rochester Pops Orchestra (Frederick Fennell, conductor).
Mercury disc CDS/1495
Harvest Hymn (1905–32) [3'43"]. Strings of the Sydney Symphony Orchestra (John Hopkins, conductor). Schirmer. 16 Aug. 1971.
World Record Club disc S/5257
Harvest Hymn (1905–32) [3'23"]. Wind, harmonium, piano, horn, trumpet, string sextet from the Sydney Symphony Orchestra (John Hopkins, conductor). Schirmer. 16 Aug. 1971.
Duke of Marlborough Fanfare [2'05"]. Brass of the Sydney Symphony Orchestra (John Hopkins, conductor). Schott. 5 May 1971.
World Record Club disc S/5257
Duke of Marlborough Fanfare [2'12"]. English Chamber Orchestra (Benjamin Britten, conductor).
Decca disc SXLA/6410
Scottish Strathspey and Reel (1901–11) [7'50"]. Male voices of the Oriana Singers, Sydney Symphony Orchestra (John Hopkins, conductor). Schott. 22 Feb. 1971. *World Record Club disc S/5257*
The Lonely Desert Man sees the Tents of the Happy Tribes (1911–49) [3'00"]. Pearl Berridge (soprano), David Parker (tenor), Ronal Jackson (baritone). Sydney Symphony Orchestra (John Hopkins, conductor). MS. 9 Feb. 1972.
World Record Club disc S/5257

The Valley of the Bells (orchestration of Ravel's *La Vallée des cloches*) [5'20"]. Sydney Symphony Orchestra (John Hopkins, conductor). Durand. 9 Feb. 1972.   *World Record Club disc S/5257*

Willow-willow (1902–11) [3'58"]. Peter Pears (tenor), English Chamber Orchestra (Benjamin Britten, conductor).   *Decca disc SCLA/6410*

I'm Seventeen Come Sunday [2'54"]. Peter Pears (tenor), Ambrosian Singers, English Chamber Orchestra (Benjamin Britten, conductor).
                         Decca disc SXLA/6410

Psalm XLVII ('O Clap Your Hands') (1958) [3'17"]. Adelaide Singers (Patrick Thomas, conductor). Leeds.   *ABC recording PRX/5600*

Lord Maxwell's Good Night [3'24"]. John Shirley-Quirk (baritone), English Chamber Orchestra (Benjamin Britten, conductor).   *Decca disc SXLA/6410*

The Lost Lady Found [2'48"]. Ambrosian Singers, English Chamber Orchestra (Benjamin Britten, conductor).   *Decca disc SXLA/6410*

Lisbon [1'21"]. Members of the English Chamber Orchestra (Benjamin Britten, conductor).
                         Decca disc SXLA/6410

Walking Tune (1900–05). Philadelphia Wind Quintet.
                         Columbia disc MS/6584

Lincolnshire Posy (1906–37). Eastman Rochester Wind Ensemble (Frederick Fennell, conductor).
                         Mercury disc MG/90173

Lads of Wamphray March (1904–05). The Goldman Band.   *W & G disc DL/8931*

Faeroe Island Dance. Cornell Wind Ensemble (Smith, conductor).   *Cornell University recording no. 8*

Early One Morning. Stokowski's Symphony Orchestra (Leopold Stokowski, conductor).
                    RCA-Victor recording LM/1238

Let's Dance in the Green Meadow [3'00"]. Benjamin Britten, Viola Tunnard (pianos).
                         Decca disc SXLA/6410

Leprechaun's Dance [2'49"]. Percy Grainger (piano; duo-art piano roll).   *Everest disc X-913*

Sussex Mummers' Christmas Carol [2'32"]. Percy Grainger (piano; duo-art piano roll).
                         Everest disc X-913

Australian Up-country Song (1905–28) [2'08"]. Adelaide Singers (Patrick Thomas, conductor). Allan. 2 Aug. 1970.   *ABC tape*

There Was a Pig [1'54"]. Ambrosian Singers (Benjamin Britten, conductor).   *Decca disc SXLA/6410*

Brigg Fair. Elizabethan Singers (Louis Halsey, conductor).   *Argo disc ZRG/5496*

Bold William Taylor. Peter Pears (tenor), Benjamin Britten (piano).   *Argo disc ZRG/5439*

Bold William Taylor [3'34"]. John Shirley-Quirk (baritone), English Chamber Orchestra (Benjamin Britten, conductor).   *Decca disc SXLA/6410*

Two songs: *The Pretty Maid Milking the Cow, The Sprig of Thyme* [3'55"]. Peter Pears (tenor), Benjamin Britten (piano).   *Decca disc SXLA/6410*

Margaret Sutherland

(*b.* 1897)

Laughton Harris

Now one of Australia's senior composers, Margaret Sutherland has played a vital role in the developing tradition of composition in her country. She was one of the first of a generation of Australian composers whose music seemed to break through the inertia of dependence on an outworn nineteenth-century musical tradition, showing a new awareness of the sound world of the post-Debussyan era. Her creative vigour, apparent as early as her Sonata for Violin and Piano 1925, has given heart to many a young composer, as has her lifelong involvement in the performance and promotion of new music.

Margaret Sutherland's creative development has been in many ways a sad reflection of the lot of Australian composers in the first half of this century, when problems of an indifferent public and profound sense of isolation were magnified many times over. Scores and performances of many key twentieth-century works were scarcely less difficult for composers to obtain than performances of their own work, of which there was a mere trickle. Little wonder that many left Australia to work out their artistic salvation in the United States, England or on the Continent. Commissions were rare indeed, and one of Margaret Sutherland's last completed works, her String Quartet (1967), was unbelievably her first work to be commissioned. For a woman to achieve professional standing as a composer in Australia was of course almost unheard of. Yet this was the goal Margaret Sutherland pursued with sure-footed conviction, and apart from two brief periods abroad, in 1923 and 1951, her battle was on the home ground, in Melbourne.

Against such odds, Margaret Sutherland's remarkable achievement owes much to her family background, extensive musical experience from an early age and, above all, the vivid world of her own musical imagination, fed by an acutely perceptive ear.

Born in Adelaide in 1897, Margaret Sutherland went to Melbourne with her family four years later when her father George Sutherland was appointed leader writer on the *Age*. Both her parents were keen amateur musicians and almost all the Melbourne branch of the Sutherland family was involved in music or the arts. It was a family environment which could scarcely have been more favourable for the development of her musical gifts.

In 1914 scholarships in composition and piano took her to the Albert Street (Marshall Hall) Conservatorium to which Marshall Hall was reappointed as director in January of that year. Despite his untimely death after barely six months in office, Marshall Hall's stimulating influence remained with Margaret Sutherland, as did that of her piano teacher Edward Goll who founded his master school of pianoforte playing at the University Conservatorium in 1914.

A different formative influence was provided by Henri Verbrugghen, the Belgian conductor and violinist who was appointed to the State Conservatorium in Sydney in 1916. Verbrugghen's frequent concert tours to Melbourne with his String Quartet stimulated Margaret Sutherland's interest in chamber music, a field in which she has been most notably successful as a composer. Certainly the impact of live musical performance loomed much larger in her life than any formal study of harmony or counterpoint at the Conservatorium, formidable as was its reputation for imparting such mysteries.

By the early 1920s Margaret Sutherland had decided that for her composition mattered above everything, and that the psychological and physical demands on a concert pianist were not to be compared with the deeper satisfactions of fashioning her own sound world. 'To pluck music from the air ... that was what made my heart beat faster. And that was what I longed passionately to have time and opportunity to do.'[1]

In 1923 she left Australia for a period of two years, spent largely in Paris, Vienna and London, attending concerts, writing music and above all, listening. But a profound nostalgia for her country remained, and she returned to Australia with some relief in 1925, her musical horizons immeasurably widened. While in London she studied composition with Arnold Bax and completed a Sonata for Violin and Piano which was later published in 1935. Bax's remark that this work was 'the best sonata he had seen composed by a woman' seems now a little two-edged. Certainly Margaret Sutherland was to suffer increasingly a feeling of discrimination against herself as a woman composer, and perhaps with some justification.

The pungent quartal harmony of the Violin Sonata anticipates her later style. In its slow movement the recurrence of a haunting four-bar theme against an ever-changing harmonic background is the first of many highlights in her work achieved by the simplest of means. Above all, the remarkable cogency of this work already reflects the composer's capacity for deep assimilation of her musical material.

From an early stage Margaret Sutherland became aware of the important role of what she called 'chant intérieur' in her whole creative process. She later gave a vivid account of her experience of this phenomenon:

> Many composers are almost at the mercy of insistent chant intérieur ... It is as if the composer who has developed the art of dealing with floating ideas (taking them, shaping them, giving them a home and an identity) has to pay the penalty for having them constantly at his door. They are like mendicants who have put a cross on his gate for others to follow in their footsteps. They come in scores, begging him to do for them what he has done for their forerunners, any time of day or night; they are no respecters of visiting hours ... they are rough-hewn, crude and unfinished. The composer reverts to them as a French polisher will give a rub to his latest piece of work, or a gardener will pull out a few weeds. They are with him constantly, jogging his elbow, prodding him ... he is in fact their slave in a sense, and how they know it! Composing then is ... a form of intuition. It is a sudden awareness of something newer and more vital, or more arresting about one of the floating images of the chant interieur.[2]

But it was some years before the early promise of her Violin Sonata was to be fulfilled. Her marriage in 1926, and the demands of a growing family of two children, gave less time for composition. In fact it was not until after 1948, when she and her husband had parted, that her composition blossomed with renewed vigour in the most productive phase of her life.

In the meantime Margaret Sutherland resumed piano teaching and continued to take an active part in chamber music. During the 1939–45 war she became a member for the Council for Education, Music and the Arts, and for many years was on the Australian UNESCO Music Committee. As a council member for the National Gallery Society, Margaret Sutherland played a key role in 1943–4 in the promotion of a plan for the Victorian Arts Centre, a vision she has had the satisfaction of seeing materialize only in the last few years.

The works written during the period before 1948 include the orchestral *Suite on a Theme of Purcell* (1939), a Concerto for Strings (1945), several song cycles, piano music, and of course much chamber music. Margaret Sutherland has had little patience for the vogue of what she called 'dressed up English folk song' so fashionable in the years between the wars. Instead, for her first orchestral work she turned to Purcell whose rich harmonic language and telling use of dissonance she much admired. The opening bars of a 'Ground for harpsichord' in Purcell's *Musick's Handmaid* (1689) provide a point of departure for all seven movements which make up the suite: theme, variation, scherzo, air, gigue, passacaglia and finale. Related to her love of Purcell is also a fascination for passacaglic structures and associated procedures which result in some of the most original passages in her music, as in the following extract from the 6th movement of her Suite. Here the wayward chromaticism of the oboe and cor anglais parts produces an intriguing slanting of the E minor tonality.

Fig. 7 Passacaglia, from *Suite on a Theme of Purcell*, Bars 18–22

There is a strong flow of musical ideas in these works of the thirties and forties, along with a classical concern for the all-pervasive development of the motivic material. This is nowhere better illustrated than in the early songs. Behind the apparent simplicity of her *Five Songs* (1936) the musical thought is elegantly controlled and concentrated. Certainly what gives many of these works a personal stamp is the strong and individual thrust of the harmony, and tonally based as much of her work tends to be, the new and subtle ways in which tonal ambiguities are set up. The vacillating resolution of the closing bars of the first movement of the Concerto for Strings (1945) antedates by several years a rather similar alternation at the conclusion of Vaughan Williams's Sixth Symphony. It would be strange indeed if, as in the String Quartet (1939), echoes from Debussy, Stravinsky and Bartok were not occasionally to be heard. The remarkable fact is that Margaret Sutherland managed to use so many of the current techniques, including bitonality, added note clusters, fourth chords and inflected scales, in fresh and original ways. Nor need we wonder at the thirty years time-lag for such influences to reach Australian shores when a similar period has been cited for musical influences to cross the English Channel— in a westerly direction!

The years following a brief trip to England in 1951 were particularly fruitful. The bulk of Margaret Sutherland's major orchestral compositions were completed in the next decade, and range over a wide variety of familiar forms, yet always with an individual voice. They include a tone poem *The Haunted Hills*, a much neglected Violin Concerto, the Concerto Grosso for strings, keyboard and percussion, and an orchestral suite, *Three Temperaments*, the last-named providing an interesting cross-section of the composer's mature style. Her handling of the orchestra has a well-considered clarity and economy in which individual timbres are often highlighted and deftly contrasted. Characteristic also is the lithe and linear tendency of many of the musical ideas, and above all the remarkable capacity for well-focused musical argument. In the first movement the composer's imagination is kindled yet again by the use of *ostinato*. The poignant lyricism of the second movement recalls movements in similar vein in the Violin Concerto and the Concerto Grosso, while the swiftly moving canonic textures of the third movement provide a brilliant conclusion to the cycle.

Margaret Sutherland's mature style of the fifties and sixties shows a growing concern for economy and coherence. Her keyboard and chamber music of this period is at its best when she is wringing the utmost from the smallest segment of her musical material. The piano pieces, *Chiaroscuro I and II*, and *Voices I and II* (1968) are tautly constructed by means of continuous variation and expansion of a few terse melodic-rhythmic cells whose structure is typified in the closing bars of *Voices II* (Fig. 8). Here the main motivic material of the movement (a, b and c) is briefly restated in its simplest terms.

Fig. 8 *Voices II*, Bars 89–93

In *Extension* (1967) fragments which have been developed in turn converge on a theme that pays homage to Bartók:

Fig. 9 *Extension*, Bars 82–85

In 1964 Margaret Sutherland completed her chamber opera, *The Young Kabbarli*, which was first performed in Hobart in the following year. Its theme, the conflicting worlds of Aboriginal and European, is conveyed by abrupt mosaic-like juxtapositions of the musical material, including the use of such disparate elements as the didjeridu and Irish folk melody. Scored for an orchestra of two flutes, two oboes, bassoon, horn, percussion, piano, viola and double bass, the opera's spare but telling instrumental textures reflect Margaret Sutherland's lifelong involvement with chamber music.

The *Six Australian Songs* (1967)—settings of poems by Judith Wright—show the same motivic concentration of her later piano works. Here too is the individual and at times immensely imaginative harmonic style which takes her to the brink of atonality. It was the composer's intention that the voice be integrated into the texture as a whole, though never submerged: 'the voice takes its place in the web'.[3] These settings, like so many of her earlier songs, are both well wrought and sensitive. Their changing moods match well the sense and rhythm of the words.

Margaret Sutherland was virtually untouched by the wave of serialism that caught up so many of her colleagues in the late fifties. Her approach to tonality, however, has always been somewhat ambivalent, and in her later works an increasing tonal freedom can be seen. In her *Blake Songs* (1950) the effect of what she refers to as 'telescoped tonalities' is achieved by means of polytonal inflection of the harmony and also by an alternating resolution in the closing bars of the first song of the cycle, 'Memory, hither come'. This latter technique occurs fairly commonly throughout her later work.[4] Certainly tonality is left far behind at the conclusion of her second string quartet, *Discussion*, when the individual strands move rapidly through a cycle of fourths in closely packed imitation.

Fig. 10 String Quartet no. 2, *Discussion*, Bars 322–325

The slow movement of her String Quartet (1967) is one of Margaret Sutherland's most freely chromatic movements. It is also one of the most assured and eloquently expressive movements of her output.

Fig. 11 String Quartet no. 3, opening bars of second movement

In 1969 Margaret Sutherland was awarded an honorary Doctorate of Music from the University of Melbourne in recognition of her contribution to Australian music. Commonwealth recognition came in the following year when she received an O.B.E. For much of her life Margaret Sutherland has been in the vanguard of composers who, in spite of the cultural youth and isolation of their country, came to terms with some of the main musical currents of the first half of this century. At a time when the transplanted European musical culture seemed in danger of stagnation, theirs was an uphill task which required not only real creative gifts, but courage, persistence and determination as well. All these Margaret Sutherland possessed in full measure.

Notes

1. Margaret Sutherland, 'Young days in music', *Overland*, Dec. 1968, p. 27.
2. J.D. Garretty, Three Australian Composers, M.A. thesis (University of Melbourne, 1963), p. 55.
3. *ibid.*
4. Compare also the closing bars of: Concerto for Strings, 1st movt; 'Winter Kestrel' from *Six Australian Songs* (1967); 'The oceans clapped their hands' from *A Company of Carols* (1966) and *Voices II* (see Fig. 8).

Select Bibliography

Covell, Roger. *Australia's Music: Themes of a New Society*, Sun Books, Melbourne, 1967, pp. 152–4, p. 261.

McCredie, Andrew. *Musical Composition in Australia*. Advisory Board, Commonwealth Assistance to Australian Composers, Canberra, 1969, pp. 8–10.

Murdoch, James. *Australian Composers*. Macmillan, Melbourne, 1972, pp. 181–6.

Sinclair, J. 'Margaret Sutherland—Australian Composer', *Australian Journal of Music Education*, April 1969, pp. 57–8.

Sutherland, Margaret. 'Young days in music', *Overland*, Dec. 1968.

List of works

Opera
The Young Kabbarli (Casey) (in one act) (1965)

Ballet
Dithyramb (short ballet for pf; orchestrated ?1941) (1937)
The Selfish Giant

Incidental Music
Incidental Music to *A Midsummer Night's Dream*

Orchestral Music (see also Ballet)
Pavan (1938)
Prelude and Jig for str (1939)
Suite on a Theme of Purcell (1939)
Concertino for pf and orch (1940)
Concerto for str (1945)
Rondel (1945)
Adagio for 2 v and orch (1946) (see also Chamber Music)
Threesome for junior orchestra (1947)
Ballad Overture for junior orchestra (1948)
Four Symphonic Concepts (Studies) (1949) (movements subsequently performed under the titles *Triptych* and *Vistas*)
Bush Ballad (?1950)
The Haunted Hills (1950)
Open Air Piece (1953)
Violin Concerto (1954)
Concerto Grosso (1955)
Outdoor Overture (1958)
Three Temperaments (1958)

Movement (1959)
Concertante for ob str and perc (1961)
Fantasy for v and orch (1962) (see also Chamber Music)

Chamber Music
Sonata for v and pf (1925; publ. Paris, 1935)
Trio for cl va and pf (1934)
Fantasy Sonatina for sax and pf (?1935)
House Quartet for cl (or v) va hn (or vc) and pf (1936)
Rhapsody for v and pf (1938)
String Quartet no. 1 (?1939)
Sonata for vc (or sax) and pf (1942)
Ballad and Nocturne for v and pf (both 1944: originally coupled—later separated)
Adagio and Allegro giocoso for 2 v and pf (?1945) (see also Orchestral Music)
Sonata for cl (or va) and pf (1949)
Trio for ob and 2 v (1951; publ. Melbourne 1951)
Contrasts for 2 v (1953)
Discussion (String Quartet no. 2) (1954)
Quartet for Eng hn and str (1955)
Six Bagatelles for v and va (1956)
Sonatina for ob (or v) and pf (?1957; publ. Melbourne 1958)
Divertimento for str trio (1958)
Little Suite for wind trio (?1960)
Fantasy for v and pf (?1960) (see also Orchestral Music)
String Quartet no. 3 (1967)
Quartet for cl and str (1967)
Simple string pieces for school class work (publ. Sydney 1967)

Piano Music (see also Ballet)
Burlesque (2 pf) (?1927)
Two Chorale Preludes on Bach's Chorales (publ. Melbourne 1935)
First Suite (publ. Melbourne 1937)
Second Suite (publ. Melbourne 1937)
Miniature Ballet Suite (publ. Melbourne 1937)
Miniature Sonata (?1939; publ. Melbourne 1940)
Six Profiles (?1946)
Sonatina (publ. Melbourne 1956)
Pavan (2 pf) (publ. Melbourne 1957) (see also *Three Temperaments* for orch)
Canonical Piece (2 pf) (publ. Melbourne 1957)
Sonata (publ. Melbourne 1966)
Extension (1967)
Chiaroscuro I and *II* (1968)
Voices I and *II* (1968)
Miscellaneous short teaching pieces

Harpsichord Music
Three Pieces

Choral Music
The Passing for SATB and orch (?1939)
A Company of Carols (Bassett, Casey, Dobson, Lindsay (2)) for SATB and pf (1966)
Miscellaneous short settings (unison, 2 and 3 part women's and girls' voices and SATB) of Austin, Cuthbertson, Garran, Lewis, Martyr, Palmer (2), Shaw Neilson (4), Sutherland, Wolfe (2) and Wright.

All SATB items unaccompanied: most of the remainder with pf.

Vocal Music (voice and pf unless otherwise indicated)
Songs for Children (Martyr) (?1929)
Three Songs (Thompson) for voice, v and pf (1930)
Five Songs (Shaw Neilson) (1936; publ. London 1948)
The Gentle Water Bird (Shaw Neilson) for voice, v (or ob) and pf
The Orange Tree (Shaw Neilson) for voice, cl and pf (?1938; publ. Melbourne 1954)
Four Blake Songs (?1950)
The World and the Child (Wright) for mezzo sop and pf or str quartet (1960)
Sequence of Verse into Music (Casey) for speaker, fl, va and bn (1964)
Six Australian Songs (Wright) (1967; publ. Melbourne 1967)
Miscellaneous settings (c 1925–c 1950) of anon., E. Brontë (2), Esson, Flecker, Hunt, Landor, Levy (2), Martyr (2), Shakespeare (2), Shaw Neilson, Stewart, Thompson, Wilmot and Wright
Arrangements of old Australian bush ballads (14) (trad: collected Palmer) (publ. Melbourne 1950).

Acknowledgement is made to David Symons who generously made available the list of Margaret Sutherland's works which he has recently compiled.

Discography

The Young Kabbarli. New Opera of South Australia (Patrick Thomas, conductor).
        EMI disc Q4OASO—7569
Dithyramb (1937). Australian Youth Orchestra (Sir Bernard Heinze, conductor).
        Philips disc S/10839/L
The Haunted Hills (1950). Melbourne Symphony Orchestra (John Hopkins, conductor).
        Festival disc SFC 800/20
Concerto Grosso (1958). Sybil Copeland (violin), John Glickman (viola) Max Cooke (harpsichord), Strings of Melbourne Symphony Orchestra (John Hopkins, conductor).   *ABC recording RRCS/387*
Three Temperaments (1964). Melbourne Symphony Orchestra (John Hopkins, conductor).
        ABC recording RRCS/145
Sonata for clarinet and piano. Jack Harrison (clarinet), Stephen Dornan (piano).
        Festival disc SFC 800/25
Trio (1954). Jiri Tancibudek (oboe), Sybil Copeland (violin), John Glickman (viola).
        Brolga disc BXM-02
Six Bagatelles (1956). Sybil Copeland (violin), John Glickman (violin).   *W & G disc AL/660*

The following works have been recorded either on disc or tape by the A.B.C. These discs are available only in approved circumstances (for use in educational institutions, diplomatic and Broadcasting Union exchanges and internal A.B.C. usage). They cannot be purchased commercially.

Suite on a Theme of Purcell. Melbourne Symphony Orchestra (John Hopkins, conductor).
Outdoor Overture. Queensland Symphony Orchestra (Patrick Thomas, conductor).
Concerto for strings. Strings of the Queensland Symphony Orchestra (Patrick Thomas, conductor).
Sinfonia Concertante for oboe and strings. Jiri Tancibudek (oboe), Melbourne Symphony Orchestra (Patrick Thomas, conductor).
Concerto for violin and orchestra. Leonard Dommett (violin), Melbourne Symphony Orchestra (Patrick Thomas, conductor).
Discussion for string quartet (1954). [7'30"]. Walter Gerhadt, Harold Fairhurst (violins), David Powell (viola), Ernest Greaves (cello). MS. 1959.
        ABC recording PRX/4389 (ABR only)
Quartet for cor anglais and string trio (1956) [15'00"]. Walter Gerhadt, Harold Fairhurst (violins), David Powell (viola), Ernest Greaves (cello). MS. 1959.
        ABC recording PRX/4389 (ABR only)
Sonata for viola and piano (1949). [8'49"]. John Glickman (viola), Margaret Sutherland (piano). MS.
        ABC recording PRX/5598 (ABR only)
The Gentle Water Bird [3'53"]. Muriel Luyk (mezzo soprano), Sybil Copeland (violin), Margaret Sutherland (piano). MS. 1959.
        ABC recording PR/2971 (ABR only)
Four Blake Songs [9'10"]. (i) Memory hither come—1'15"; (ii) Piping down the valleys wild—1'39"; (iii) How sweet I roamed—2'34"; (iv) The jocund dance—1'12". Muriel Luyk (mezzo soprano), Margaret Sutherland (piano). MS. 1959.
        ABC recording PR/2971 (ABR only)
Miscellaneous Songs [9'49"]. (i) The old prison—3'33"; (ii) Winter kestrel—1'27", (iii) How sweet I roamed—2'59"; (iv) Piping down the valleys wild—1'50". Muriel Luyk (mezzo soprano), Margaret Sutherland (piano). O.U.P.
        ABC recording RRC/69 (ABR only)
Miscellaneous Songs [6'54"]. (i) For a child—1'28"; (ii) In the dim countries—1'58"; (iii) May—1'58"; (iv) Song be delicate—1'30". Muriel Luyk (mezzo soprano), Margaret Sutherland (piano).
        ABC recording PRX/5597 (ABR only)
Extension (1967) [6'15"].
Voices I (1968) [5'25"].
Voices II (1968) [4'20"].
Chiaroscuro I (1968) [5'15"].
Chiaroscuro II (1968) [5'00"]. Stephen McIntyre (piano). 6 September 1971   *ABC tape*
Sonatina for violin and piano [6'30"]. Beryl Kimber (violin), Margaret Sutherland (piano). 1959.
        ABC recording PRX/4389 (ABR only)
Adagio and Allegro [6'15"]. John Glickman, Sybil Copeland (violins), Margaret Sutherland (piano). MS.   *ABC recording PRX/5598* (ABR only)

Clive Douglas
(1903—77)

Gregg W. Howard

The music of Clive Douglas in large part exemplifies the self-conscious search for a uniquely Australian musical identity, a concern which was to some extent shared by most other Australian composers in the period from the thirties to the late fifties (although none emulated Douglas's thoroughgoing commitment to this search). This preoccupation has now waned, however, and in the mid-sixties the internationalist banner was raised aloft and borne along by a new generation of Australian composers to whom such a concern appeared conservative and parochial. Douglas has given expression to this concern in his writings as well as in his music:

> The absence of a national music adds to the difficulties which confront an Australian composer who attempts to infuse his music with a recognizable Australian identity ... A musical idiom must be found which is so entirely Australian that no other influence can be felt ... [I]n the mystical 'dream-time' of antiquity can be found the all important link—the tribal ceremonial chants of the brown man [i.e., Aboriginal].[1]

It is in his attempts to apply this solution in his work that Douglas makes his most interesting contribution to Australia's musical history, and at the same time leaves himself most open to attack on theoretical grounds, for in so doing, he casts his lot with Jindyworobakism and is thus vulnerable to the general objections to that cultural movement.

Jindyworobakism developed as a literary-nationalist movement in the forties and attempted to breathe new life into Australian writing through an identification of literary subjects with indigenous Aboriginal traditions and myth, and through a closer identification with the unique Australian landscape. The movement was short-lived, for its theoretical basis was insecure and the products of its creative efforts failed to excite general literary admiration. In objection to the movement, it is arguable that the identification of white, middle-class Europeans with the complex and perhaps even psychologically inaccessible culture of the Australian Aboriginals could not hope to be other than superficial and culturally exploitative. The presence of a European population in Australia for less than two hundred years, most of which period was spent in conflict with or general ignorance of the 'alien culture' of the

Aboriginals was hardly an auspicious basis for cultural identification. The same theoretical objection may be directed at Jindyworobakism in music.

Douglas identifies himself with this cultural movement through his use of Aboriginal myth and legend as the programmatic basis for works such as the early operetta *Kaditcha* (1938), through the programmatic use of episodes in Australian history, as in *Sturt 1829* (1952), and in weaving melodic and rhythmic material of Aboriginal derivation into the musical fabric of works like the tone poem *Carwoola* (1939) and the symphony *Namatjira* (1956). In addition, *Terra Australis* exemplifies the interest of the composer in evoking in tonal terms the spirit and antiquity of the Australian outback centre and its landscape.

It is in his attempt at absorbing Aboriginal musical elements into symphonic music, however, that Douglas explores the most radical and perhaps controversial possibility in Jindyworobak music. As late as 1967 Roger Covell admitted this possibility in discussing potential sources of influence on Australian music:

> The value of Aboriginal music as a source for Australian composers will not lie in direct imitation but in the assimilation of those elements of it—notably of rhythm, scale structure and microtonal intervals—which seem to explore territories of music relatively untouched by the standard varieties of European music.[2]

Covell's meaning is somewhat unclear for he does not seem to be arguing for the use of *recognizably* Aboriginal elements ('assimilation' rules this out), and yet, if the influence of the elements of rhythm, scale structure, and interval is to be *un*-recognizably Aboriginal, one is justified in asking how the use of such elements will differ in any significant sense from the standard practice of contemporary composers, for whom the investigation of the whole gamut of musical materials provides the means of compositional innovation and development (as was already the case in 1967 when Covell wrote). In short, it is arguable that contemporary composers have nothing to learn about musical materials from Aboriginal musical practice. Similarly, objection can be made to the practice of Douglas in incorporating Aboriginal melodic and rhythmic elements into his music simply on the grounds that despite the efforts to which the composer has gone, the aural result is generally not recognizably different in quality from that achieved by the exponents of European primitivism in the early part of this century. The same rhythmic and melodic materials were accessible to them sixty years ago, and the fact that they were rediscovered in Australia in mid-century does not *per se* endow them with any deeper cultural attachment or more specific national flavour than at the time of the inception of their European use. Thus, for example, the *ostinato*-like motives which are to be found in *Namatjira* (Figs 12 and 13) can not be said to contribute to the music anything distinctively Australian or Aboriginal despite their indigenous origin.

Three possible consequences may result from the attempt to incorporate Aboriginal musical elements into Western art music: (1) the derived material may be so abstracted from its original form as to lose its recognizable identity; (2) in an attempt to accommodate this fact, the composer may contrive the musical expression to the extent that the derived material is caricatured; and (3) the material may be allowed to retain its recognizable identity and is 'framed' by rather than integrated into the musical fabric. (George Dreyfus's recent Sextet for didjeridu and Wind Quintet could be regarded as falling into this last category.) The results of Douglas's use of

Aboriginal music are generally consistent with the first of these three alternative possibilities.

Fig. 12 From *Namatjira*

Fig. 13 From *Namatjira*

For the sake of completeness, it should be added that in the political climate of the early seventies, the ideological implications of the use of Aboriginal music for the purpose of Western composition can no longer be disregarded as they were in less politically sensitive periods; and for this reason alone, it is unlikely that thoughtful composers will seek in future to exploit Aboriginal culture as a source of musical materials.

The search for Australian musical identity as exemplified by Douglas's work has been dwelt upon because it is the most characteristic and individual feature of this composer's music. Clive Douglas, however, had a productive compositional life stretching from the mid-thirties and thus his music exhibits a variety of other interests and directions, the most recent of which suggests an abandonment of his former preoccupations. It must be said, though, that in general all his work displays a structural weakness which is often insufficiently compensated for by his skill and imagination as an orchestrator. This fact may throw some light on his interest in programmatic writing (which interpreted broadly, makes up the bulk of his musical output), for a programme to a large extent independently determines the dramatic structure of a work (albeit not always successfully). *Sturt 1829* is an example. It is programmatic in the sense that it presents a tableau-like series of musical impressions of the major events of Charles Sturt's epic journey to the mouth of the Murray River. In his attempt to sketch musically scenes and events, and to develop literal associations with the historical story, Douglas has lost the sense of musical relationship of one part to another. The sections are inadequately delineated thematically and in terms of their dramatic function. The result is a work in which the range of dramatic expression is too consistently narrow and this is in part a consequence of the absence of thematic or motivic material with potential for development and transformation. A brief examination of some of the characteristic features of this work will serve to illustrate these points and give the reader some appreciation of Douglas's style and compositional procedure.

Perhaps the most initially striking feature of the work is Douglas's extensive use of rhythmic *ostinato*. The work opens with an *ostinato* accompaniment (in lower woodwinds, brass, and lower strings) to a sinuous solo flute theme (Fig. 14). Such regular, pulsing figures return frequently throughout the work, generally serving as accompaniment to freer material, and often relegated to brass and lower woodwind. Syncopated effects are frequently applied (Figs. 15 and 16). Regrettably, the

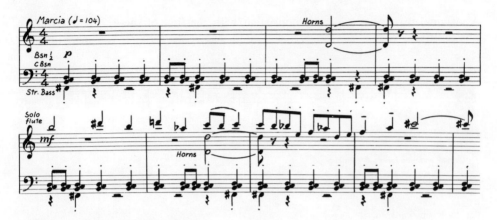

Fig. 14 *Sturt 1829*, extract from Bars 1–9

Fig. 15 Extract from Bars 54–57

Fig. 16 Extract from Section 15, Bars 9–12

composer's reliance on simple rhythmic *ostinato* tends to produce throughout the work a rhythmic sameness, a feeling of inevitability rather than surprise. In much the same way, melodic and harmonic materials are limited in their effectiveness by over use. The strongly chromatic but rhythmically square opening flute theme (Fig. 14) is the archetype of melody in this work, returning again and again in varied forms but always retaining the stamp of its origin. Melodic variation is an important tool of any composer, but here the chromatic and rhythmic character of the material results consistently in too close an identification of themes rather than successful variation of them. What militates most strongly against interesting melodic variation, however, is the harmonic vocabulary in which parallel movement is the chief organizing principle. Much too extensive a use is made of parallel tritone progressions (Fig. 17), movement in fifths (Fig. 18), and quartal harmony (Fig. 19). It may be argued that this overall limitation of vocabulary (harmonic, rhythmic, and melodic)

Fig. 17 Bars 18–21

Fig. 18 Bars 26–30

Fig. 19 Section 13, Bars 1–4

causes the work to founder as a structural unit, despite the consistently brilliant hand of the composer as orchestrator. Never can the work be accused of lacking textural clarity; nor can the composer be charged with insensitivity to the use of the orchestral palette. But ultimately, it is the architecture which causes this work to fail, and architecture grows directly out of style.

A like problem is apparent in *Essay* for strings (1952). This work contains recurring melodic motives with developmental potential, but of which little is made until the very end when a broad thematic idea emerges only to be cut off prematurely and unexpectedly. Much of the work tends to be directionless and there is no adequate sense of structural logic apparent to the listener. As in *Sturt* and in the later work *Three Frescoes* (1969) (which is an example of Douglas's compositional investigation of serialism), climax is seen as a function of force rather than of dramatic logic.

Melody in general lacks distinction, and in *Three Frescoes* and the Symphony no. 3 (1963), there is an uneasy compromise between tonality and free serialism which tends to compound the problems of thematicism, structure, and dramatic development.

In conclusion, what can be said of the thirty-five years of Douglas's creative activity? There can be no doubt that he has done Australian music a service by his commitment to composition in a period which was not noted for its enlightened attitude to Australian composition. In addition, his interest in and respect for Aboriginal music and folk-lore, which dates from the early thirties, is remarkable when seen in the light of W.E.H. Stanner's characterization of Australian attitudes to Aboriginal affairs and culture as 'the great Australian silence'[3]—a period of general apathy and ignorance. For these reasons, he has earned a place in Australia's cultural history, but chiefly for the independent path which he trod in his search for an Australian music identity free from the preoccupations of the old world.

Notes

1. Clive Douglas, 'Folk-song and the Brown man: A means to an Australian expression in symphonic music', *Canon*, 10 (1956), 81.
2. Roger Covell, *Australia's Music: Themes of a New Society* (Melbourne, 1967), p. 72.
3. W.E.H. Stanner, *After the Dreaming: The Boyer Lectures*, 1968 (Sydney, A.B.C., 1969), pp. 18–29.

Select List of Works

Operas

Ashmadai Op. 12, operetta in one act (1935)
Kaditcha Op. 19, operetta in three scenes (1938)
Eleanora Op. 26–28, operatic trilogy (1940–43)

Symphonies

Symphony no. 1, *Jubilee*, Op. 48 (1951)
Symphony no. 2, *Namatjira*, Op. 67 (1956)
Symphony no. 3, Op. 86 (1963)

Miscellaneous Orchestral

Carwoola Op. 22, symphonic poem (1939)
Sturt 1829 Op. 53, symphonic poem (1952)
Essay for strings Op. 55 (1952)
Wangadilla Op. 57, suite for orchestra (1954)
Olympic Overture Op. 64 (1956)
Terra Australis Op. 76, for narrator, soprano, chorus, and orchestra (1959)
Variations Symphoniques Op. 80 (1961)
Three Frescoes Op. 90, for orchestra (1969)
Discourse for strings Op. 94 (1971)

Discography

Boonoke (1965)—1'38"; *Waitangi Dance*—2'02". West Australian Symphony Orchestra (John Farnsworth-Hall, conductor).   *HMV disc OCLP/7632*
Carwoola, Op. 22 (1939) [13'15"]. Victorian Symphony Orchestra (Clive Douglas, conductor). 1955.
                                 ABC disc COL/2152
Sturt 1829, Op. 53 (alternative title *Kaiela*) (1954). Victorian Symphony Orchestra (Clive Douglas, conductor). 1954.   *HMV disc OALP/7511*
Essay for strings, Op. 55 (1952) [10'03"]. Strings of the Melbourne Symphony Orchestra (Tibor Paul, conductor). Allan. 6 Feb. 1969.
                              ABC recording RRCS/380
Wongadilla, Op. 56 (1955) [30'25"]. Victorian Symphony Orchestra (Clive Douglas, conductor). MS. 19 May 1955.   *ABC recording PR/2327*
Festival in Natal, Op. 57 (1954) [7'55"]. Victorian Symphony Orchestra (Clive Douglas, conductor). MS.   *ABC recording PRX/4783*
Olympic Overture, Op. 64 (1956). Sydney and Victorian Symphony Orchestras (Sir Bernard Heinze, conductor). 1957.   *HMV disc OALP/7526*
Suite: Coolawidgee, Op. 66 (1957) [15'00"]. Strings and woodwind of South Australian Symphony Orchestra (Clive Douglas, conductor). MS.
                               ABC recording PRX/4783

Symphony no. 2, *Namatjira*, Op. 67 (1956) [27'00"]. Victorian Symphony Orchestra (Clive Douglas, conductor). MS. 1957.   *ABC recording PRX/4137*
Terra Australis, Op. 76 (1959) [29'21"]. Keith Hudson (narrator), Glenda Raymond (soprano); Melbourne Oriana Choir, Victorian Symphony Orchestra (Clive Douglas, conductor).   *ABC recording PRX/4668*
Sinfonietta: Festival of Perth, Op. 79 (1961) [16'45"]. Victorian Symphony Orchestra (Clive Douglas, conductor).   *ABC disc 2XS/2687*
Variations Symphoniques, Op. 80 (1961) [12'12"]. Victorian Symphony Orchestra (Georges Tzipine, conductor). MS. 1961.   *ABC disc PR/3280*
Divertimento no. 1, Op. 83 (1962–63) [15'05"]. Arnost Bourek (flute), Edwin Denton (oboe), Phillipe Miechel (clarinet), Eugene Danilov (clarinet), Glen Spicer (bassoon). MS   *ABC recording RRC/31*
Three Frescoes, Op. 90 (1968) [20'48"]. Sydney Symphony Orchestra (Moshe Atzmon, conductor). Allan. 6 Feb. 1969.   *Festival disc SFC 800/19*
Five Pastels, Op. 51 (1952) [14'35"]. Molly McGurk (soprano); Strings and celeste of the West Australian Symphony Orchestra (Georg Tintner, conductor). MS. 12 Feb. 1972.   *ABC tape*

John Antill

(*b*. 1904)

Patricia Brown

By now the problems surrounding creative musical development in Australia up to and including the mid-twentieth century have been thoroughly investigated.[1] Continuing geographical isolation from the wellsprings of European musical initiatives, conservative policies of musical institutions and promoting bodies, lack of systematic public and private subsidy for composition—these and many other factors had contributed to a general state of near-atrophy in Australia's creative musical development by the end of the Second World War.

It was at this time that the still rather enigmatic personality of John Antill came to the attention of Australian music, largely as a result of the international acclaim won by his work *Corroboree*. If it is possible for a composer's reputation to be sustained chiefly by one composition, then Antill is a one-work composer. Apart from this orchestral score, few of his large body of compositions are heard today in either live performance or via broadcasting. By contrast *Corroboree* has remained one of the most frequently performed works on A.B.C. radio since its première in 1946[2] even though it is now very rare to find a public performance of the work, either as an orchestral suite or as a ballet.[3]

More will be said about *Corroboree* and its significance later. Let us look first at the man and his achievement without assuming that *Corroboree* must remain the only unit of measure.

When talking to Antill one cannot help being struck by a double-edged attitude which in fact indicates the difficulty of setting his work in any convenient historical or structural pigeon-hole. On the one hand he has a genuinely quiet, unassuming and almost deferential attitude to being considered a composer; on the other, he is painfully and perhaps regretfully aware of the deprivations and obstacles his composing generation encountered in Australia in terms of lack of encouragement and financial support. Not surprisingly, this brings a strong reaction when comparisons with the contemporary situation are broached. Young Australian composers are now undoubtedly better off both financially and in the reassurance that their communities accept and even occasionally need them. The lack of this kind of support meant that Antill was never able to devote himself entirely to composition. In the face of continuing public indifference and lack of financial and organizational support he channelled most of his energy into providing scores for dedicated and enthusiastic amateur groups. This attitude is characteristic of the man. In this way he has written no fewer than thirty-two ballet scores alone, ranging from large works to quite small ones.

Here we come up against another aspect of Antill's composition. He has never drawn up a list of his works and is genuinely unable to give a precise account of his large output. Most of his work is still unpublished and as hand-copied orchestral and choral parts have a recurring historical tendency to disappear, it is not surprising to find that much of his music has been lost. Of the already mentioned ballet scores only six remain.

For this reason the list of works given at the end of this chapter is simply an attempt to show something of the breadth and variety of the composer's output.[4] Yet even now the record must remain incomplete. Prior to a recent change of address Antill destroyed a huge amount of his early work. On another occasion twelve string quartets which no longer measured up to his critical standards met a similar fate.

Fortunately, enough of his juvenilia remain to show us the seeds of later preoccupations. The most striking of these is his theatrical orientation. His father loved opera and even though Antill's childhood visits to the theatre were infrequent, his ability to interpret scenes visually and vividly resulted in his writing several plays which he also set to music at a very early age. By the time he was sixteen he had written two operas, one (*c*. 1920) based on Keats' *Endymion*.[5]

This ability to visualize things in theatrical terms is almost second nature to him. His collection of scores contains his own sketches and paintings depicting set designs, stage movements in relation to musical timing,[6] and so on. He also has a self-made model stage complete with set and costume designs. When he is engaged on a theatre work he keeps one eye on the set to ensure that the work evolves in relation to production and stagecraft.

Antill's oratorio, *The Song of Hagar to Abraham the Patriarch*, for which he has a particular fondness, provides us with a not untypical example of his achievements and disappointments. As it was originally designed for television, Antill painted all the rolling background scenes to ensure that the visual backdrop would be exactly in keeping with his overall conception of the work. The poem, by Ethel Anderson, is based on the biblical story depicting the desert wanderings of Hagar and Ishmael. From a handwritten note which prefaces the unpublished vocal score Antill describes it as '... a song written in the tradition of those archaic marriage songs sung by prehistoric Semitic tribes; similar songs are said to be assembled in the Song of Solomon. In it the early Gods Elohim and Jaweh are named, and the dethroned God Azazel appears. Hagar herself represents the archetype of the disposed [*sic*] woman still faithful to a great vision. She illustrates the Apocryphal text, "Many waters cannot quench love, nor can the sea drown it".' Unfortunately, as has happened too frequently with Antill's works, the projected television production never took place, thereby leaving an essentially visually oriented work to be assessed as a rather pale 'straight' oratorio.

John Antill was born in the suburb of Ashfield, Sydney, on 8 April 1904. Both his parents were English. His mother came to Australia at the age of four after a six-month sailing voyage. His father came from Bristol at the age of eleven. Antill admits that attending St Andrew's Anglican Cathedral choir school in Sydney was an asset, as it enabled him to devote several hours a day to the study and practice of music, and in addition allowed him to become familiar with a wide variety of choral and instrumental traditions. In the meantime he wrote various compositions which were greeted with enthusiasm by his suburban music teacher. He himself received no further practical help or direction. A few years later some of his self-taught efforts were shown by his then clarinet teacher to Arthur Benjamin, and a scribbled reply by that experienced composer, which I came across among some of Antill's early manuscripts, includes the following rather cryptically illuminating advice to the self-taught boy:

> After going through the pieces I would recommend that the author should learn Harmony. Would also recommend that Mr. Antill should have 12 months under Mr. Alfred Hill and tell him that you want to learn composition. Let him see the pieces. There are parts in the pieces that I cannot quite grasp. Whether they were put in for an object, this does not appeal to me and should not have been done. Perhaps Mr. Antill had some of this work done to suit the piece as he thought. It would be far better to hear the pieces played. Still it is remarkably well done, considering no tuition on this work. Would certainly carry on for the 12 months. The pieces were nicely arranged.

At sixteen Antill became an apprentice mechanical draftsman in the New South Wales Railways Department, but at the end of his five-year apprenticeship he decided to devote himself to music. Having won a scholarship to study composition with Alfred Hill at the New South Wales State Conservatorium in 1925, he set about learning his craft thoroughly, which included familiarizing himself with every instrument of the orchestra. After these student years he joined the New South Wales State Orchestra and the then Sydney Symphony Orchestra and also joined several touring opera and ballet companies. In these his love for the theatre was further nourished, not only through his playing in the pit, but also through his tenor singing on stage, his conducting, his work as chorus master and his experience backstage.

This absorption in as many aspects of the theatre as possible is again typical of the man's approach to a set work. Before embarking on a major score he will spend as long as he feels it necessary to steep himself in the hinterland of the subject. For example, his reading and anthropological studies into the tribal life and customs of the Australian Aboriginals were to occupy almost twenty years prior to the composition of *Corroboree*. From his personal experience in the field of radio broadcasting at the Australian Broadcasting Commission during the thirties and forties, he also drew up for publication a 'Design for Broadcasting' which was a collection of his detailed observations on the best methods of broadcasting music at that time.

This association with the A.B.C. was to be a long one: For thirty-six years until his retirement in 1969, Antill held the posts successively of Chorus Master, Presentation Officer, Assistant Federal Music Editor and later Federal Music Editor for the Commission. 'This meant that every composition, either local or from overseas, submitted to the A.B.C. found its way to Antill's desk for approval to broadcast ... for many years he was the virtual arbiter of the selection of new music broadcast by the A.B.C.'[7] Obviously this was a position of responsibility. Although Antill was not entirely responsible for the extreme conservatism of the A.B.C.'s music broadcasting policies at this time, Murdoch is probably correct in claiming that Antill's generally conservative bias was another factor in contributing to Australia's isolation from contemporary musical developments overseas. Yet Antill never used his position to promote his own music. If anything, the promotion and performance of his own music suffered as a result of his employment with the A.B.C. Looking through his scores one is dismayed at the number of works, complete with his own carefully copied manuscript parts, which had been promised a performance they were never to receive.

Antill was born much too soon to be a part of the new and exciting wave of younger composers in the sixties. Belonging as we have seen to an earlier, post-colonial generation which had enjoyed no commissions and little encouragement or interest from the public at large, he had to put aside ideas of overseas travel and additional study for a career in composition. Without the aid of L.P. discs and tape recorders, he and his contemporaries living in Australia had little chance of following current European musical development. Consequently Antill taught himself everything by reading and listening, and firmly believes that no craftsmanlike composition is possible without a thorough grounding in the traditional disciplines of musical theory.

The strong conservatism which characterizes Antill's approach to composition as well as his attitudes to most manifestations of twentieth-century music is perfectly understandable in view of the era in which he grew up. It is also related to the fact that the bulk of his music is firmly indebted to traditions such as the English choral movement and the more readily accessible styles of European orchestral writing of the late nineteenth and early twentieth centuries. This becomes apparent in a work such as the oratorio *The Song of Hagar* or the choral *Festival Te Deum*, the former presenting a gentle panorama of male and full choruses, solos and orchestral writing and the latter remembering the post-Handelian choral style.

In view of his almost compulsive necessity to continue composing, it is not surprising that Antill's music covers a wide range, with each work reflecting something of the social and musical climate which nourished it. Even though the attached list of compositions represents the first attempt to account for as many of the composer's extant works as possible, it represents only a fraction of Antill's output. Predictably, dramatic works including ballets, operas, oratorios, music for films, television and radio plays are strongly in evidence. Like many other mid-twentieth century composers Antill found the discipline of writing for films a useful if not always entirely rewarding experience (as in the case of documentary films for which he wrote more than twenty scores).[8] His compositions include choral works and songs of various kinds, orchestral suites, overtures, fanfares, music for pageants, symphonies, concertos and chamber music. These works help us to construct a clearer picture of Australia's music-making at a time prior to the wider and more concrete recognition of Australian composers.

Whatever the craftsmanlike merits or weaknesses of many of his other works, the impact of the pounding rhythms and rich orchestration of *Corroboree* when it first fell on the ears of Australians in 1946 was unmistakable. Here at last was a work in totally Western idiom and instrumentation, paying a remote yet sincere homage to Aboriginal culture and possessing a recognizably Australian identity. Antill originally wrote it as an orchestral suite. But he also envisaged its performance as a ballet based on the theme of tribal initiation. This score, as might be expected in a work founded on driving rhythmic impetus and vivid orchestral colour, calls for a very large orchestra. The percussion section includes the native bullroarer and thora sticks in addition to relatively standard instruments such as Chinese temple blocks, castanets, ratchet and sleigh bells. The accompanying illustration taken from the final section of the full manuscript score of *Corroboree*, shows something of Antill's harmonic vocabulary, rhythmic impetus and orchestral colour which are at the very heart of this work.

Fig. 20 Page 192 of manuscript full score of *Corroboree* in the hand of the composer (photograph by Roger Covell)

The story of Antill's boyhood experience of a ceremony of Aboriginal dances at La Perouse, Botany Bay, his notation of those melodies and rhythms, his composition of the score of *Corroboree* during the thirties and forties and the subsequent championing of the score by Sir Eugene Goossens, later conductor of the Sydney Symphony Orchestra, is now well known.[9] At its première during a Sunday afternoon concert on 18 August 1946 it created something of a furore. Comparisons of the Australian work with Stravinsky's brilliant *Rite of Spring* score of more than thirty years earlier are inevitable,[10] even though Antill denies having had any knowledge of Stravinsky's work at that time. *Corroboree* was subsequently performed in its orchestral version in Britain and the United States. In 1950 it was staged by the National Ballet with choreography by Rex Reid and design by William Constable.

Just as Stravinsky refused to repeat *The Rite of Spring*, Antill knew that he could not go on re-composing *Corroboree*. Antill admits to a lifelong fascination for rhythmic drive and precision in music: it comes, then, as a surprise that the rhythmic aggression and tensions exploding in this work are conspicuously absent from most of his other compositions. In this sense *Corroboree* stands like Ayers Rock among the soundscapes of the gentler works which both precede and follow it.

Since his retirement from the A.B.C. Antill has been active on several music boards (including the Fellowship of Australian Composers which he was instrumental in initiating in 1947) and continues to adjudicate throughout Australia for the A.B.C.'s annual instrumental and vocal competition. In 1970 he received an O.B.E. Although he feels disappointment in not having been able to reach as many people through composition as he would have liked, he nevertheless expresses the hope that he may have inspired some listeners through his own music, his conducting (of which he was very fond and regrets his limited opportunities in that field) and work in many branches of musical activity. He is at present writing a score inspired by a recent visit to Fiji. There, at the invitation of the Fijian Government, he prepared and conducted local choirs during the First South Pacific Festival of Arts.

How then can one try to formulate Antill's creative achievement and contribution to twentieth-century Australian composition? Just a few of the ways in which he has been described include: 'one of the forgotten men in Australian music' and 'a conservative',[11] 'a composer who has declined to repeat himself' and 'a musician employed by the A.B.C.... a kind of musician-laureate for state occasions',[12] '... part of a trend [along with] the rise of interest in anthropology [and] the discovery of Aboriginal art',[13] a composer responsible for a brilliant restatement of Australian Aboriginal culture in Western terms,[14] and the first to inform a broad public that Australian composers did exist.[15]

All these labels possess some truth, but no single one can hope to embrace the composer's total achievement. *Corroboree* is undoubtedly the work which brought his name to an Australian and overseas public. It seemed at the time to be a musical catalyst releasing new forces and possibilities in relation to a recognizably Australian school of composition, to the extent that contemporary Australian music can be claimed to date from this score. Yet Antill was no prophet or messiah. 'No one writes à la Antill'[16] and to this day he has remained a rather solitary figure, still composing abundantly, still able to hear the work which brought him fame, yet with most of his music still unpublished and largely overlooked.

Notes

1. Most notably in Roger Covell's *Australia's Music: Themes of a New Society* (Melbourne, 1967); also in such general historical works as Geoffrey Serle's *From Deserts the Prophets Come: the creative spirit in Australia 1788–1972* (Melbourne, 1973).
2. Even allowing for the A.B.C.'s necessity to provide specified Australian content in its broadcasting, the frequency of *Corroboree's* performance sets something of a record for an Australian work.
3. One notable exception was the performance of the full ballet in 1970 by the Australian Contemporary Dance Company as part of the Sutherland Shire's Captain Cook Bi-Centenary celebrations. Another was the performance of the orchestral suite at the opening of the Perth Concert Hall in 1973.
4. My thanks are extended to Mr Antill for kindly allowing me to examine all his scores at his home. It is on the basis of these works and others held by the A.B.C. Federal Music Library, Australasian Performing Right Association and music publishers that the concluding bibliography has been compiled.
5. This was later produced by the New South Wales National Opera in 1953.
6. As for example the set design sketches and timed moves accompanying the score of his opera *The Music Critic* (1953). More decorative illustrations may also be found in both copies of the full score of *Corroboree* (one in the possession of the composer, the other held by the National Library of Australia, Canberra).
7. James Murdoch, *Australia's Contemporary Composers* (Melbourne, 1972), p. 9.
8. On one occasion he was asked on a Friday to write a score, conduct it and have the completed product ready for the film screening in Paris three days later. That commission was fulfilled.
9. See e.g., Murdoch, pp. 11–12.
10. See Covell, *Australia's Music*, p. 154.
11. Murdoch, p. 9.
12. Covell, discussing *Corroboree*, p. 157 and p. 155.
13. Serle, p. 133.
14. Donald Peart, 'The Australian Avant-Garde', *Proceedings of the Royal Musical Association*, 93rd Session, 1966/67, 1.
15. Serle in discussing the impact of *Corroboree*, p. 204.
16. Murdoch, p. 9.

Select Bibliography

Covell, Roger. *Australia's Music: Themes of a New Society*. Sun Books, Melbourne, 1967.
Covell, Roger with Sargent, Margaret and Brown, Patricia. *Music in Australia: needs and prospects.* 2 vols. A report prepared for the Australian Council for the Arts. Unisearch, Sydney, 1970.
McCallum, Lester. 'John Antill', *Canon*, viii, 9 (April 1955), pp. 353–6.
McCredie, Andrew. *Music by Australian Composers*. 3 vols. Survey No. 1. Commonwealth Assistance to Australian Composers, Canberra, 1969.
Murdoch, James. *Australia's Contemporary Composers*. Macmillan, Melbourne, 1972.
Peart, Donald. 'The Australian Avant-Garde', *Proceedings of the Royal Musical Association*, 93rd Session, 1966/67, pp. 1–9.
Serle, Geoffrey. *From Deserts the Prophets Come: the creative spirit in Australia 1788-1972*. Heinemann, Melbourne, 1973.
[Author not named] 'John Antill's Song of Hagar', *Canon*, xiii, 6 (January 1960), p. 140.

Select List of Works

Operas
Endymion (*c.* 1920) performed 1953
The Music Critic (1953)
Christmas (1959)
The First Christmas (in one act) (1969)

Oratorio
The Song of Hagar to Abraham the Patriarch (1958)

Ballets
Corroboree (1946)
Wakooka (1957)
Snowy full orchestra and soprano voices (1961)
Black Opal SATB choir and timpani (1961)
G'Day Digger

Film and Television Music
Port Jackson (1948)
The Land that Waited (1963)
The Tempest music for Shakespeare's play (1963)
Everyman music for the morality play (1964)
Dark Rain [Documentary]
Dreaming Time Legends [ABC-TV ballet]
Mantle of Safety
The River
Salute to Danger
The Sands of Yellow Rock

Radio Play
Hassan

Symphony
Symphony on a City (1959)

Concertos
Concerto for harmonica and orchestra (1961)
Concerto/Sonata for harmonica and orchestra (1961)

Overtures, Fanfares, Pageants
Overture *'for a Momentous Occasion'* (1957)
Music for a Pageant of Nationhood (1963)
Paean to the Spirit of Man (1968)
Jubugalee (1973)
Australian Scene, Fanfares, Anthem
Outback Overture

Miscellaneous Orchestral and Instrumental
Corroboree: Orchestral Suite no. 1 (1946)
Corroboree: Orchestral Suite no. 2 (1950)
Variations for orchestra (1953)

A Sentimental Suite for Orchestra (1955)
Nullarbor Dream Time improvisation for violin on G
   string (1956)
The Unknown Land suite for string orchestra (1968)
Variations on a Theme of Alfred Hill (1970)
Australian Rhapsody
Capriccio
Singing Dust: 'To Henry Lawson' for strings and
   narrator

Choral
Cantate Domino SATB choir, brass and organ (1970)
Festival Te Deum
The Lovers Walk Forsaken
My Sister the Rain women's chorus and strings
Cradle Song women's chorus and strings

Solo Songs
Five Australian Lyrics for bar and pf or str orch (1953)
Five Songs of Happiness for high voice, pf and ob
   (optional) (1953)
Barbara's Song
In an Old Homestead Garden
Prospector's Song
Song of a Silver City
Songs of Praise
Songs of Righteousness
West Bound

Select Discography

(Contents are restricted to commercially released discs,
and therefore exclude records such as those of the
'Australian Composers' series released privately by the
A.B.C. for educational institutions only)

Concerto for harmonica. Lionel Easton (harmonica),
   Sydney Symphony Orchestra (John Antill, con-
   ductor).   *RCA disc SL 16372*
Corroboree ballet suite. London Symphony Orchestra
   (Sir Eugene Goossens, conductor).
                     Top Rank International disc
                     TRC 1032 (EV 6003: 3003)
                     (World Record Club disc S/2414)
Corroboree ballet suite. Sydney Symphony Orchestra
   (Sir Eugene Goossens, conductor).
                     HMV disc OALP 7503
Corroboree ballet suite. Sydney Symphony Orchestra
   (John Antill, conductor).   *HMV disc OASD 7554*
Five Australian Lyrics: 'The Wanderer', 'Sunset Song',
   'The Stones Cry Out', 'A Prayer', 'A Song of the
   Storm'. Stewart Harvey (baritone), Henri Penn
   (piano). *Australian Music Today* Vol. I, Side 2.
                     World Record Club disc A-601
Overture *'for a Momentous Occasion'*. Sydney Sym-
   phony Orchestra (John Antill, conductor).
Seven Contemporary Songs by Australian Composers.
   Bernadette Quin (soprano), Dorothy White (piano).
                     Brolga disc BM-14

Robert Hughes

(*b.* 1912)

Peter Tahourdin

Robert Hughes has an established place in the annals of Australian music alongside such composers as John Antill, Clive Douglas and Margaret Sutherland. His reputation is founded on a firm base of expert craftsmanship in the service of an honesty of mind and integrity of purpose that lifts his music above the changing whims of fashion. His acknowledged output is not large and is confined almost entirely to orchestral works, but through it there runs a consistency and security of technique that commands admiration and respect. As may be expected from a composer of his generation and background, his style is firmly rooted in European techniques that developed out of late nineteenth-century romanticism during the first forty years of the present century. Though quite clearly conservative, Hughes's style is not based on a self-conscious imitation of 'prestige models', but is rather an imaginative and intelligent synthesis of a number of disparate influences that, taken together, yield a distinctive and individual musical personality.

Robert Hughes's reputation, however, does not rest on his work as a composer alone, for he has been a tireless fighter on behalf of other composers and has continuously advocated the need for Australian music to take its place in the musical life of the country on equal terms with the accepted international repertoire. His has not simply been a fight for the new versus the old, for the acceptance of contemporary music as a whole, but rather for the acceptance of the composer and his work as an integral part of the cultural fabric of Australian society. Nowadays it may seem strange that such a fight should have been necessary, that a country could be said to have a valid musical life at all if the work of its composers went largely unperformed and unacknowledged. The fact that the prejudices which brought this about are rapidly disappearing, that a composer today can count on rather more than tacit acceptance, is in large measure due to the untiring efforts of Robert Hughes and others of his generation.

Hughes was not born in Australia but came to Melbourne with his family from Fifeshire in Scotland in 1929 at the age of seventeen. An interest in music did not become apparent until he was about fourteen years old when he took piano lessons and began to compose. His early musical tastes were formed by visits to concerts and recitals in Aberdeen, at which he heard many of the leading performers of the day in the standard concert and operatic repertoire. Opera at this time attracted him particularly and to this day he has a special affinity with music drama and theatre. Indeed, had the conditions been right in Australia forty years ago, Hughes might have emerged as a leading opera composer, instead of turning his talents towards concert and symphonic music.

In addition to attending concert and operatic performances in Aberdeen, Hughes became acquainted at the age of sixteen with Marshall Gilchrist, organist of Saint Machar's Cathedral, who instructed him in harmony and offered him encouragement and advice at a time when his creative ability was starting to emerge and to assume a sense of direction and purpose. So it was something of a reversal of fortune for him to find himself a year or two later in Melbourne, where the musical life was neither as sophisticated nor as varied as it had been in Aberdeen. In addition there arose the need to earn a living, and for the next ten years Hughes worked as a costing clerk and studied accountancy, whilst continuing to compose and to play the piano at weddings and other social functions in his spare time.

During this period the pattern of Robert Hughes's life was centred around his day-to-day job, with music occupying him only in the evenings and at weekends. But in the few years immediately before the Second World War his industry began to pay dividends and the Australian Broadcasting Commission performed a number of his early works. It was partly as a result of this awakening of interest in his work as a composer that Hughes felt the need to improve his technique and undertake formal studies once again. He was granted a bursary to study with Arthur Nickson at Melbourne University Conservatorium of Music, and from him he received a knowledge of harmony and counterpoint that helped to broaden his outlook and add a further dimension to his compositional style. But this period of study was short-lived. Hughes joined the army and for the next five years served first in Australia and then in New Guinea—the only musical bright spot being the broadcast performance of an orchestral work of his by the B.B.C. over its Pacific network.

With the war over, Robert Hughes's career took a giant step forward when he joined the staff of the A.B.C. and became its music editor and arranger in Melbourne. In those days the A.B.C.'s Melbourne orchestra was not the full-sized body it is today, and Hughes's principal task was to arrange works from the standard repertoire to suit the reduced forces available. He has been with the A.B.C. for more than twenty-five years, and during this time he has worked not only as an editor and arranger but has also composed a quantity of incidental music for radio and television, as well as numerous scores for documentary films. It is this practical side of Hughes's work that is perhaps the most important single factor in his musical style, and it is not without significance that he no longer acknowledges any of his music composed before he was appointed to the staff of the A.B.C. Hughes has learnt from daily experience to judge his effects to a nicety, to ensure that whatever he writes will be telling and effective within the context in which it occurs. A look through any of his scores will show that, though the texture may be active and ornate, it is never opaque, never overburdened; each strand takes its place as an organic part of the whole and is scored so as to ensure it will be clearly heard.

It was during this postwar period, too, that Hughes emerged as a dogged fighter for Australian music. In the late fifties he became Director of the Australasian Performing Right Association and also, together with other senior composers, founded the Fellowship of Australian Composers. He began a long campaign to bring about an active policy of financial support by the Federal Government for Australian composition.

In the end, of course, a composer stands or falls by his music alone, and Robert Hughes must be judged on the sixteen or so works he has composed since 1948. During this quarter century of sustained creative activity Hughes's style has changed very little. Its roots lie principally in English music of the first three decades of this century—the sweep and sustained drive of Elgar, the reflective lyricism of the English pastoral composers, allied to the rhythmic vitality of Walton. But over and above this is an exoticism that stems from the use of chromatically inflected modal scales that have a central European flavour to them, producing melodic writing that twists melismatically around narrow intervals—the augmented second, or minor third, being markedly prominent. It is these chromatically convoluted melodies, not infrequently moving in parallel thirds, that give to Hughes's music its particular stamp and fingerprint. The contrapuntal interplay of parts gives rise to the harmony (a legacy perhaps from the composer's studies with Arthur Nickson), together with the use of parallel-moving chords built in thirds. Motoric rhythms in *ostinato* patterns generate much of the music's momentum and help to build climactic tension. In fact Hughes has said that he regards rhythm as of primary importance, as a generative and unifying factor in his music.

Of the composer's major works the First Symphony stands out strongly for its command of large-scale symphonic form and for the craftsmanship and vision that lie behind it. It originated as a three-movement work and in this form won the Australian section of the Commonwealth Jubilee Competition in 1951, receiving its first performance in Melbourne the following year under the direction of Sir Bernard Heinze. Four years later a slow movement was added and Norman Del Mar conducted a broadcast performance of this version for the B.B.C. In 1971, however, Hughes received a Commonwealth Fellowship and undertook such a thorough reworking of the Symphony that it may now be regarded as a new composition. In its present form it is a substantial work in four movements and serves as a major testament from one of Australia's most distinguished composers.

The first movement reveals the principal features of Hughes's mature style with remarkable clarity. The slow introduction begins with a passage for horns (Fig. 21) that recalls the gentle, reflective vein of the English pastoral school, later recurring in altered form on the woodwind immediately after the central climax (Fig. 22). Following the opening for the horns is a melodic fragment for the first oboe (Fig. 23) that is highly characteristic in its winding chromaticism and which generates much of the melodic material of the movement. The second subject of the subsequent *allegro*, derived from the initial horn passage, has a veritable Elgarian sweep about it and is richly sonorous in its scoring for unison first and second violins (Fig. 24); a few pages later this is transformed into a delicate, polymodal, contrapuntal interplay between oboe, clarinet and bassoon (Fig. 25). Against this is set a rhythmic *ostinato* for the second violins (Fig. 26) that illustrates the motoric rhythm that underlies this *allegro* and which contains within it a drive and energy that propels the movement forward. Finally, it is clear that the overall structure is expertly planned to lead naturally to a sustained climax that is well placed some two-thirds of the way through to give the movement a fine balance and proportion.

Fig. 21

Fig. 22

Fig. 23

Fig. 24

Fig. 25

Fig. 26

Whilst the Symphony must surely be regarded as Hughes's most ambitious and successful achievement in orchestral writing, his smaller works should not be overlooked, for they, too, show a fine command of colour and formal cohesion, albeit on a smaller and less exalted plane. The Sinfonietta, composed for the centenary of the Hallé Orchestra in 1957 and dedicated to Sir John Barbirolli and the Orchestra, is a four-movement work that is thoroughly characteristic of Hughes's style. Both the *Essay* of 1953 and *Synthesis*, commissioned by the A.B.C. for its Youth Concerts in 1969, are single movement works for large orchestral forces. *Synthesis* in particular has a bite and piquancy that show a fresh subtlety of colouration—the use of divided strings and the more delicate of the percussion instruments is a striking addition to the composer's palette and is a technique that is carried forward in the more recent *Sea Spell* of 1974.

Robert Hughes, now in his early sixties, has already made a substantial contribution to Australian music. What comes next can only be a matter for speculation, but it would be interesting to discover if his early interest in opera could be reawakened. There can be no doubt that the technique is there, and a full-length opera by one of Australia's most prominent composers could only be a valuable addition to this—in Australian terms—much neglected medium. Musical theatre in Australia needs its more senior composers, as well as its advanced younger ones. Equally speculative, of course, is any attempt to predict how succeeding generations will assess the music of Robert Hughes. But if honesty, integrity, fine craftsmanship and a courageous spirit have any meaning, then Hughes's future place must surely be an honoured one.

Publishers

Chappell, A.P.R.A.

Bibliography

Portrait in *Musical America*, lxx (Jan. 1950), p. 75.
Canon, vi (1952), p. 51f.
Wagner, W. 'Two Symphonies by Australians played in Sydney', *Musical America* lxxii (November 1952), p. 25f.
Hince, K. 'Robert Hughes', *Canon*, viii (1954), p. 211.
Scherek, J. 'Robert Hughes: An Australian Composer', *Canon* ix (1956), p. 189f.
Kennedy, M. 'Robert Hughes' "Sinfonietta"', *Musical Times*, xcix (1958), p 34.
Canon, xiii (1959), p. 63.
Simon, D. and Burke, A. 'The Forbidden Rite', *Music and Dance*, liii (1962), p. 6.
Hughes, R. 'The Forbidden Rite—Notes on the book and music', *Music and Dance*, lii (June 1962), p. 14.
'Music of Robert Hughes'. Australian Composers' Seminar (Hobart, 1963, UNESCO), p. 24f.
Garretty, J.D. Three Australian Composers, M.A. thesis, University of Melbourne, 1963, pp. 105–43.

List of Works

Stage Music
Hamlet incidental music (1952)
The Forbidden Rite dance drama for T.V. (1961)
Untitled comedy with music in three acts (1972–75)

Orchestral Music
Festival Overture (1948)
Suite *Farrago* (1949 revised 1965)
Symphony (1951, revised 1971)
Serenade for small orchestra (1952)
Essay for orchestra (1953)
Linn-o-Dee (1954)
Xanadu ballet suite (1954)
Overture *Masquerade* (1956)
Sinfonietta (1957)
Fantasia (1963, revised 1967–68)
Flourish (1968)
Synthesis (1969)
Ballade for string orchestra (1969)
The Forbidden Rite Suite (1971)
Sea Spell (1974)

Chorus and Orchestra
Five Indian Poems (1971)

Chamber Music
Serenade for solo cl harp and str qu (1952) (cf. *Serenade* for small orchestra)
String Quartet (1953)

Discography

Sinfonietta (1957) [17'00"]. Melbourne Symphony Orchestra (Willem van Otterloo, conductor). Chappell. 21 Oct. 1967   *World Record Club disc S/2495*
Sinfonietta (1957) [17'32"]. Sydney Symphony Orchestra (Nicolai Malko, conductor). Chappell. 1961.
RCA Red Seal disc L/6233
Symphony no. 1 (1951) [29'00"]. Sydney Symphony Orchestra (Joseph Post, conductor). MS. 27 July 1971.   *Festival disc SFC 800/23*
Masquerade Overture (1956) [6'00"]. West Australian Symphony Orchestra (Verdon Williams, conductor). Chappell. Feb. 1971.   *ABC tape*
Fantasia (1963; revised 1968) [8'35"]. Melbourne Symphony Orchestra (Willem van Otterloo, conductor). Chappell. 5 July 1968.
ABC recording RRCS/125
Synthesis (1969) [9'30"]. Melbourne Symphony Orchestra (Willem van Otterloo, conductor). Chappell. 13 Aug. 1969.   *ABC recording RRCS/380*
Farrago Suite (1949; revised 1965) [11'42"]. Sydney Symphony Orchestra (Joseph Post, conductor). MS.
ABC recording PRX/5614
Essay for orchestra (1953) [9'30"]. Melbourne Symphony Orchestra (Tibor Paul, conductor). MS. 5 Feb. 1969.   *ABC recording RRCS/380*
Essay for orchestra (1953) [9'25"]. Melbourne Symphony Orchestra (Nicolai Malko, conductor). 1958.
ABC recording PRX/4783
Ballet suite: *Xanadu* (1954) [16'28"]. West Australian Symphony Orchestra (Verdon Williams, conductor). Chappell. 12 Feb. 1970. *ABC recording RRCS/382*
Ballet suite: *Xanadu* (1954) [16'15"]. Sydney Symphony Orchestra (Joseph Post, conductor). Chappell. 1955.
HMV disc OALP/7511
Flourish (1968). [52"]. Tasmanian Symphony Orchestra (Patrick Thomas, conductor). MS. 2 May 1968.
ABC recording RRC/72

Raymond Hanson

(1913–76)

Malcolm John

A fourth generation Australian, Hanson was born of musical parents and took to music with missionary zeal. Schooling during the Depression was limited so he spent much time composing and performing his own works and won a composition scholarship in 1939. Early influences were Grieg and Chaminade, Bach, Handel, Beethoven and Brahms, and in Sonata for Piano (1938–40), *Idylle* (1942) and *Episodes on Tarry Trowsers* (1948) can be seen the lyrical, sensuous qualities of the first two, whilst the structural strengths of the 'Three Bs' have been a constant challenge. As a rehabilitation student after the war Hanson received disciplined tuition from Dr Alex Burnard for two years. He then joined the staff of the New South Wales State Conservatorium of Music in 1948. In this role as teacher he has influenced Meale, Butterley, Conyngham, Burrows, Woodward and many other outstanding musicians who have sought his advice.

Hanson's fascination with harmony—the triad in particular—was reinforced upon reading Hindemith's *A Composer's World* and *Craft of Musical Composition*. His music has its roots in the past; even at its most complex and dissonant the 'third' relationships are present. He admitted to being a romantic individualist and his style is not as predictable as, say, Rachmaninov's, nor as eclectic as Williamson's. He does not belong to a 'school'. And like the thorough craftsman that he was, he chose words and medium with serious integrity, respecting the characteristics and techniques of the instruments. His music evokes a strong emotional response but does not pander to emotionalism; there is a reserve of feeling, a sense of understatement.

In his settings of Rossetti and Gilmore as well as Tagore, Hanson reveals a preoccupation with metaphysical delights and a deep concern for life's spiritual potential. The words of Thomas Gray and Dylan Thomas, both of whom depict so well inner, secret states of exaltation, are illuminated by his music. His acknowledged physiological tenseness is revealed in the conflicts within much of his music, a constant austerity which relaxes not into sunny humour (although by nature the composer was a most easygoing and likeable man) but into introverted visions of exalted states of being. His last opera is based upon the Rum Rebellion, and ought to present ample opportunities for externalizing this conflict.

If Tagore was a constant source of inspiration so was the piano. With his friend Igor Hmelnitsky championing the Piano Sonata, and Albert Landa performing the 1972 Piano Concerto, his empathy with the instrument is clear. Hanson tackled most media, however: string quartet, wind quintet, song, ballet, film documentary, brass band, concerto, oratorio, and opera. His constant love of jazz and his respect for two more 'Bs', Brubeck and Burrows, was a further source of ideas, particularly in the Trombone Concerto. Although he enjoyed twelve-bar blues he had little time for 'pop' music, feeling that there is oversimplification of musical thought, although often sincere. Neither had he time for Stockhausen or even the seemingly objective precision of strict serial techniques, although most of his own music is atonal.

Hanson found people exciting; 'Joe Blow is important', and in spite of the seriousness and complexity of his music he felt a common understanding with Everyman. His ambition was to be himself, and Tagore's 'The Gardener' or the Psalmist of King James' Version of the Bible, where there is humility but no blood, mystery, yet touching the common man, come nearest to expressing his philosophy on life. In considering three representative works one sees a highly individual style emerge. The composer saw his music as ruggedly lyrical, metamorphic, organic and linear rather than structured or fragmented. A solidity exists even in the many lighter textures, and a brooding, massive quality pervades much of his music.

Piano Sonata 1938–40 (revised 1963)

This violent, uneven and brilliant work is comparable with Copland's piano sonata, and Barber's sonata for piano, in that hidden within the storm of dissonance is a searcher for truth, volatile and persuasive. The first strokes and the brief motive which follows give a clue to the composer's delight in fast chromatic alteration and polytonal inflections (Fig. 27).

Fig. 27 The motive from the opening of the Piano Sonata

A left-hand melodic passage, treated sequentially, and right-hand *ostinato*, leads to a further three strokes, this time in broader seconds, fourths and octaves, and a new section with its ♫♩ and ♫♪♩♪ patterns, and indulgent sevenths moving under a wandering atonal melody develops with harmonic inconsistency whereby one measure, the C C sharp B of the germ supported by closely dissonant Rawsthorne-like sevenths and seconds, is followed by diatonic chords descending in Phrygian style A G F (E) D^7/C. Thence, sequential development, moving through strong modulations, leads to G minor.

If the warp of this complex fabric is terse (developments of thematic fragments and free chromatic harmony balanced against measured tonality), then the woof is a variety of accompanying *ostinati*—an aspect of Hanson's pianistic style (Fig. 28).

Fig. 28 An aspect of Hanson's pianistic style

The enunciation ends with the broad strokes, sonorous and extended, while the left hand again alters the germ as pedal—now E flat, F sharp, E natural. A short and rather formal development begins quietly. There is a desire to clarify and consolidate using recognizable modulations—A flat, E flat, B flat—and the second section material. Soon, extreme dynamic variation $PPP < sf$ with rich four- and five-note chords in both hands pursue a breathless dotted-note rhythm arriving quickly at a tolling motive on D flat, built upon the original germ (Fig. 29).

Fig. 29 The tolling motive

Forced enharmonic tension, with the dotted note against the reiterated D flat (C sharp) exhausts this section and the recapitulation returns with new urgency. Abrupt shifting from one area to another and the inability to sustain a development for long is apparent. Tone-clustered sevenths add to the sombre mood and the bridge passage returns a min or third higher. Majestic strokes in fourths and seconds over a D pedal open the way for the brooding introspection of the slow movement. The second section, used up in the development, does not reappear.

An oscillating 12/8 motive in thirds (right hand) moves like a hot, dry wind over the stark left-hand melody based on the previous pedal. Strong perfect fourths and fifths in the restless ♩.♩. rhythm add to the desolation. The right hand takes over the close melody and a human warmth enters into the barren landscape. The triplet motive broadens and light rippling of sixths brings us to a new region. Its lush fruits—dominant ninths, tenths, thirteenths, are lost to the wanderer, who reiterates his plaintive calls in a different key (Fig. 30).

This type of added tonal harmony is found extensively in Hutchens and Hyde, yet here it is not only colour or mood but a personal pilgrimage; cf. Ives' *The Unanswered Question* for trumpet and muted strings. But whereas Ives is radically innovative—near static rhythms, extreme textures—Hanson is closely linked with the past, not only in chordal structures but in triplet and dotted note patterns. At last we enter this new region (a desolate land or heart, depending on your viewpoint) where several rushing thirds support the right-hand melody, transformed from the theme in E major. The mystery deepens with the B flat + A flat augmented chords (version of eleventh) followed by F sharp[7] and resolution into E flat[6]. The

Fig. 30

order and sensuous joy delight the wanderer. Suddenly, the vision disappears, and big chords bring about a hasty conclusion based on the questioning C-F sharp interval.

Hanson grasped the significance of serialism but not in its strictest form—as epitomized in Webern and Boulez—it was not his way. The power of contrast, to reflect human states of mind, inherent in a freer atonal extension of diatonic material was essential for him.

The rhythm of the original motive (Fig. 27) receives textural and time transformation in the Finale. 5/8, 6/8, 7/8 fluctuations, pianistic sixths and octaves and a sheer lack of tonal centre free the Prokofiev-like bounding rhythm and idiomatic sounds already accepted, so that the ear hears only spontaneous creation. Thematic development leads to thick chords, while the left-hand E, G sharp, F suggests a further transformation of the germ. It is also obvious that third relationships, here C sharp minor/F minor, are heard now as integral parts of Hanson's style. A lyrical second subject alludes to the tolling motive, gentler here, and the F sharp E (F sharp) D (E) germ grows into a melody, develops with strength, and recalls the joy of the discovered regions of the slow movement (Fig. 31).

Fig. 31

A persistent trill on D and cascading chords with fluctuating 5/4 establish a short middle section, the main feature of which is the playing with enharmonic alterations about the trill. After a brilliant cadential passage the jaunty first theme is recalled; down a third in E. Elaborated with imitation, augmentation, and some mirror formations, the sonata builds to a bravura close in B flat.

The Immortal Touch (1952) from 'Gitanjali' by Rabindranath Tagore

This oratorio for soprano, bass, mixed choir and orchestra is in nine sections. Hanson's austere yet evocative harmony is polychordal rather than polytonal. The sounds of his poetic framework reinforce the moment. Structure is not ignored but is secondary to the motivating power of the text. Germinal motives recur, usually fleetingly (Fig. 32).

Fig. 32

1. Choir:
    'Thou hast made me endless . . .'
A long pedal-point on D, with strings fluctuating between major and minor thirds, underpins with endless clashes and descending Phrygian phrases the humanity of the measured voices, where dark hues are achieved by spreading added-note structures over a wide canvas.
    'This little flute of a reed thou hast carried over hills and dales and hast breathed
    through it melodies eternally new . . .'
Here the bass pivots about B then down in thirds, F to D; a symbolic return.
    'Still thou pourest and still there is room to fill . . .' The texture is vocally sensitive, with recurring open triads and creating a mood of personal awareness and frail dependence. The orchestra is more positive in its recognition of 'thou' but seldom influences the voices.
2. Bass:
    'When thou commandest me to sing it seems that my heart would break with
    pride . . .'
The rich orchestral response is open and vigorous; cf. Elgar's *Dream of Gerontius* or Ireland's *These things shall be*. Phrases are compact and intense with tonality shifting about B and C minor, while dotted notes and a medium *tessitura* give serious dignity to a flexible *arioso*. A preference for augmented and added-note chords, combined with a fluent chromatic bass, forms a springboard for free non-diatonic progressions. Here, two flutes, spiritual messengers, hover over the strings and voice (Fig. 33).
3. Soprano:
A limpid siciliano, 'My song has put off her adornments . . .', is based upon the perfect fifth and recalls Berlioz in its confirmation of transparent orchestration and wandering melody. The texture is sometimes complex, yet with surprisingly disarming results, as in this passage suggestive of polytonality (Fig. 34).
    Stepped rising thirds and leaping minor sixths—vocal coloratura in another age —are here pervaded by a gentle lyricism, with falling cadential fourths and oscillations about a momentary centre, paralleling Bellini recitative.
4. Choir:
Open triads, moving smoothly from F sharp minor through A flat major in six measures, illustrate points of style already mentioned, allowing the voices to express unworthiness; the poet's inability to reach to the depths of life.
    '. . . among the poorest and lowliest and lost'.
This phrase, reiterated four times, casts fresh light upon states of being, cf. Christ's Sermon on the Mount, which are incomprehensible in worldly terms. The original motive appears fleetingly in a mood searching and straining for understanding, assisted by a rising fourth falling second motive. Dissonances are mild; the delicate

Fig. 33

Fig. 34

woodwinds comment. A highly dissonant final *ritornello* resolves into unison spread over five octaves.

5. *Bass:*

The positive core of the poem lies here:

'Leave this chanting and singing and telling of beads . . .'

Terse and declamatory, syncopated brass chords puncture the self-indulgence of the religious sentimentalist. The original motive appears once, subtly hidden in the sub-structure and covering several measures with the B minor to C minor link again apparent (Fig. 35). The final section of twenty measures—'Meet him and stand by him in toil and sweat of thy brow'—is noble acknowledgement of the power of tonality. Cumulated motives are hammered out in richly textured sound with heartfelt conviction.

6. *Soprano:*

Surely Hindemith's tonal concept of tension and relaxation are felt in this short paraphrase. The luminous, less austere mood, with Straussian filagree never too voluptuous, retains the innocence of the earlier song—also ♩♪♩ patterns—and uses triadic melody.

Fig. 35

'There are times when I languidly linger and times when I awaken and hurry
in search of my goal . . .'
The sensuousness portrayed by a slower harmonic rhythm, first inversion harmonies
and soft dissonance, does not detract from the direction and agility of the singer,
although this section is the least inspired. The accompaniment murmurs and oscil-
lates about clear diatonic centres.

7. Bass:
Strange sonorities reminding one of Holst's *Uranus* or Messiaen's first movement
in his *Quartet for the End of Time* reiterate in measured dotted rhythms the slow,
steady pulse of the universe.
'I am here to sing thee songs,
   in this hall of thine I have a corner seat . . .'
The sheer power of harmony, gained through linear progression, relentlessly and
joyfully climaxes with:
'Honour me, commanding my presence'.

8. Soprano:
The singer leaps the octave in expectation, then like the descending steps of earth-
bound music sinks quietly back at the phrase's end. The sparse orchestration leaves
the voice free for spiritual utterance.
'I am only waiting to give myself up at last into his hands.' Again, fluctuating
thirds, melodic oscillation and a free ternary structure are characteristic of the
composer's awareness of the existence of divine truth and his unfulfilled search
for it.

9. If the influence of Sibelius can be seen in the spare texture of the previous song,
in the finale the patriotic brilliance of a Shostakovitch is apparent. The rushing
semiquavers and hammering bursts of brass join with a swinging 6/8 using
'Let my country awake'

in a sincere attempt to match in sound and words a spiritual awareness of the best in Mankind. Then, in extended *fugato*, coupled with long phrases in chorale style, fragments from other movements coalesce with the intervallic relationship of the third prominent.

'Into that heaven of freedom, my father,
Let my country awake . . .'

Vocally and orchestrally exciting, and too burning a personal issue for pompous indulgence, the oratorio ends broadly and positively in E major.

String Quartet (A.P.R.A.) 1967

Briefly, this work shows another side of Hanson's nature. Apart from fine craftsman-ship and awareness of sonorities, the working out of motives, avoidance of tonal implications, and use of techniques such as imitation, pairing, displacement, frag-mentation and transformation are emphasized. Although the texture is thick and the approach thematic rather than melodic, Hanson's characteristic harmonies appear. The rhythmic ambiguity of 6/8 3/4 in the opening Scherzo shows a wit not often heard in his music. There is some working out of motives at (40) (Fig. 36).

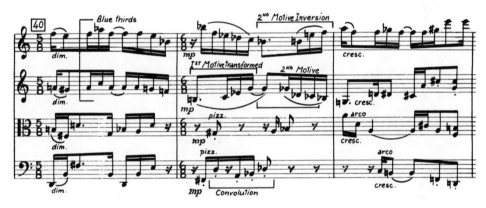

Fig. 36

Episodic, self-contained and organic in structure, there are definite points of recall. In the Variations the atonal theme is completely transformed in the 3rd Variation and the Schoenbergian preoccupation with rhythmic interest and interplay but without the surprise and drama associated with the Austrian—takes Hanson deeper into new waters. The *Toccata* with its pulsating dotted rhythms and glimpses of individual melodies amid complex harmonies and interplay reminds one of the composer's love of Beethoven's *Grosse Fuge*, with its vigorous dotted rhythm and demanding technique. His love of the late quartets is clear.

'I would like to memorise Beethoven's Op. 131 in time
for the end.'

Epilogue is forty measures of intense reflection, explicably tonal, using the discord in a pointilistic manner; ruminating and lyrical. Bitonal elements create luminous sonorities which please rather than distress the ear (Fig. 37).

The music dies away with an augmented triad combined with the tritone as if to say 'I have succeeded in using a new technique, touching Serialism, but have retained my individuality and my own brand of uncompromising lyricism'.

Fig. 37

Publishers

Ricordi, Allans, Nicholsons, Southern Music, Peer International.

Bibliography

Best, M. *Australian Composers and their Music*. Adelaide, 1961, p. 28.
Covell, Roger. *Australia's Music: Themes of a New Society*. Sun Books, Melbourne, 1967, pp. 160–1. (See also *Canon*, v (1952), p. 474; *Music and Dance*, lii (July 1961), p. 12.
Murdoch, James. *Australia's Contemporary Composers*. Macmillan, Melbourne, 1972.

Select List of Works

Opera
The Golden Ring (one act) (1958)
The Lost Child (one act) (1959)
Jane Greer (two acts and Prologue) (1974)

Ballet
Dhoogor (1941–45)

Orchestral
Concerto for violin (1946)
Novelette (1946)
Concerto for trumpet (1947)
Symphony in one movt (1951–52)
Concerto for trombone (1954)
Gula (1967)
Movement (homage to Alfred Hill) (1969)

Chamber Music
Sonata for violin and piano (1940)
Sonata for flute and piano (1940)
Legende for violin and piano (1947)
Sonatina for viola and piano (1954)
String quartet (1967)
Divertimento for fl ob cl a sax and bn (1971)
Dedication 2 fl and cl (1973)

Piano Music
Sonata (1938–40)
Six Preludes (1940)
Sonatina (1949)
Idylle (1952)
Episodes on Tarry Trowsers (1948)
Numerous miniatures including *On Holidays*, *Quizzic*, *Procrastination* and teaching pieces such as *Five Portraits* (1948)

Organ Music
Sonata (1952)
Three Preludes (1964)

Vocal Music
Several major sets of songs include *Seven Settings of Tagore* (1959–60), as well as settings of Karl Hanson and Dame Mary Gilmore.
The Lord Reigneth cantata for contralto, organ and strings (From the Psalms) (1966)
Fern Hill for soprano and orchestra (Dylan Thomas) (1969)

Choral Music
The Immortal Touch oratorio (1958)
The Web is Wove unaccomp. chor. (1968)

Discography

Concerto for trumpet (Lovelock: Concerto for trumpet). John Robertson (trumpet), Sydney Symphony Orchestra (Joseph Post, conductor).
RCA disc SL 26371
Fern Hill   Festival disc SFC 80021
I Dreamt That She Sat by my Head. Tagore.
Brolga Recordings

Dorian Le Gallienne
(1915—63)

Noël Nickson

'The death of Dorian Le Gallienne means that we have lost one of the outstanding artists of our time, one whose dedication to art, complete and entire, was an inspiration.'[1] Le Gallienne was an original. All who knew him liked him for what he was—a genuinely sensitive musical man of individual taste, independent mind, and deep spiritual strength. These qualities are observed in his many works, more consistently and generously in those of his later years. As ailing health sapped his physical strength, so his intellectual and creative powers increased. During the ten years leading to his death at the age of forty-seven Le Gallienne produced a number of major works in which he found an acceptable reconciliation of his conservative nature and his deeply personal experience of contemporary society.

Seeking success in large-scale forms Le Gallienne revived the problem of the romantic symphonists: how to develop lyrical ideas in traditional dramatic contexts. The relationship of style and idea had always concerned the hypersensitive composer whose creative imagination had potential beyond the capacity of the tonal methods with which he was familiar. Organization of time and rhythm was the basis of his structural problem which, the evidence shows, he resolved to his satisfaction from about 1953. Returning to Australia at this time from a second period of study in Britain, a new note of authority, confidence and clarity is heard in his music.

Five major works of Le Gallienne demonstrate his peak period—Sinfonietta (1951–56), Overture in E flat (1952), Symphony (1952–53), Duo (1956) and Trio (1957). As the Symphony has been unaccountably neglected since its first performance twenty years ago, the present discussion will be limited to the Sinfonietta, the Symphony and the Symphonic Study (1963). These three works merit consideration ahead of the film music and other instrumental pieces. Critical research into the chamber music and vocal works must be deferred for an independent study.

The Sinfonietta makes a good point of departure from the general to the specific. A three-movement work, its first and last notes bridge a five-year span. At the outset the conflict of style and idea threatens to be troublesome, but in the end the problem is almost overcome. It is interesting to note that the first two movements of the Sinfonietta were written, if not actually completed, during 1951–52, and the last movement several years later.[2] In the years between Le Gallienne became involved with the Overture in E flat and the Symphony. Thoroughly absorbed in the Symphony, he worked through the four movements, scored them out and heard the piece performed publicly in Melbourne on 5 September 1955. What he learnt and gained in so doing returned him to the Sinfonietta a mature composer. There is not only a change of utterance in the finale; there is also a change of heart.

It is easy to identify influences in the Sinfonietta—Poulenc, Bartók, Hindemith, Shostakovich and Vaughan Williams for some—and one can accept the characteristic tunes and episodes if the ear and the heart respond to spontaneous lyricism and sincerity. One might also adopt a gentle attitude towards the Sinfonietta, knowing the composer's health problem, his deeply sensitive self-consciousness, and that the piece was so much part of the man he was at the time.

Scored for small orchestra in B flat (double wind, two horns and strings) Sinfonietta has individual themes which form its most pleasing features, although the style of other composers show through. But the problem of the work is one of rhythm, primarily harmonic rhythm. Further, the almost total absence of dotted rhythms in the essential ideas and extensions of them becomes increasingly evident as the work progresses.

To illustrate, harmonic movement is almost totally abandoned in the contrasting subject area of the exposition of the first movement (Allegro 4/4). From [2] to [5] of the score, fifty-five measures in triple time, where the harmony consists of D flat–A flat open fifth for nineteen measures, B natural–G flat (F sharp) for twenty, A–E for four, and D flat–A flat again for twelve. After this the revival of harmonic movement is of necessity immediate in order to propel the argument forward, but even so harmonic rhythm throughout is exceptionally slow-moving for symphonic organization. The lyrical style of Le Gallienne's thought at this time dictates a sacrifice of this kind. When the bass is allowed thematic material it assumes importance and relevance, but throughout the movement the support bass is weak. Two further instances of inertia of harmonic rhythm occur later in the same movement, these three passages accounting for more than half its length.

This was Le Gallienne's problem at that time, a problem which he tried to alleviate by almost total concentration on lyrical expression, sharp tonal conflicts in contrapuntal texture, and changing time signatures. The movement has its life, a happy but changeable one. The composer shows his real power in the transitions and in the development, where a fine augmentation of the opening reveals greater breadth and stature. The movement opens as follows—

Fig. 38

which, after one of the very static sections referred to above, moves into an augmentation of strong conviction supported by a bouncing *ostinato* pattern.

Fig. 39 Sinfonietta, opening bars

The second movement (*Andante molto tranquillo*, 6/8) is more personal.

Fig. 40 The second movement of the Sinfonietta, Bars 1–6

The composer takes up residence in G. The rate of harmonic change is more appropriate to the pastoral style and the melodic paragraphs are mature and well filled out. The use of instrumental colour and texture is more significant, and tonality more flexible though well controlled. The composer continues to avoid accepting responsibility for the bass as an essential sponsor of time in music, but allows the cellos the leading role in the tenor register in the central episode of the three-section form.

The tonal system which interests the composer is clearly one based on relationships of keys a third apart. To a degree this can be observed in the first movement but it is more convincing in the second. G and B majors, dissolving into E for the central episode, lead on round the flat side to a return in B flat and D, before returning to the tonic which itself was a third off the prime key of the first movement.

Composed several years later, the finale (*Allegro con spirito*, 2/4) shows a great advance in mastery of materials. B flat is restored buoyantly and sharply tinselled with new chromaticism in melody and harmony. Pedal points are almost abandoned, but *ostinato* occurs and dactylic rhythms in seconds stutter *falsetto* through the middle section with strong persistence. The opening is a marked change from the tone and texture of the earlier movements.

Fig. 41 The opening bars of the third movement of the Sinfonietta

The themes are more motivic than tuneful, transitions more concentrated and tense. The construction is compact and mature, while the time problem is almost overcome in the forward thrust and energy of creative concentration. The answer has been found in escape from diatonic definition, a new tonal freedom, bitonal contrapuntal textures, and reduced delay in transition. Everything falls into perspective with bounding excitement and energy. The only remaining question is how to write the coda. In later works the composer finally solved this question. Le Gallienne was now in full possession of his creative faculties and master of his materials.

The composition of the Symphony between the second and third movements of the Sinfonietta seems to have occupied the composer continuously over several years. He was now free of major distractions (apart from his job as music critic) and free of that ambivalence which was always a part of Le Gallienne to be reckoned with.

The attempt to write a symphony at this time may have been due to the wisdom and encouragement of Gordon Jacob, with whom Le Gallienne had been studying in London in 1951–52. Perhaps Jacob directed Le Gallienne towards traditional symphonic discipline as a challenge to his vitally creative mind and emotional maturity. Further, Le Gallienne needed a large orchestral work to put him in the front line of Australian composers. He was now ready to match his powers with the traditional symphony and all it meant to composers, conductors and audiences of that time.

For an Australian to write a good symphony was arresting in itself. Of notable Australian composers born between 1910 and 1920 and resident in the country, only three beside Le Gallienne wrote symphonies between 1945 and 1955,—Hanson (in one movement, 1951–52), Hughes (Symphony no. 1, 1951 rev. 1971), and Penberthy (the first and the second, 1948 and 1953). On completing his symphony Le Gallienne had advanced beyond his contemporaries and established himself as a leading Australian composer. Unfortunately the symphony finished in 1953 has been unjustly neglected. It is a strong, individual and convincing composition which from the outset should have attracted the attention of commercial recording and publishing industries.

Like the Sinfonietta the Symphony carries no key description on its title page. Although there are no key signatures used here or in the Sinfonietta, Le Gallienne accepted tonality in the wide terms of his day. The Symphony is in E major and minor. Many chords suggesting other keys are shaded in or stressed in recognizable but fleeting definitions according to structural focus and emotional tension—tonality is very flexible, even unstable—but E is the tonal centre of the Symphony as a whole and everything is heard in relation to it. Le Gallienne's practice of tonality in this work has some resemblance to that of Vaughan Williams in his Fourth Symphony, and to Honegger, Hindemith, and other twentieth-century composers, but the Australian composer lacked their experience and lucidity. Although allowing traditional common chord structures into his tonal parameter, Le Gallienne worked strenuous two- and three-part contrapuntal textures over them, taking care that superimposed vertical contacts avoided agreement with supporting triadic conventions.

This was not always the case in Le Gallienne's music. Such a description makes his writing sound more simple than it is. Often in the Symphony it is very complex—in the outer movements loud and complex. Nevertheless conflict between harmonic and contrapuntal texture is a feature to be met with *in extenso* in Le Gallienne's music. It exemplifies one of the antitheses to be found in the musical exercise of the man, between the nature of his technique and ideas. The evidence is less in the Symphony than in the Sinfonietta, though harmony as a structural attribute of form and expression is more purposeful in the Symphony, and the power of utterance overrides the mechanical procedures which make its existence possible.

The relationship of keys a third apart is more intense and indeed more intimate in the symphonic work. The music moves with nervous restlessness but insistent determination around focal points, neither major nor minor. Shifts on the basis of this relationship are heard not only between the four movements but also within each movement, where striking adjustments of tonality are achieved between ex- positionary business statements and recapitulatory retrospects or fulfilments. The Symphony is a very strong work—powerful, intransigent, monumental—'the most accomplished and purposive symphony written by an Australian'.[3]

Fig. 42 First movement of the Symphony, Bars 1–8

At the outset the first movement (*allegro* 3/4, but changing time signature thirteen times in the first twenty-five measures) establishes a tense and turbulent emotional situation. Themes and motivic figures pass rapidly, each with its own identity, but sufficiently compatible within a broad uniformity of style. The formal features of a traditional twentieth-century symphonic movement are observed amid music stirred up by strident conflicts of horizontal and vertical tensions and driven by emotional power from beginning to end. Whatever Le Gallienne's health and temperament at the time of composing this movement, he delivers his address in passionate excitement, pausing for no echo, and barely hesitating for breath.

The instrumentation is careful but colourful, with edge on the tone and attack on the ear. His development is a process of extension of melody in time. This is not music for lazy pedal-points; there is only one weak section in this regard, prior to the return—five measures on C, seven on A, and thirteen on F sharp. However, through these twenty-five measures there are clever *stretti* in simultaneous augmentation and diminution. Entries crowd in on each other pressing for home. But the passage is contrived where imagination was most needed. Apart from this instance the composer has consciously extended his skill in bass writing which frequently gives just enough harmonic implication when dissonant counterpoint is overlaid. Dotted rhythms are almost entirely absent, in fact the even groups of eighth-notes are perhaps the one single deficiency throughout Le Gallienne's music, which superficially and fundamentally restrict the stature of his invention. In both his ideas and his working of them, the rhythmic regularity of the minor incidents and the major events tends to become predictable, and thus to reduce tension when the composer feels it most. Nevertheless, the movement is admirable, sincere and thoroughly positive. For the time of its composition it demonstrated two things— that Le Gallienne had become astonishingly free in his thinking, and unexpectedly demonstrative in self-revelation.

The second movement (*presto* 12/8) is fantastic and mysterious. Never rising above *mezzo-forte* it moves *moto perpetuo*, a will-o' the-wisp, evasive, mocking. It is one of those movements in which a composer distends his keys a fraction above and below so constantly as to defeat a search for pedantic definition. The movement is a scherzo in which B major and minor colours a hazy backdrop of fleeting phosphorescence and shimmering images. The trio section is tied to an inner pedal third of D-F sharp (apart from several momentary changes of one or other note by a half-tone). The scherzo returns, followed by a slightly shortened presentation of the trio, this time with B-D sharp sounding continuously. In the whole movement the four-pulse time signature is constant, and melody prevails. Variety is achieved in unpredictable phrase lengths and speedy contrasts of idea and texture. The movement holds together well, is successfully scored, and effectively balanced.

The slow movement (*Lento* 4/4) is in A flat, enharmonic notation for G sharp, the mediant major of the first movement and the relative minor of the second. Here the pedal-points of the opening and closing sections spell repose and quiet, but there is a deep sadness in the melodies. This poignant expression is achieved through the melody-harmony relationship, the one liberated from sweet diatonicism and the other insistent on traditional authority. A very slow harmonic rhythm saves the composer's soulful lyricism from sentimentality. It is a total personal experience revealed in the music. Though splendidly prepared, the ponderous *fortissimo* climax relieves not the heart. Release is frantically sought but not found. Submission brings the only relief. The music gradually fades to the point at which it began.

Instrumentally the two central movements are the most successful. Primary colours are well chosen, structural details suitably concealed. The time problem is satisfactorily resolved, and form and content maturely matched. In both these movements style and idea are essentially one. Le Gallienne has achieved his ambition and proved himself a real composer. From this moment his voice is that of the convinced creative artist, secure in craft and original in thought.

The finale (*Allegro molto*, 6/4) resumes the physical energy and drive forgotten since the first movement thundered to a sullen standstill. Symphonic life since that moment has not been easy nor happy, but bluster and fearful anticipation had been put aside for a deeper and more individual experience too personal for cold words to capture. Now once more into the tumult.

The composer finds himself again in a situation where he needs muscle and spiritual strength, but this time the direction is reversed. In the first movement he faced outwards to go forward, this time he looks straight at himself. The ideas are quite different. The themes are more conjunct though reaching still further into chromaticism. The movement begins and ends in E, but the textural complexities of the structural fabric give few clues.

Although the music is still lyrical, as it always was with Le Gallienne, melodic extensions and additions are the manner of his development aided by all the contrapuntal devices including canon, augmentation, and diminution. Melody is never absent, which can be a composer's disability in symphonic organization. From the outset nervous figures attract attention, stir up irritating fuss, take over the words from the argument.

Fig. 43 Finale of the Symphony

But the lyrical muse nourishes the soul of this artist and never lets him down. There are moments of great beauty, touches of colour not to be forgotten, and a splendidly timed passage of quite simple scoring and thematic transformation leading back to the inevitable return. The coda, a disappointment in the Sinfonietta, is more expertly handled here. If Le Gallienne had memories of earlier failures, at this point he erased them with a precisely controlled ending of loud augmented recalls of the opening phrase of the first movement transformed into chords of revelation, translucent and transcendent. Never losing his vision or his identification with it, the composer closes the Symphony victoriously. The creative spirit is exalted in its destiny.

Sufficient to leave the Symphony at this point. Harmony is the propeller of symphonic development in the romantic and twentieth-century tradition. The problem of harmonic choice and timing is one Le Gallienne lived with in all his large-scale compositions. Try as he did to disguise it with counterpoint, figurative overlay, aggressive dynamics, distorted tonal contrivances,. he was too good a composer to believe that the total solution could be found in subterfuge. He had still to strive to master it. Perhaps if he reduced his texture, took out the harmonic weight from the middle orchestra, concentrated still more on line and time relations, in fact on counterpoint which in the right situations produced its own harmony and dictated its own rate of change, then he might find the full subjective experience for which he yearned. The Symphonic Study shows that this was the direction he was now to take.

In 1960 Le Gallienne left Australia for a year to live in Greece. The working holiday was remarkable for its effect on him. It was not the first time he had been there, but at the age of forty-five he was going at a most important time in his life. Greece symbolized the classic concept of art as Le Gallienne had always imagined it in the universal experience of man. There he saw the answers to the questions which had occupied his mind for years. The superb humanity and spirit of marble sculpture, the refined delicacy and optical illusions of ancient architecture, the magnificent logic of grand columns, and the deep colour of famous ikons. The impact was stunning. Enriched with a new sense of order and beauty and a new understanding of himself, Le Gallienne returned to Melbourne to continue work on a second symphony, excited but much weakened in health. He died in 1963 leaving the first movement almost completed. Posthumously named 'Symphonic Study', it was his last work.

Symphonic Study (*Allegro moderato*, 4/4) is a vindication of Le Gallienne's life's experience. All the features of his music are now reduced to a common level. A traditional formal principle is acknowledged. Dotted notes remain absent, but the bass line is now mature and the rhythm never shuffles. The composer knew just what he was doing. He approached the heart of his own human experience and bared what he found there. Rarely has such deep feeling been shared so consciously. Classical economy is written over the score.

The music moves almost entirely in two or three parts. There is little harmony in an organized functional sense. The score is full of open spaces except for four pages in the middle of the work (*meno mosso* 3/4) lasting nineteen measures. The themes of the movement are essentially lyrical but with motivic features to which attention is frequently drawn. Texture is light, doubling reduced. Only the essentials are now necessary.

Symphonic Study marks a purification of Le Gallienne's style. Extravagance of feeling and display has been pruned, brilliance of colour is reduced although the edge is still sharp. The humble sincerity of the committed artist is exposed for what it is.

What the second symphony might have become is beyond conjecture. The single movement is evidence enough that given ten more years this man would have surpassed the finest music of his contemporaries and gained a reputation far beyond the shores of Australia.

Fig. 44 Symphonic Study, Bars 1–6

Le Gallienne was an outstanding artist of his time, 'one whose dedication to art, complete and entire, was an inspiration'[4] to all those who heard his music and were privileged to have enjoyed his acquaintance.

All of the music of Dorian Le Gallienne has been deposited with the State Library of Victoria. It is housed in the Manuscripts Section of the Latrobe Library.

Some of the material is impossible to date accurately and even to identify as the MSS. include loose pages without numbers and titles, some rough sketches in score on unconnected pages and passages in reduced score, some completed scores, works of which there are all or some instrumental parts and no score, and unfinished works in rough score or with incomplete or uncompleted parts and no score. In addition, as the composer often sketched hastily in pencil, the original or photocopy of the original is sometimes faint and not always decipherable. A further problem is that of handwriting.

A number of the MSS. are in the composer's hand but carry a title and/or date in another hand. Some works exist only in instrumental parts in handwritings other than the composer's. Quite an amount of the material in the Latrobe Library is photocopied from pages which are not contained in the collection. Much work lies ahead to bring brighter light to the Le Gallienne MSS. and papers, and to penetrate the workings, range, and power of his musical mind.

To the present time the work of two people is due for acknowledgement—Miss Margaret Dixon of the State Library of Victoria, who compiled the lists of music deposited in the Library, and the composer Mr Robert Hughes of the Australian Broadcasting Commission, Melbourne, who has done what he can to bring order out of, not actually chaos, but haphazard disarray. Robert Hughes has made it possible to publish a number of Le Gallienne's works in performing editions.

The dates given in the list of published works are dates of publication. Those in the list of unpublished works are dates of composition given by Garretty (see note 2), and/or M. Dixon ('List of music deposited with the Victorian State Library' 23 December 1963, 22 August 1964, unpub.).

Notes

1. Anon., 'Vale', *Adult Education* (Council of Adult Education, Melbourne), Sept. 1963, vol. vii, no. 1, p. 5.
2. J. D. Garretty, Three Australian Composers, M.A. thesis, University of Melbourne, 1963, 2 vols, i, 145.
3. Roger Covell, *Australia's Music: Themes of a New Society*, Melbourne, 1967, p. 162.
4. 'Vale', *op. cit.*, p. 5.

Published Works (alphabetical list)

A Jinker Ride for piano (Allans, Melbourne, 1965).
Duo for Violin and Viola (Melbourne University Press, 1963).
'Farewell! Thou art too dear for my possessing': Sonnet no. 89 Shakespeare for voice and piano. [Published under the auspices of the Lady Northcote Permanent Orchestra Trust Fund] (Allans, Melbourne, 1954).
Four Divine Poems of John Donne for voice and piano (Allans, Melbourne, 1967). 'A Hymne to God the Father'; 'Death be not proud'; 'At the round earths imagin'd corners'; 'Batter my heart, three person'd God'.
Four Nursery Rhymes with pianoforte accompaniment (London, Augener, 1955). 'I had a little nut tree'; 'There was a king'; 'Peter White'; 'Grey goose and gander'.
'Go, Heart', unison song for voice and piano (Allans, Melbourne, 1956).
'I bind unto myself today' (The School Anthem), *Methodist Ladies' College*, (*Hawthorn*) *Song Book*, for three voices and piano, words by St Patrick, trans. by C.F. Alexander. (Priv. publ. M.L.C., Hawthorn, 1960).
Nocturne for piano (Allans, Melbourne, 1964).
Sinfonietta for orchestra, study score. [Australian Music Fund] (Allans, Melbourne, 1956).
'Solveig's Song' from Ibsen's *Peer Gynt*, for voice and piano. [Published under the auspices of the Lady Northcote Permanent Trust Fund] (Allans, Melbourne, 1954).
Sonata for piano [Australian Music Fund] (Allans, Melbourne, 1969). Only three movements complete, the finale was never written.
Sonata for violin and piano [Australian Music Fund] (Allans, Melbourne, 1969).

Unpublished Complete Works

Stage Music
BALLET MUSIC
Contes Héraldiques (The Sleepy Princess) (1947) [A.B.C., Sydney]
Voyageur (1954) [Ballet Victoria, Melbourne]

INCIDENTAL MUSIC, VOCAL AND INSTRUMENTAL
Twelfth Night (Shakespeare) (1945)
Othello (Shakespeare) (1946)
Macbeth (Shakespeare) (1949)
The Rivals (Sheridan) (1950)

Peer Gynt (Ibsen) (1950)
The Caucasian Chalk Circle (Brecht) (1959)

Film Music
The Prize (1960) [dir. Tim Burstall]
Sebastian and the Sausages (1961) [puppets, Peter Scriven]
Dance of the Angels (1962) [ceramic figurines, John Percival]
The Crucifixion (1963) [bass reliefs, Matcham Skipper]

Orchestral Music
Sonatina for two pianos (1941) orch. arr. Verdon Williams, undated
Overture in E flat (1952) [A.P.R.A., Sydney] (hire library, Allans, Melbourne)
Symphony (1953) [A.B.C., Sydney]
Symphonic Study (1963) [A.B.C., Melbourne]

Chamber Music
Sonata for flute and piano (1943)
Fugue for string quartet [?]
Trio for oboe, violin, and viola (1957)
Two Pieces (1959)
1. violin, cello, clarinet, percussion, and harp
2. two clarinets and string quartet

Piano Music
Symphonic Study (1940)
Sonatina for two pianos (1941)
Three Piano Pieces (1947)
Legend for two pianos [?]
Sonatina [1963?] one movement completed by Robert Hughes

Choral Music
Three Psalms (1948), for chorus and organ [Psalms 93, 142 and 47]
O Rose thou art sick [?], W. Blake, unacc.
Matthew, Mark, Luke and John [?], unacc.
Most blessed of mornings [?], unnamed text, unacc.

Vocal Music
Fear no more the heart of the sun (Shakespeare) (1943)
No longer mourn for me (Shakespeare) (1946)
How oft, when thou, my Music (Shakespeare) (1946)
Beloved, let us love one another (*The Bible* John 1) [?]
Five Songs for Male Voice [?], un-named texts
Bear away Death; Give and take; Orpheus, thy charm hath flown; Come Folly, sweet Folly; So meets and sips my soul.
Moonlight (H. McCrae) (1948)
The Cactus of the Moon (N. Keesing) (1956)
Three Songs (1957)
The Ghost (Omi Okura trans. C.A. Walsh); Winter (J.C. Hobson); Cranes (T.W. Earp).

Unpublished Uncompleted Works

Incidental music
Little plays of St Francis (1942)
Vocal music
The Apparition (J. Donne) (1956?)

Discography

Overture in E flat (1952) [8′20″]. Victorian Symphony
Orchestra (Clive Douglas, conductor). MS. 1961.
ABC recording PR/3280
Overture in E flat (1952) [8′20″]. West Australian
Symphony Orchestra (Georg Tintner, conductor).
Allan. Feb. 1971. *ABC tape*
Symphony in E (1953) [29′23″]. Victorian Symphony
Orchestra (Walter Susskind, conductor). MS. 1961.
ABC recording COL PRX/3902
Sinfonietta (1956) [12′40″]. Melbourne Symphony
Orchestra (John Hopkins, conductor). Allan. July
1966. *World Record Club disc S/FRAM*
Ballet Suite: *Voyageur* (1954). Ballet Guild Orchestra
(Harold Badger, conductor).
W & G disc AL/660
Contes Héraldiques (1947) [28′45″]. Victorian Sym-
phony Orchestra (Clive Douglas, conductor). MS.
1961. *ABC recording 2XS/1343*
Duo for violin and viola (1956). Sybil Copeland
(violin), John Glickman (viola).
W & G disc CL/660
Sonata for violin and piano (1945) [11′45″]. Thomas
Matthews (violin), Eileen Ralf (piano). MS. 1961.
ABC recording PRX/5334
Four Divine Poems of John Donne (1947–50) [11′35″].
(i) 'A Hymn to God the Father'—3′04″; (ii) 'Death
be not proud'—3′13″; (iii) 'At the round earths
imagin'd corners'—3′14″; (iv) 'Batter My Heart'—
2′04″. Lauris Elms (contralto), Marie van Hove
(piano). Allan. 4 June 1965.
World Record Club disc A/602
Solveig's Song (1946)—2′05″; Four Nursery Rhymes
(1945)—3′32″. Vera Cappadona (soprano), Valda
Johnstone (piano).
ABC recording PRX/5597 (ABR only).

Film Music

The Crucifixion (orchestra conducted by George
Dreyfus)
Dance of the Angels (orchestra conducted by the
composer)
Sebastian and the Sausages (orchestra conducted by
the composer)
The Prize (orchestra conducted by George Logie-
Smith)

James Penberthy
(*b.* 1917)

John Meyer

James Penberthy was born in Melbourne in 1917, but by virtue of more than twenty years residence in Perth prior to his move to Sydney in 1974, he has gained particular recognition as the most prominent composer to be associated with the western capital. In spite of his close personal attachment to the landscape and peoples of Western Australia, however, he has more than a merely parochial significance. His earlier works in particular align him with composers like Antill, Douglas and Sculthorpe, all of whom have consciously striven in various and often quite diverse ways to create a body of music that is specifically Australian both in inspiration and spirit.

It was in Melbourne that Penberthy received his professional training as a composer—at the Melbourne University Conservatorium of Music,[1] where his contemporaries included Don Banks, Peter Sculthorpe, Keith Humble and George Dreyfus. Between 1951 and 1953 he studied in England, France and Italy under a Victorian State Government scholarship. Perhaps as important a circumstance as any for the setting of the direction that Penberthy's music was to take, however, was not his academic training but his practical involvement in the theatre as musical director of the National Ballet from 1947 to 1950. During the next decade ballets and operas formed the bulk of his output. It was also in this period that he established himself as a musical nationalist, since almost all his theatrical works were based on Aboriginal stories or legends, or on other subjects with specifically Australian associations.

The extent of the influence of Aboriginal culture on Penberthy's early music is immediately apparent from a glance at the list of his works. Among his ballets, *Euroka* (1947), *Brolga* (1949), *Boomerang* (1951), *The Whirlwind* (1954) and *Kooree and the Mists* (1960) are based on Aboriginal stories or legends, while the operas *Larry* (1955), *The Earth Mother* (1957–58) and *Dalgerie* (1958) are all concerned with aspects of the uneasy relationship between the Aboriginal and European races. In the field of instrumental music a similar influence is apparent. The Second Piano Concerto (1955) is subtitled *Aboriginal*; *Julunggul and Kadjari* (1957) is described as a 'ritual dance' for orchestra, while the Sextet (1954) for flute, oboe, clarinet, horn and two bassoons uses Aboriginal themes and rhythms as the basis of its material.

In order to examine in greater detail the music from this phase of Penberthy's career, let us consider in turn a ballet, an opera, and a symphony. The story of *Kooree and the Mists* concerns a young Aboriginal girl who seeks refuge from evil spirits among the mists rising from a paperbark swamp after a hot day. The ballet's subject lends itself to music of an impressionistic character, and the rising of the mists is aptly represented by slow-moving chromatic chords and darkly coloured orchestration, resulting in a sombre, brooding atmosphere typical of Penberthy's early music. As a consequence of the comparative dearth of original or striking thematic invention, however, the atmospheric passages in *Kooree and the Mists* are more effective than the purely melodic ones. One cannot escape the feeling that the best ideas in the work are basically derivative, whether the source be Delius, Satie or Poulenc. A similar impression is made by the Sixth Symphony (1962), where the strongest influence is that of Stravinsky, but the contrasts in texture and mood are far greater than in the ballet, and the work as a whole makes a more striking impact. The symphony is subtitled *The Earth Mother* and is closely related to Penberthy's three-act opera of the same name, an 'aboriginal folk-lore tragedy' dating from 1957–58. As a starting point for his music, Penberthy takes a popular Aboriginal song from the north-west of Western Australia; its melody is heard at the beginning of the overture and recurs as a leitmotiv throughout the opera. The song describes the Earth Mother as a hole in the ground out of which everything grew—in other words, the source of creation. In the opera, however, the idea of the Earth Mother is transformed into an ironic, pathetic symbol of primitive in-nocence corrupted by European civilization: an Aboriginal city prostitute in love with a half-caste who has successfully found his place in the bewildering new world imposed on their race by the white settlers. They have a child, but tragedy strikes with the sudden revelation that they both had the same mother.

In *The Earth Mother* such traditional devices of European opera are used in a new, localized setting. Just before the dramatic discovery of the lovers' true relation-ship, there is a comic scene in a shearing shed, based on an authentic folk ballad, *The Ballad of Crooked Mick* (the words are traditional, but the music is Penberthy's), so that the tragedy strikes with even greater force after this passage of light relief. The conventional love duet is here too, forming the central point in the second act. Much of the music, both here and in the rest of the opera, is in a continuous, de-clamatory style, but there are also more conventionally melodic moments like *The Ballad of Crooked Mick* and another ballad sung by the prostitutes as they hang out their washing.

An exotic flavour is imparted to the opera by the use of Aboriginal motives and rhythms, and by imitations of the didjeridu. In Penberthy's better-known opera *Dalgerie* (1958)—with a libretto drawn from Mary Durack's novel *Keep Him My Country*[2]—the composer inserted a sequence of authentic native dances, and in the 1973 production at the Sydney Opera House these were performed by Aborig-inals from Arnhem Land and the Kimberleys.

The Symphony is more elemental than the opera; the thick orchestration and violent outbursts of the first and fourth movements are intended to represent the rugged, primitive aspects of nature, and the dramatic gestures of these movements are obviously theatrical both in inspiration and in effect. The first movement portrays the creation of the earth and the birth of man and is based on the 'Earth Mother' theme, while the wild and stormy beginning of the finale, 'with its jagged harmonies and the impression of wind and sea, was suggested by the rock formations on the western tip of stormy Cape Naturaliste'.[3] The slow movement draws on the opera's love duet, but here the music becomes a sad expression of the destruction of Aboriginal culture in the wake of the white man's invasion. The finale of the Sixth Symphony introduces recollections of the earlier movements, such recollections persistently interrupting the stormy passages. At the end, the 'Earth Mother' theme makes a last appearance before being swamped by the final overwhelming climax.

Another cyclic instrumental work is the Viola Concerto (1962), which has a summarizing epilogue at the end of the third movement. This work's emotional atmosphere, however, is completely different—not surprisingly, considering the nature of the solo instrument. Whereas the shadow of Stravinsky seems to hover over the Sixth Symphony, Bartók is the composer most readily brought to mind by the Viola Concerto, which was written for the Hungarian violist Paul Komlos. The work is generally intimate and restrained, although there are some abrasive harmonies and orchestral effects in the finale, a sprightly dance-like movement with a repetitive main idea and a short, partly accompanied cadenza. The focal point of the work is the Andante, a sustained meditative aria for the viola, framed and interrupted by a tense, declamatory idea, and with its melancholy character heightened by sinking harmonic progressions and a questioning cadential figure (derived from the recitative) at the close.

The Viola Concerto is perhaps the most impressive example of that combination of lyricism and emotional warmth that is the hallmark of Penberthy's music, at least until about 1965. Within the admittedly conservative, romantic style of this period, he wrote a number of works that impress by their workmanship and sincerity. The central aria of *Dalgerie*—'Keep him my country'—makes a moving effect, as does the *Cantata on the Hiroshima Panels*, the first of three works ($E = MC^2$ and *Hiroshima* being the others) that derive their impetus from the memory of the bombing of Hiroshima. Scored for soprano, tenor, baritone, chorus and orchestra, this work is occasionally reminiscent of *The Dream of Gerontius* in general atmosphere and in its alternation between declamation and arioso; indeed, Penberthy uses exactly the same vocal forces as did Elgar, although it is the baritone who has the most solo work. The favouring of this voice and of its orchestral equivalents is once again indicative of Penberthy's somewhat brooding, darkly-coloured style.

During the sixties Penberthy's hitherto prolific output tapered off considerably, partly as a result of his concentration on teaching and journalism, and of the prominent part he was playing in the establishment of the Western Australian Opera Company and the State Branch of the Fellowship of Australian Composers. A more important reason, however, was an event that ultimately had a decisive influence on the new direction his music was to take. This was the 1965 Hobart seminar for composers, from which he saw developing an unmistakable confrontation between the avant-garde and traditionalist streams of Australian composition. While recognizing that his music to this point had been basically traditional, and realizing the necessity of moving forward, Penberthy could not entirely accept the more radical ideas of the extreme avant-garde; he desired rather to find a middle position. For a while his creativity was stifled by the impact of the seminar (at which his comic opera *Ophelia of the Nine Mile Beach* was performed, together with Sitsky's *The Fall of the House of Usher* and Sutherland's *The Young Kabbarli*), but then he began experimenting with newer methods of composition. $E = MC^2$ (1967), a song cycle for soprano and tape recorder combining mathematical processes with *musique concrète*, and *Colours, Numbers and Objects* (1968) mark the real turning point in his career. The latter was Penberthy's first major orchestral work for some years, but although it appears to strike out in a completely new direction, its reliance on an extra-musical stimulus links it closely to his earlier instrumental music. A series of colours, numbers and objects were noted on the manuscript and set the music in motion, but only the colours are revealed to the listener. The music is not worked out in a thematic sense but relies on textural impact, each of the seven short movements having its own distinctive scoring and sound pattern. Recollections of previous movements in the final section (*Spectrum*) illustrate Penberthy's fondness for cyclic devices, already demonstrated in the Sixth Symphony and the Viola Concerto.

Because each texture is confined to a single movement—apart from the reminiscences in the finale—there is a greater sense of unity in *Colours, Numbers and Objects* than in *Happening 1970*, an overture composed for the Festival of Perth. In the latter work a large orchestra is used in an uninhibited and seemingly arbitrary manner, the composer having departed almost completely from his earlier emphasis on lyricism and relying now on sound effects and textures 'aimed at the brain and nerves rather than at the heart'.[4] The overture consists of two short sections entitled *Happening* and *Phonelude* respectively; the first depicts a 'hippy' scene and is designed as a musical expression of the irrational imaginative effects of drug-taking, while the second section uses solo viola and cello to represent a telephone conversation between two of the hippies. So unlike Penberthy's earlier music as to be almost unrecognizable as a piece by the same composer, *Happening 1970* nevertheless shares with such works as the Sixth Symphony and the *Cantata on the Hiroshima Panels* the sudden outbursts and rapid changes of texture that have become increasingly characteristic features of his style. Such extremes of expression are usually more satisfactorily handled in his vocal works, however, than in his orchestral music, where the effect is more diffuse as the result of the absence of a supporting text.

In his more recent works, Penberthy has tackled the problem of achieving structural coherence through two contrasting methods; firstly, by an increased use of mathematical formulae, and secondly, by a continued reliance on extra-musical ideas and concepts. Both approaches may be seen in *Spheres, Ellipses, Labyrinths*, a work for twenty-one solo strings composed in 1971. The musical ideas are based on the shapes suggested by the title; in the first section two large circles are constructed by means of a contrary-motion pattern, involving considerable use of microtones, while in the second section eight ellipses, built up in similar fashion, overlap with each other to form a palindromic structure. Finally, twelve string parts are played rapidly together, but with freedom of tempo for each player; the consequent mass of notes (with pitches derived from a computerized list) constitute the labyrinths of the title. The ensemble includes a string quartet that functions as a concertino, commenting in each section on the shapes constructed by the central body of strings (twelve violins and two violas), while another unit of two cellos and a double bass acts as virtually a second concertino, providing a bass line throughout the work.

It is noteworthy that since Penberthy's change of direction in the 1960s he has retreated almost completely from the theatre. Since 1965 he has composed no operas and only one ballet—*Picture of Dorian Gray* (1970), scored for piano, harpsichord, tape and organ. To a certain extent this reveals a more realistic approach than in his earlier career—notwithstanding the circumstances that encouraged him to compose operas and ballets—an approach that now recognizes the difficulty of making significant headway in Australia as a primarily theatrical composer. It could be suggested that this has been paralleled by a more realistic, albeit experimental, musical style; yet despite his increasing interest in electronic devices and the computer, Penberthy has remained attached to romantic concepts. In almost every work one can find him attempting to portray extra-musical ideas, or reacting to a philosophical or metaphysical stimulus.[5] Various literary forms have continued to attract him. In 1971, for example, he composed two song cycles with texts based on the writings of the Indian philosopher Krishnamurthy: *Commentaries on Living* for announcer, chorus and large orchestra, and *Commentaries on Love* for soprano and string orchestra. But even in purely instrumental forms, Penberthy's attachment to romanticism has remained strong. His Trumpet Concerto (1972) was designed, no less than any other of Penberthy's concertos, with the personality and ability of the player concerned in mind, and attempts to portray a sensitive man—represented by the soloist—having to face a chaotic and destructive world. Hence the trumpet has a number of melodic solos, contrasted with more agitated passages for the orchestra, and the outcome is that the concerto has a much more traditional character than most of Penberthy's recent works.

At the time of the Trumpet Concerto's first performance, it appeared that Penberthy might be returning to his earlier style, but it can be seen now that the work constitutes only a temporary reversion. Since then he has continued to pursue his interest in the computer, which helped him to produce such works as the orchestral *Men and Women* (1970), the virtuosic Saxophone Concerto (1970) and *Spheres, Ellipses, Labyrinths*. More recently he has been attempting to evolve a computer programme devised to produce a series of nine orchestral works, each with the title *Beyond the Universe* and each with the same basic programme but with alterations to one or more parameters such as rhythm, pitch or instrumentation.

To evaluate Penberthy's place in Australian composition is no easy task; any assessment at this stage in his career must inevitably be a tentative one and subject to revision in the future. In the national context he has appeared so far to be a relatively minor figure, yet some of his works compare favorably with those of better-known and more lauded contemporaries, and it may be that his move away from Perth will bring him greater recognition than has hitherto been the case. His output has been prolific and inevitably varied in quality, and it covers virtually every form and medium. Despite his recent experiments in the more radical methods of composition, it may in fact be his earlier, more traditional music—often reflecting his sometimes aggressive, yet basically sensitive, personality—that is likely to be regarded in time as his most characteristic contribution to Australian music.

Notes

1. In 1974 Penberthy was awarded the degree of Doctor of Music from Melbourne University.
2. The novelist is incorrectly named as Mary Cusack in Roger Covell, *Australia's Music: Themes of a New Society* Melbourne, 1967, p. 261.
3. Composer's programme note for first performance, A.B.C. Subscription Concert, Perth, 5 October 1967.
4. Composer's programme note for first performance, Australian Composers' Workshop concert, Festival of Perth, 26 February 1970.
5. Penberthy has found great inspiration in the work of Gwen Harwood, the Tasmanian poet. Examples of her influence are to be found in *Commentaries on Living*, Symphony no. 8 (*Choral*), Love Song (Sydney Opera House Commission) and the libretto of the new three-act opera *Stations*. (Editor's note)

Select List of Works

Operas
The Whip (1952)
Larry (1955)
Ophelia of the Nine Mile Beach (1955)
The Earth Mother (1957–58)
The Bullock Driver (1958)
Dalgerie (1958)
The Miracle (1963)
The Town Planner (1965)

Ballets
Euroka (1947)
Brolga (1949)
Boomerang (1951)
Cinderella (1953)
The Whirlwind (1954)
A Bunch of Wild Flowers (1954)
Sunflower (1955)
The White Kangaroo (1956)
The Beach Inspector and the Mermaid (1958)
Kooree and the Mists (1960)
Fire at Ross's Farm (1961)
Revenge (1962)
Woodara and the Gilgaree (1962)
The Little Man, also known as *Roundelay* (1963)
The Christmas Dinner (1964)
Waves, also known as *Sea Drift* (1964)
Australian Wildflowers (1965)
Mods and Rockers (1965)
Picture of Dorian Gray (1970)

Symphonies
Symphony no. 1 in G minor (1948)
Symphony no. 2 (1953)
Symphony no. 3, *Uranus* (1956)
Symphony no. 4, *Under the Sea* (1960)
Symphony no. 5 (incomplete) (1960)
Symphony no. 6, *Earth Mother* (1962)
Symphony no. 7, *Little Symphony* (1965)
Symphony no. 8, *Choral* (1972)

Concertos
Piano Concerto no. 1, *Kaleidoscope* (1947)
Oboe Concerto (1953)
Piano Concerto no. 2, *Aboriginal* (1955)
Bassoon Concerto (1954)
Flute Concerto (1955)
Cello Concerto (1962)
Viola Concerto (1962)
Saxophone Concerto (1970)
Trumpet Concerto (1972)
Trombone Concerto (1973)
Piano Concerto no. 3 (1974)

Miscellaneous Orchestral Works
Colours, Numbers and Objects (1968)
Happening 1970 (1970)
Men and Women (1970)
Spheres, Ellipses, Labyrinths (1971)
Squares, Spirals, Spears (1972)
Beyond the Universe No. 1 (1973)

Chamber and Instrumental
Sextet for flute, oboe, clarinet, horn, two bassoons (1954)
String quartet no. 1 in D minor (1959)
String quartet no. 2 (1963)
String quartet no. 3 (1965)
Spectra—suite for percussion (1974)
String quartet no. 4 (1974)

Choral
Cantata on the Hiroshima Panels (1959)
The Swan of the Bibbulmun (1960)
Bedlam Hills (1962)
Hiroshima for unaccompanied choir (1970)
Commentaries on Living (1970)
Heroes for unaccompanied choir (1974)

Vocal
Four Indeterminate Songs on E = MC² (1967)
Commentaries on Love (1971)
Odyssey 71 (1971)
Love Song (1973)

Discography

Symphony no. 6 (*Earth Mother*) (1962) [20′40″]. West Australian Symphony Orchestra (Thomas Mayer, conductor). MS. 28 Nov. 1968.
ABC recording RRCS/46, Philips disc 6508002
Viola Concerto (1962) [15′15″]. John Gould (viola), West Australian Symphony Orchestra (Sir Bernard Heinze, conductor). MS. Feb. 1969.
ABC recording RRCS/136
Saxophone Concerto (1971) [7′50″]. Peter Clinch (saxophone), West Australian Symphony Orchestra (Verdon Williams, conductor). MS. 3 Feb. 1971.
Festival disc SFC800/26
Bedlam Hills (1962) [7′29″]. Adelaide Singers, South Australian Symphony Orchestra (Patrick Thomas, conductor). MS. *ABC recording RRC/28*

Colours, Numbers and Objects (1969) [14′15″]. West Australian Symphony Orchestra (Thomas Mayer, conductor). MS. May 1970.
                              ABC recording RRCS/621
Happening 1970 (1969) [10′31″]. West Australian Symphony Orchestra (Thomas Mayer, conductor). MS. 26 Feb. 1970.   *ABC recording RRCS/385*
Ballet suite: *Koree and the Mists* (1958) [17′55″]. South Australian Symphony Orchestra (Patrick Thomas, conductor). MS.   *ABC recording RRC/28*
The Swan of the Bibbulmun (1962) [20′30″]. Lyric Singers, West Australian Symphony Orchestra (Thomas Mayer, conductor). MS. 7 Mar. 1968.
                              ABC recording RRCS/125
Ballet suite: *The Beach Inspector and the Mermaid* (1958). West Australian Symphony Orchestra (Thomas Mayer, conductor). MS. June 1970
                              Philips disc 6508002
Scherzo (1968) [0′45″]. Tasmanian Symphony Orchestra (Patrick Thomas, conductor). MS. 2 May 1968.
                              ABC recording RRC/72
Cantata on the Hiroshima Panels (1971) [16′18″]. Jane Carter (mezzo soprano), Malcolm Potter (tenor), Robert Dawe (baritone), Adelaide Singers, South Australian Symphony Orchestra (Patrick Thomas, conductor). MS. Sept. 1970.
                              Festival disc SFC 800/18

Felix Werder

(*b*. 1922)

Maureen Thérèse Radic

Felix Werder is now fifty-five. He has lived in Australia since he was nineteen, but he was born on 24 February 1922 of German parents in Berlin. It is to this European heritage that Werder attributes what he terms his 'philosophy', or his particular view of life, which he claims is bound up inextricably with his work as a creative musician. In all the years that have passed since he arrived here as a political prisoner in 1941 to be interned at Tatura, Victoria, Werder says he has found no reason to alter that 'philosophy'.

He attended the Grosse Hamburger in Berlin for his ordinary schooling, but his early musical education was supplied by his father, Boaz Bischofs Werder, then cantor at a leading Berlin synagogue, who pressed the child into service as his copyist for the routine compositional work demanded by his position.

His family, middle class, respected, drew about them members of the intelligentsia as well as artists and musicians. The influence of the Schoenbergs,[1] of Dr Sundberg,[2] Arnold Nardel,[3] and Stuckenschmidt,[4] experienced directly by the child through their visits to his father, did not cease when the circle of friends was broken in 1934, but continued to be felt in the instruction given by Bischofs Werder to his son in London when the family settled there to avoid the rising danger of the Nazi party in Berlin.

The practical training, the copying and reading of scores, continued with his father in his work for the Aldgate[5] synagogue, but it was coupled now with hours of listening to his father expound his views on music, religion and life, as they walked between the synagogue and their house at Bow. The arguments of Werder Senior, absorbed in silence, made such an impression that thirty years later Werder still attributed his own theories of aesthetics to his father's teachings.[6]

In London Werder argued his way in and out of various musical institutions to which his father sent him to gain a formal education. The same thing happened with his studies in architecture. Then, with the outbreak of the Second World War came the arrest of the heads of families still retaining German citizenship, and Werder chose to accompany his father to imprisonment in Australia.

Until mid-1944 Werder was kept at Tatura, where there were two internment camps, housing two thousand German prisoners, among them an unexpectedly large number of academics who proceeded to organize an informal 'university' in which Werder became involved. When it was discovered that there were also fine musicians amongst the internees, someone donated instruments for their use. The lack of music to perform sent the instrumentalists to Werder who wrote from memory fragments of Handel and Mozart scores and, later, imitations of seventeenth- and eighteenth-century music, which convinced the performers of his talents and revealed to Werder the fact that his ability was not the ordinary 'tool-of trade' he had been led to believe, but a rarity even among musicians.

In 1944 Werder joined the Australian army, being discharged in 1946. In Sydney he found work making music arrangements for radio and playing double bass in a nightclub. Later he became a carpenter in Melbourne but the long hours of physical work followed by equally long hours of composition left him exhausted. Taking advantage of an army rehabilitation course, he trained as a teacher of music in schools with the Education Department. His demonstrations of systems of teaching music not known here resulted in an appointment to Melbourne High School, but after a year he disagreed with the authorities on the relative importance of music in education and spent the rest of his five bonded years with the department, moving from one school to another until he left in disgust. Since 1956 he has been a lecturer for the Council of Adult Education and since the early sixties he has been music critic for the *Age*.[7]

During his earliest years in Australia Werder says he composed in a variety of imitative styles but that gradually he rediscovered the theories expounded by his father's friends. In the Europe he had left, Bartók and Schoenberg had long since been heard, assessed, absorbed. In Australia they seemed unknown, but it was to their example that he now turned. The compositions Werder subsequently submitted to the Australian Broadcasting Commission and other bodies were returned as unplayable and too 'avant-garde' to be acceptable to the public, though Werder knew himself that his work was almost reactionary even then. He went on writing, but his own stringent standards resulted in the destruction of literally hundreds of scores he later felt were not of high enough quality to be kept. Today he still continues this practice so that any list of even his past works is rapidly outdated.[8]

Werder feels that it was the acceptance of his work by Sir Eugene Goosens which saved him from abandoning composition altogether. On the advice of Szymon Goldberg,[9] Werder sent Goosens a manuscript and a letter explaining his doubts about his ability as a composer. Goosens, then conductor of the Sydney Symphony Orchestra, performed Werder's *Balletomania* score[10] as his reply in 1948. At last someone whose opinion he respected had seen some worth in his work and for Werder that was enough.

In the late fifties Werder began to feel that he had written himself out. It was then that Walter Susskind, the conductor of the Victorian Symphony Orchestra at the time, suggested to him that he needed a period of renewal, a time to discover what other composers were doing and why they were doing it. Werder began an intensive study of the Bartók scores.

By this time single performances of Werder's works were receiving press notices, the influences in his works discussed and his reputation as a composer built upon music written years before its first hearing. Werder was rightly distressed by this time-lag. Over the years there have been many opinions formed and expressed in this way concerning the quality of Werder's work. Most of these are cautious or tentative, mainly because the sheer volume of his output makes any one work, or even a series of works seem, at present, unrepresentative, though the opposite view has been taken at times that all his compositions sound like part of one huge work. Less open to mere opinion are the discernible intra-musical influences evident in his music.

Dorian Le Gallienne, as witness to the early works which no longer exist, spoke of Werder's use of strict twelve-note theory, and of his lucid counterpoint, but he found it difficult to discover Werder's 'emotional message', disliking his 'structure for its own sake' and in *Monostrophe*, for example, he perceived a chromaticism with 'quite a lot of post-Tristan romanticism about it'.[11]

Roger Covell[12] has defined the main influences in Werder's work as the modern contrapuntal technique of Hindemith, the serialism of the Schoenberg school, and the compression, the use of dissonance and the tight measured stressing of Bartók. Behind these he feels there is the influence of the Hebraic modes and in the background the lingering effect of the German late romantic tradition. Andrew Mc-Credie[13] also finds there are responses in Werder's music to the work of Mahler, to the second Viennese school and to Krenek. To these Larry Sitsky[14] adds the influence of Handel, Mozart, Monteverdi, Gluck and the Gabrielis.

Hince[15] believes that not many techniques are foreign to Werder but that he is essentially a romantic, a melodist whose ideas issue naturally in long strands of intricate counterpoint. He regards Werder as a man of long and extended ideas, and dislikes (for example, the short allusive ideas of *Laocoon*), though he sees the continuity of the musical argument existing here as in much of Werder's music.

But Werder himself is impatient of this analysing of the trace elements in his work, saying that such things no longer matter to him since he has outgrown them years ago. He admits some truth is to be found in claims for various influences but that it is unimportant now to look for such things in his more recent work. Any composer, he says, has to begin by learning from others through a process of selection and rejection until he finds his own personal voice. Even then some of his preferences are bound to remain with him and mark the subconscious shaping of his works as in his own case.

Time and again, in his lectures for the Victorian Council of Adult Education and in his capacity as music critic for the *Age*, Werder has verbalized the forces he believes underlie all his music. His radical views and forceful language established him as a storm centre in Australian music in the sixties, but apart from his functioning as a needed irritant in a complacent society, Werder also used these platforms to inform the public of his musical intentions, which were not to entertain but 'to educate, to edify'.

From the time of the 1963 Hobart Conference, when Werder acted as catalyst for the first hesitant gathering of Australian composers seeking a way to express their views, he has remained the most vocal of all our composers. The hiatus between his theories and his music is apparent, but as usual with Werder the more one tries to understand his 'philosophy' the clearer his musical intentions become. It is an intensely personal music encased in a technical virtuosity of such compression that the ear tires rapidly in following its manoeuvres. For this reason his shorter works (for example, the quartet from no. 5 on, *Concert Music for 5* (1964), *Trilude for Violin* (1968), *Scherzi* (1972)) have always tended to appeal more. He creates tension so quickly in his works and remains on a high plateau for so long that emotionally one becomes detached through exhaustion. For these reasons Werder's work has often puzzled his audiences; they lack the stamina to follow his ideas through. Werder seems to expect from them the quick-wittedness and musical erudition he possesses himself.

When asked which of his works embody his ideas best he points to the (at present) twelve quartets. These, he says, show his progression over the years, and it is legitimate to regard them as his best works, but adding a note of caution that this body of work exists because demand was there. He wanted actual performances of his music, not just manuscripts left unheard, so he wrote for the combinations available, using material he calls 'fragmental', 'theatrical'. These two words he uses to describe (a) his use of unthematic starting material and (b) his idiomatic use of the geometrics of that material. He feels he is basically an operatic composer who has had so little chance to develop that form that all the material normally destined for its place in the terms of theatre end in instrumental drama. In the case of his symphonies he feels this does not succeed precisely because he spurns the symphonic form with its germination principle as 'Hegelian'. His own work, he says, resembles more Joyce's concept of the 'stream of consciousness' technique, though by virtue of Werder's acute early training there is a terseness and order in his use of even this technique that belies his stated intentions.

Fig. 45 From String Quartet XII

Of the five symphonies (presently existing) only one, that known as *Laocoon*, the third, has been heard. It is an impressive, hyperactive score in one movement, but its basis in the philosophy of Lessing, as in the case also of *Dramaturgie*, is elusive.

It becomes increasingly apparent that Werder is probably right in believing that the cost factor involved in the presentation of large-scale works, especially opera, will continue to limit the scope of Australian composers. That opera happens to be his true milieu is Werder's greatest problem. Development through repeated performances and an assured and competent staging of new works seems to be impossible at present. The result is that few composers are willing to spend the necessary time in such composition. Yet Werder has written seven operas: *Kisses for a Quid* (1960), *Private* (1969) (for T.V.), *The Affair* (1969) (Fig. 46), all of which have been performed, as well as *The General* (1966), *Agamemnon* (1967), *The Vicious Square* (1971) and *The Conversion* (1973). At present he plans a full-scale work within the form without thought of production, simply because he wishes to attempt it at least once. He cannot afford the time to follow his real inclinations and must turn to chamber music and to commissioned works for special soloists in order to be heard.

Fig. 46 From *The Affair*

   In recent days he has turned to electronic music, but he maintains that even in this field he is simply making use of yet another available instrument, one which he strives to use as a practical performing medium. The works in this area are designed for synthesizer and a number of conventional instruments, usually those without a notable repertoire, since Werder finds the players of woodwind and percussion, for example, eager to develop the arduous techniques he requires in order to find a relevant music for themselves. He enjoys the exchange of ideas in rehearsal and performance and the response of young audiences to this music. The result is an eagerness on his part to develop the live performance further, the composer taking the part of the leading player-director somewhat in the manner of seventeenth- and eighteenth-century tradition.

   The idea, however, of using newer sound sources merely for effect enrages Werder. He is most emphatic that content alone is of importance and novelty or shock effects are childish tricks if the content of a composer's work is not fixed on principles he himself understands and uses as the very fabric of his life. In his own case this has always been his 'religious' feeling towards man, what he calls his 'humanism', that belief in man as man, not as a fated or tragic creature that he expresses in often ironic

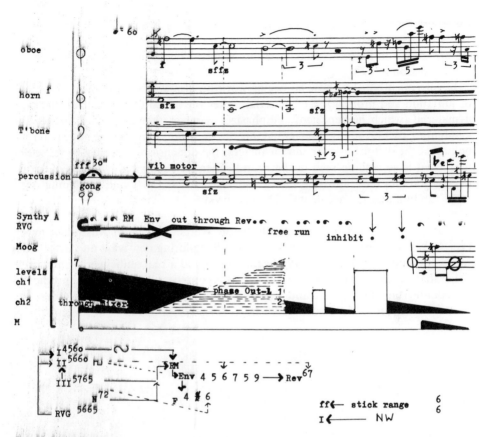

Fig. 47 From *Syntronic*

terms. It is precisely this irony that is unexpected in the unrelenting terms of his music. It is not a quality found so consistently in any other Australian composer's work and is therefore the aspect of his work least understood by his listeners who are so unprepared for it.

Werder today still regards Mozart as his musical deity, Monteverdi as his teacher, Aristotle and Lessing as his mentors in aesthetics. He laces his reviews and his lectures with references to Pythagoras and Plato and will talk of Grunwald and Hindemith in a linked metaphor. To Australians his European breadth of reference and the virtuosity with which he uses it are bewilderingly unfamiliar. His 'Gothic' use of English only emphasizes the feeling that he is somehow out of context. At one time he felt this himself and almost left this country for Germany because his music was accepted there more readily than in Australia. His visits to Europe in recent years have made him aware that he can never be anything less than a 'European' but that he is also an Australian and that his roots have somehow become entangled in this society.

Werder is a mid-career composer and only now, with the support of a five-year Fellowship from the Australian Government is he able to work in some degree of financial security and to work to some extent as he wishes. Always ready to champion the cause of Australian contemporary music, he now battles for assured performances and proper standards to make effective the use of public monies in the support of composers such as himself. In January 1976 he took a group of Australian musicians known as 'Australia Felix' to West Germany where they gave concerts, lectures and broadcasts in Berlin, Nuremburg and Munich. The group has been invited for a return season in 1978.

He is frequently asked how he begins work on a new piece, the method he uses for initiation and protraction of material. After the initial choice of idea and type of material (which he repeatedly emphasizes is never thematic) he examines the possibilities of everything that could be drawn from it in mathematical terms, looking at the distortions, the mirror images, the dimensions he refers to as 'sculptural', that is something seen in the round. Then he begins his selection of actual useable permutations, allowing mood and taste to take over and remaining open to the random and the accidental. The end product may bear little resemblance to his original master plan.

Whatever the verdict may eventually be on Werder's place in Australian music it certainly cannot be made now when he is still exploring new ways and when Australian contemporary music is only beginning to find a real audience. What can be said is that he must be considered already as a composer of genuine importance in this country on many levels and that his influence is considerable. Werder was created a Member of the Order of Australia for services to music in January 1976.

Notes

1. Arnold and his nephew Joseph. The general cultural climate, particularly with regard to art as well as music, formed the centre of debate within this circle, though Werder says it was Nardel rather than the Schoenbergs who acted as its centre.
2. Werder refers to him as then experimenting with a quarter tone piano, possibly an attempt to improve on the Behrens-Senegalden model (Berlin 1892).
3. The art historian, then considerably older than Werder's father.
4. The music critic and scholar.
5. Not to be confused with Aldersgate.
6. These are expounded in his unpublished book A Sense of Style (typescripts dated 1964, 1966) and his Essays (typescript, 1966) based upon lectures given for the Victorian Council of Adult Education.
7. Werder had deputized as music critic for extended periods before he was appointed to Le Gallienne's position following the latter's death. This accounts for the confusion of dates to be found in some of the writings about Werder.
8. Confusingly, new works sometimes fill the numberings of destroyed early works.
9. Making Australia his home during the war, Goldberg was later to become conductor of the Netherlands Chamber Orchestra.
10. Written at eighteen, this work was later destroyed by the composer.
11. See reviews in the Age: 13 August, 27 September 1962; 8 March, 8 June 1963.
12. Roger Covell, Australia's Music: Themes of a New Society, (Melbourne, Sun Books, 1967), pp. 188–9.
13. Andrew McCredie, Musical Composition in Australia, p.70; Catalogue of 46 Australian Composers and Selected Works, pp. 19–20. The Composers and their Work, pp. 19–20. Australian Government Publications, (translated into French and German) Government Printing Office, Canberra, A.C.T., 1969.
14. Larry Sitsky, Current Affairs Bulletin, vol. 46, no. 3, entitled New Music, pp. 1–47 (entry on Werder p. 43), University of Sydney 29 June 1970.
15. See the Australian, 7 September 1968.

Select List of Works

Compiled by Maureen Thérèse Radic from verbal information and written lists provided by the composer 1975. Where opus numbers are missing, material deleted by the composer is indicated

Paisago for string orchestra (1939)
Piano Sonata no. 1 (1939)
Actomos choral prelude for strings (1948)
Symphony no. 1 (1948) (revised 1967)
Divertimento for woodwind (1951)
Piano Sonata no. 2 (1951)
Shir Hashirim cantata for mezzo and str (1953)
Sonata da camera for v va clar (1953)
Piano Quartet (1954)
Four Songs (Palmer) (1954)
Psalm for viola (1954)
Flute Concerto (1954)
String Quartet no. 4 (1955)
Three-part Fantasias for string trio (1955)
Piano Concerto (1955)
Concert Music for violin (1956)
String Quartet no. 5 (1956)
Brand symphonic fragment (1956)
Nietzsche Poems (for Maureen Forester) (1956)
Sonata for cello (1956)
Symphony no. 2 (Sinfonia) (1956)
Abstract for three orchestral groups (1958)
Violin Sonata (1958)
Trio for violin, piano and cello (1958)
Quintet for clarinet, horn and string trio (1959)
Psalm 127 (for the Adelaide Singers) (1959)
Flute Sonata (1960)
Flute Trio (1960)
Kisses for a Quid one-act opera (1960)
Hexastrophe for orchestra (1961)
Sonata for wind quintet (1961)
Blake Songs (written for Beatrice Oakley) (1961)
Monostrophe for orchestra (1961)
Leaves of Grass (Whitman) songs for mezzo and clarinet (1961)
String Quartet no. 6 (1962)
Madrigals for recorders (1962)
Koheleth Songs for cello (Song of Koheleth) (1962)
Prelude and Passacaglia for piano (1962)
Four Blake Songs (for Maureen Forester) (1962)
Harpsichord Sonata (1963)
Strophe for oboe (1963)
Partita for piano (1963)
Septet for flute clarinet harp and strings (1963)
Trio no. 2 for piano, viola and cello (1963)
Tristrophe for orchestra (1964)
Strophe for viola (1964)
Koncert Music for Five (1964) (re-worked 1970)
Piano Quintet (1964)
Clarinet Quintet (1965)
Sonata for unaccompanied violin (1965)
Apostrophe for wind quintet (1965)
String Quartet no. 7 (1965)
Symphony no. 3 (Laocoon) (1965)
The General opera in one act (libretto by Leonard Radic) (1966)
String Quartet no. 8 (1966)
Violin Concerto (1966)
Strophe '66 for flute, clarinet, percussion, piano and strings (1966)
Dramaturgie for orchestra (1966)
Satyricon for six horns (1967)
'Etwas Musik' for piano (1967)
Agamemnon opera (see Banker) (1967)
The Cranes of Ibicus for orchestra (1967)
En Passon for flute and strings (1967)
Electra's Strophe for mezzo and percussion (1967)
Piano trio 'La Trobe' (1967)
Aspects of the Third for solo flute
Radic's Piece cantata (1967)
Piano Sonata (1968)

Strophe '68 (Homage to Stravinsky) (1968)
Holderlin Songs (for Rita Streich) (1968)
Composition for wind instruments (1968)
Sonata for unaccompanied cello (1968)
String Quartet no. 9 (1968)
Tower Concerto for orchestra (1968)
Strophe for unaccompanied violin (1968)
The Second Paisago for orchestra (1968)
After Watteau. 'La Gamma d'Amore' for orchestra and
    mandolin (1968)
Trilude for unaccompanied violin (1968)
Klavier Musik (1968)
Trio for harp (1969)
The Affair opera (libretto L. Radic) (1969)
Activity for piano and percussion (1969)
Sound Canvas for orchestra (1969)
Triphony for flute, guitar and bongos (1969)
Private TV opera (1969)
La Trobe Second Edition for chamber orchestra (1969)
Klang Bilder for orchestra (1969)
Piano Trio (1969)
Symphony no. 4 (1970)
Triple Measure for orchestra (1970)
Two Donne Songs (for Glenys Fowles) (1970)
The Five Acts of Coriolanus (1970)
Piano Sonata no. 4 (1970)
Prom Gothic for organ and orchestra (1970)
Tetract for viola, oboe and percussion (1972)
Quartet Music X 1970
Divertimento for guitar and string quartet (1970)
Don Giovanni Retired: an Epilogue for orchestra (1971)
Wind Quartet (1971)
Symphony no. 5 (1971)
Bacon's Essays cantata (1971)
The Vicious Square opera masque in two acts (1971)
Three Night Pieces for flute and guitar (1972)
Percussion Play for solo percussion (1972)
Collector's Item for wind orchestra (1972)
Fanfare for Brass (1972)
Apopthegems for orchestra (1972)
Scherzi for bass trumpet and percussion (1972)
String Quartet no. 11 (1972)
Toccata for organ (1972)
Fantasia on the Letters ABC for piano (1972)
La Belle Dame orchestral ballet (1973)
Music for clarinet, saxophone, trumpet, trombone and
    percussion (1973)
Piano Sonata no. 5 (1973)
Quantum ballet (1973)
Oscussion for synthesizer and percussion (1973)
Sextronic for synthesizer and quintet (1973)
Carrion Comfort for cello and mezzo (1973)
Encore for unaccompanied violin (1973)
The Conversion one act opera for piano, percussion
    and bass (commissioned by National Theatre for
    1975) (1973)
Rapressentazione de Pieri for organ (commissioned by
    Sergio di Pieri) (1973)
Reigen to K.P.E. string trio (1973)
Synorgy for synthesizer, wind and organ (1974)
Syntronic for synthesizer and wind (1974)
Sans Souci flute concerto (1974)
Organ Music for Professor George Loughlin (1974)

The Tempest electronic music for VIOO (1974)
String Quartet XII (1974)
Brandenburgisches Koncert for string orchestra (1974)
Tower Sonata for brass ensemble (1975)
J + J for clarinet and percussion (1975)
Cranach's Hunt horn concerto (1975)
'Hyperion,' Holderlin Songs (1975)
Piano Concerto no. 2 (1975)
Holy Thursday for organ (commissioned by the Organ
    Society) (1975)
La Tempesta music theatre (1975)
Wesso Brunner Gebet (prayer) choral work on an old
    Bavarian text electronics and chamber music en-
    semble (commissioned by the Lutheran Church in
    Berlin) (1975)
Index 157 for chamber orchestra (commissioned by
    Lucio Berio) (1976)
Encore for violin and piano (1976)
Lustspiel for baroque ensemble (1976)
Bellyful music theatre for Victorian Opera Company
    with libretto by Leonard Radic (1976)
Jeremiad music theatre for A.B.C. Italia Prize entry
    (Libretto by Leonard Radic) (1976)
Three for Stuttgart Piano Trio (1976)

Discography

Concerto for violin. Leonard Dommett (violin),
    Melbourne Symphony Orchestra (Fritz Rieger,
    conductor).   *Festival disc SFC 80020*
Fantasia in Three Parts. Glickman String Trio.
Concert Music for Five. Adelaide Wind Quintet.
                                  HMV disc OASD 7558
Music for clarinet and string quartet. Donald Westlake
    (clarinet), Austral String Quartet.
                                  HMV disc OASD 7553
Music for clarinet, horn and string trio.
                                  W & G disc A/1635
String Quartet no. IV. Austral String Quartet.
    HMV disc OASD 7553 (deleted December 1971)
String Quartet no. VI. Austral String Quartet.
                        World Record Club disc S/2474
String Quartet no. IX. Austral String Quartet.
                                  HMV disc OASD 7563
Banker. Percussion Play 1971. Players: synthesizers,
    Felix Werder and Keith Humble; percussion, John
    Seal; Guitar, Jochen Schubert; piano, Dennis
    Henning. Concert recording. 1973.
                          Discovery Stereo disc GYS. 001
Toccata. Organ of St Patrick's, Melbourne. 1972.
                              MOVE MS Stereo 3008
The Tempest + After Giorgione's 'Tempesta' 1974
    (reverse side *Oscussion* 1971) Music by Felix Werder
    Volume 2.   *Mopoke GYS 002*

Don Banks

(b. 1923)

Philip Bracanin

William Mann has described Don Banks as 'the most distinguished living Australian composer, though perhaps not the most widely popular',[1] and the esteem he enjoys is evident through the large number of commissions he has received from over twenty different bodies. Included among these are the British Broadcasting Commission (Cheltenham Festival and Sir Henry Wood Promenade Concerts), the Edinburgh Festival Society, the London Symphony Orchestra (Peter Stuyvesant Foundation), the Staatstheater Kassel, and the English Bach Festival. Banks is a composer who has always kept abreast of new developments in music without actually being part of the avant-garde. His compositional skill is always totally in control of his vivid and unconventional creative imagination, much of it acquired during the years spent in the exacting task of writing music for film scores (seventeen full-length feature films), television shows, cartoons, documentaries and commercial advertisements.

Banks's earliest formal studies in composition were undertaken at the University of Melbourne Conservatorium of Music. In 1950 he migrated to England and for two and a half years studied composition privately with Matyas Seiber. The untimely death in 1960 of that highly respected teacher/composer motivated Banks to write the *Sonata da Camera* (1961) and dedicate it to him. Banks chose the same instrumentation as Seiber had used in one of his best works, *The Portrait of an Artist as a Young Man*, scoring it for string trio, flute, clarinet, bass clarinet, piano and percussion and featuring in the third movement (the work's last and most intensely expressive) Seiber's principal instrument, the cello. The impact of Seiber's teaching is evident in the economic approach and resultant lucid textures, but his influence can also be felt more directly in the whimsical nature of parts of the scherzando second movement. Banks also made an unconscious tribute to Seiber in the use of some thematic material in the form of a twelve-note row which Seiber had employed in his Concert Piece for violin and piano (1953–54).

Banks relates that it was not until some three years after having written the *Sonata da Camera* and when asked to provide a programme note for Seiber's work, that he realized he had made use of the same row. Actually, this row is one of three employed in the composition. It is the first derivative of the original row (all three are given in Fig. 48). The initial idea for the piece and the basic shape from which the original row and its two versions are derived is the three-note combination C, F, B, first sounded by the cello in bars 5–6. It is clear from Fig. 48 that the first derivative was formed from permutations of the basic three-note shape (C, F, B) and the second derivative from notes 4, 5 and 6 of the original row. If the original row and its first derivatives are Schoenbergian in structure, the second derivative is Webernian.

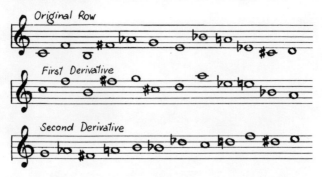

Fig. 48

Schoenberg and Webern, when composing twelve-note works, used one row for each piece. Banks's technique, based on rows derived from the original through-permutation processes, is a later method found in works by such composers as Stockhausen, Boulez and Nono. The first and third movements of the *Sonata da Camera* are composed with the original row and its first derivative, while in the second movement all three versions are used, although the second derivative predominates. A feature of the original row is its potential division into four-note groups which are reproduced as permutations when the row is transposed upwards by tones (Fig. 49).

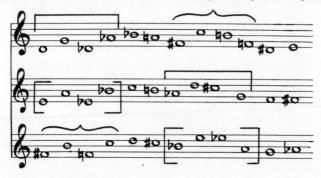

Fig. 49

Its inversion at the ninth transposition also reveals a permutation hexachordal equivalent in the second half of the row (Fig. 50).

Each of the three movements is sectional in overall design. In the first, which is in five sections with a coda, the various instrumental combinations are exposed. There are two episodes for the tutti and one each for the piano and xylophone, woodwind and string trio. The second movement, which is in three sections, approximates to a ternary design and combines a scherzando with a chorale-like passage. Although the final movement (*Lento espressivo*) gives the impression of a continuous flow, it can be viewed as consisting of six sections 1, 2, 3, 3a, 4, 5 which are recapitualated as follows 4, 3, 3a, 1, 2.

Fig. 50

As the seventeen-bar introduction which prefaces the *Sonata da Camera* exposes all the main material in the piece, a closer examination of it will give some idea of the skill of the composer.

The first twelve-note flourish (Fig. 51) is based on the original row and the attacks

Fig. 51 *Sonata da Camera*, Bars 1–17

Allegro Moderato ♩ = 108

[Musical score for Flute, Clarinet (in A), Bass Clarinet (B♭), Percussion, Piano, Violin, Viola, Cello]

❋   N.B.   This score is in concert — all notes are written at actual pitch.

making up this twelve-note chord soon become converted into a rhythmic cell. Bars 5–8 are based on the first derivative of the row. At bar 5 the cello motive introduces a simple rhythmic relationship of crotchets and dotted crotchets but the first direct statement of an important generative rhythmic idea is made in bars 7–8. Fig. 52 shows how and where the rhythmic attacks first conceived in these two bars are

Fig. 51 (cont.)

employed later in the first movement. At bar 9, the three-note combination which forms the basis of the second derivative of the row is introduced and comes to rest in bar 12 with the cello sounding D flat while the timpani progresses by a *glissando* from C to the D flat of the cello. This battle between C and D flat, which continues into the first movement, changes in the second movement to a battle between D and

Fig. 51 (cont.)

D flat, but in the concluding bars of the work the cello finally settles on D flat. The two three-note motives played by the clarinet and bass clarinet respectively in bar 14 become important material to be worked out in the final movement. Actually, this particular motto is a restatement by Banks of the 'Fratello' motive from Dallapiccola's *Il Prigionero*.

Fig. 51 (cont.)

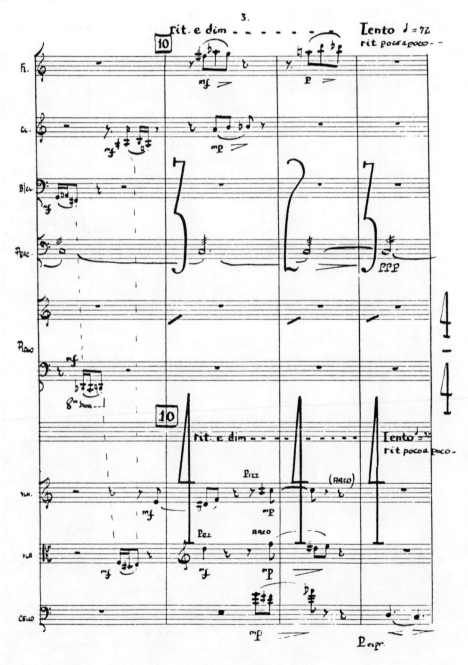

The reference to Dallapiccola's music in a work dedicated to Seiber is fitting, since on completing his studies with Seiber, Banks had moved to Florence to undertake further work in composition and orchestration with him. That Banks learnt a great deal about the craft of composition and orchestration from these two outstanding teachers is evident from a close examination of the *Sonata da Camera* as well as an

Fig. 51 (cont.)

earlier work, *Four Pieces* for orchestra (1953) written while studying with Dallapiccola.

Fig. 52 *Sonata da Camera*

During the period from 1962 to 1965 Banks wrote a number of chamber works
included amongst which are the *Three Episodes* for flute and piano (1964) and Horn
Trio (1962). In a way, the Horn Trio is a runner-up for the Horn Concerto (1965).
Both works were written for Barry Tuckwell and characteristically display Banks's
fondness for working with motivic ideas. Indeed, it is to Banks's immense credit that
the Horn Concerto, while not being modelled architecturally on the traditional
solo concerto prototype, holds its own as a worthy twentieth-century successor of
this phenomenon of the classical era. The craftsmanship and musicianly skill shown
in both solo horn and orchestral writing is matched by the refined treatment of the
thematic material, almost all of which emanates from two interval combinations—

an augmented fourth, and a tone and semitone grouping. Continuity of thought is achieved throughout and between the work's eight sections, even though each section provides a different perspective of basically the same thematic ideas. A comparison, for example, of bars 30–36 from the second section with the opening bars (324–30) of the final section demonstrates this very clearly (see Fig. 53). It is also evident from

Fig. 53 Horn Concerto: (a) Bars 30–36; (b) Bars 324–30

these excerpts that the orchestra, while essentially functioning as an accompaniment, nevertheless employs relevant material derived from, but complementary to, the main trend of musical thought which is carried in the horn part. The scoring here, as in the work generally, is lucid and appropriate to its purpose.

Fig. 53 (cont.)

As mentioned earlier, Banks has always kept pace with current developments in music, and when in 1966 he was asked to write a work for students to demonstrate some of the techniques then current he produced the work entitled *Assemblies*. The title refers to the fact that it was written for an expandable orchestra and also allows

Fig. 53 (cont.)

scope in the score for the players to improvise according to certain instructions set down by the composer. In 1968 *Tirade*, a more sophisticated work also making use of controlled improvisation, was written as a result of a commission from the Centre de Musique, Paris.

Fig. 53 (cont.)

Tirade is a triptych for medium voice, piano, harp and percussion and is a setting of three poems by Peter Porter dealing with the present, the past and the future as it applies to the Australian scene. Banks and Porter arrived at a suitable text only after working very closely together on it. Indeed, the closeness of the collaboration between poet and composer is even seen in the relationship between the instrumentation and the main ideas expressed in the text. For instance, 'the present' depicted by 'Dullsville's citizens' moving through life as in a museum, is related to a 'museum' of percussion instruments from different parts of the world—Latin America, China, Japan and Africa. He also includes a knife (the player is asked to vibrate its blade against wood) in imitation of a museum turnstile.

The main theme of the work is announced in the opening lines of the first poem.
We're in a permanent Museum
With an ever-changing Loan Collection!
This statement which is spoken in the style of a 'quasi lecture' acquires much of its impact from the apathetic mood created at the beginning of the movement. In the opening moments of the piece the instrumentalists are allowed a certain amount of freedom of interpretation, and in the section during which the description of certain 'public icons' is ridiculed they are instructed to improvise, to knock 'with fingers and knuckles on wood, skins and sides of instruments in (a) short flurried patterns, (b) repeated notes, (c) trills, etc.'. The final section of the poem deals more seriously with Australia's present situation
A northern race living in the south,
   myths in reverse, . . .
and the piece ends appropriately with an intoned
   give us our quotidian fame.
accompanied by a sustained C on the harp. The piece is in a roughly strophic variation form.

The second poem dealing with the future is somewhat more philosophic than the other two poems, and in effect refers back to a kind of Aboriginal dreamtime, the repeated-note rhythm which sounds through most of the piece on different instruments giving it an element of timelessness. This idea is coupled with the more sophisticated nature of 'the future', depicted in the score by the emphasis given to the melodic percussion instruments (harp, piano, vibraphone and glockenspiel), and the use of serial technique. The vocal line is, however, never obscured by the other parts. They fulfil the dual role of either complementing the sentiment expressed in the text, or of providing a reflective comment. This procedure often behaves like a musical enjambment and also acts as a link between stanzas or lines of the poem which is set in 'through-composed' manner. This is shown in Fig. 54. The essential material of the piano interlude is first heard as an integral part of the accompaniment to the text
A white tree is his mother, . . .
and its conclusion leads logically into the next line
He will come out of the story . . .
The third piece reaches a frenzied climax when the word 'raped' is delivered in a shrieked *glissando* beginning on a high A flat. This sums up the ultimate exploitation of Australia's raw materials by some of the nation's so-called developers. During the climax Banks asks the three percussionists to improvise a kind of pandemonium using 'all or any percussion instruments and occasional shouts of ah!' while the

Fig. 54 From *Tirade*

pianist plays forearm clusters and operates a foot-controlled electronic siren. The
pianist, who is also the director of the ensemble, determines the point of entry of the
siren and the duration of its attack and decay. By comparison with traditional means
of achieving a musical climax this may seem somewhat crude, but in the context
of this piece it is immensely effective. The introduction of the siren and the importance
given to the non-melodic percussion section calls to mind the music of Varèse, a
composer whom Banks greatly admires. *Tirade* is nevertheless a distinctive work
outwardly showing none of the influence of Varèse. Banks has absorbed the experience of this little-understood composer and produced an original piece of music.
On a superficial level *Tirade* can be placed alongside Berio's *Circles*. In contrast with
Circles, however, the text of *Tirade* remains intact throughout and Banks's treatment
of it is characteristically imaginative without being destructive. During the work
a variety of types are employed including spoken voice quasi lecture style, half
voice, whispering, normal speaking voice and falsetto.

Another work in which Banks collaborated with Peter Porter is the cantata *Limbo*
(1971), for three solo voices, chamber ensemble of eight instruments and two-channel
tape. This is a very lyrical and philosophical piece dealing with the principal idea
'nothing is ever lost', a phrase which is sung at various stages throughout the work by
the soprano. Although the work stands on its own as a cantata its impact could be
greatly assisted by lighting and projected visual images. Banks looks forward to
producing it in a theatre/music situation and considers it, along with his violin and
horn concertos, a major work.

There are many sides to Don Banks's musicianship, two of which have as yet not
been mentioned. One is his active interest in jazz which dates back to his childhood
when he was exposed to it by his father. This was carried on into his youth when

he played jazz piano in night clubs as a means of earning a living, which was also the way he financed his first trip overseas in 1950. His involvement in this field has resulted in a number of works for ensembles which include jazz instrumentalists— *Equations I, II* and *III* (1963, 1969, and 1972 respectively), *Settings from Roget* (1966), *Prelude, Night Piece and Blues* (1968), *Nexus* (1971), *Three Short Pieces* for voice and jazz quartet (1971). *Settings from Roget* and the *Three Short Songs*, two works written for Cleo Laine and the John Dankworth Quartet, provide an interesting pair in the jazz idiom. *Three Short Songs* are diatonic-jazz pieces which Banks refers to as 'kind of twentieth-century lieder', while *Settings from Roget* (Banks's own texts based on Roget's *Thesaurus*), are twelve-note jazz. The first piece, 'World', is a very strict twelve-note piece, and is based on three four-note chords with jazz associations; the second, 'Direction', is appropriately based on its retrograde inversion while the third, 'Silence', is free and is based on Messiaen's second mode of limited transposition. In the third piece two notes are pegged and played inside the piano on the strings to sound like tuned bongos, and the rasped strings on the lowest notes of the piano give explosive-like effects. There is also a visual pun on the word 'silence' when four bars are beaten after the words 'silence has come', and the jazz quartet finishes with a chord.

The other important interest is that of electronic music, and since the mid-sixties this has played an increasingly significant role in Banks's development. Indeed, in 1973 he was appointed to the Canberra School of Music as Head of Composition and Electronic Music. Besides writing purely electronic music Banks has shown a fascination for combining it with more traditional compositional procedures, as for example in *Intersections* (1969) for electronic sounds and orchestra. On the other hand, he has also applied it in an unconventional context in the audio-visual concert *Synchronos '72*. For this he collaborated with the artist Ostoja-Kotkowski to produce a work which embodies besides electronic music, tape music and laser beam projection.

Banks's considerable experience in all three areas of jazz, electronic and 'serious' art music is clearly evident in *Meeting Place* (commissioned by the London Sinfonietta in 1970), a work for jazz group, chamber ensemble and electronic synthesizer. Its six movements are varied in orchestration—the first and fourth are scored for chamber ensemble and jazz group, the second for synthesizer and chamber ensemble with flugel horn, and the fifth and sixth employ the total resource. Throughout the work there is much scope for improvisation from the jazz group but the most consistently jazz-inspired movements are the third and fifth. The mood of the third is established by the opening idea (Fig. 55) which lasts for twenty-seven bars and returns throughout the movement in *ritornello* fashion. In the fifth movement the electronic synthesizer takes on a similar function with a jazz-inspired idea which continues throughout with (at times) slight variations in pitch. Its rhythm determines that of the whole movement.

Much of the success of this work is due to Banks's ability to allude to more than one idiom simultaneously and from a mixed parentage to create a new, healthy hybrid. Consider, for example, the flugel horn theme in bars 18–19 of the second movement. It suggests at the outset the key of C minor altered in jazz-like fashion with alternating major and minor thirds, flattened seventh and raised fourth. In fact, that tonality is never actually established in the melodic line nor confirmed by its accompaniment, which incidentally combines sufficient major seconds in

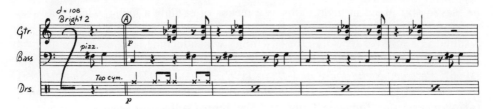

Fig. 55 *Meeting Place*, the opening coda of the third movement

Fig. 56 From *Meeting Place*, Bars 49–50

its basically non-diatonic structure to give the impression of a minor seventh or major ninth chord while not actually sounding any such chords. The remaining element in the accompaniment is the bitonal statement in the piccolo part of an F major/E flat minor arpeggio chordal combination. This material is restated in bars 22–23 as a sustained chord in the strings and in *stretto* fashion in the flutes and clarinets.

In *Meeting Place* Banks also makes use of the same material in different ways according to the idiomatic nature of its context. The opening idea of the third movement (the perfect fourth/augmented fourth chord quoted at Fig. 55) assumes an entirely different but no less appropriate character in a new context in bars 49–50 (Fig. 56) of the second movement. This passage suggests serial treatment reminiscent of Webern. Indeed, it is the almost uncanny aptness of means suited to context that makes this work worthy of a lasting place in the repertoire

Don Banks's esteem as an Australian composer was given recognition by his native country when he was commissioned by the Australian Broadcasting Commission and the Music Board of the Australia Council to write a work to mark the opening of the Sydney Opera House in 1973. In writing the piece he was affected by his return to Australia after more than twenty years overseas and the title *Prospects* was chosen as a result of looking at Australia with new eyes and seeing what the country had to offer. It is, however, not a programmatic work.

In broad design *Prospects* has an arch-like structure, Lento, Allegro, Adagio espressivo, Allegro, Adagio, with the greatest correspondence taking place between the treatment of material in sections of similar speed. In spite of this, there is never the slightest hint of any discontinuity in the overall flow of the work because motivic treatment of the same material is carried on throughout the five sections. For example, the second Allegro which is distinctly jazz-like in mood provides a new aural perspective on the ideas previously worked out during the first Allegro, and further, the main idea on which these sections are based is initially announced in bar 10 of the Lento. In fact, all the relevant material used in the piece is stated in the opening section.

Prospects is a fine example of Banks's highly developed motivic-thematic technique as well as his first-rate orchestration. The success of a composer who works motivically is directly linked with the degree of subtlety employed in the transformation of ideas. A closer consideration of some of the passages from *Prospects* will help to elucidate this aspect of Banks's music. The figure from bar 3 (Fig. 57) harmonized in parallel minor chords combined with minor seventh chords and played by the flutes and oboes is taken over in part by the horn in bars 4–5 and extended into bars 6–7. In bars 12 and 13 it becomes part of the material sounded by the oboes and clarinets. At the beginning of the Adagio espressivo (to take a further instance among many others) the solo cello theme commences with a restatement of this basic intervallic combination, rhythmically transformed and altered in shape by octave displacement. The continuation of this theme is accompanied in bars 64–65 by a rhythmically augmented and reharmonized version of the same motive that first appeared in bar 3.

Don Banks has earned the reputation of an internationally recognized Australian composer. It is, in fact, this acute awareness of being an Australian that has led him since his return to devote much of his energy to administrative work on the Music Board of the Australia Council and to develop an electronic music studio at the

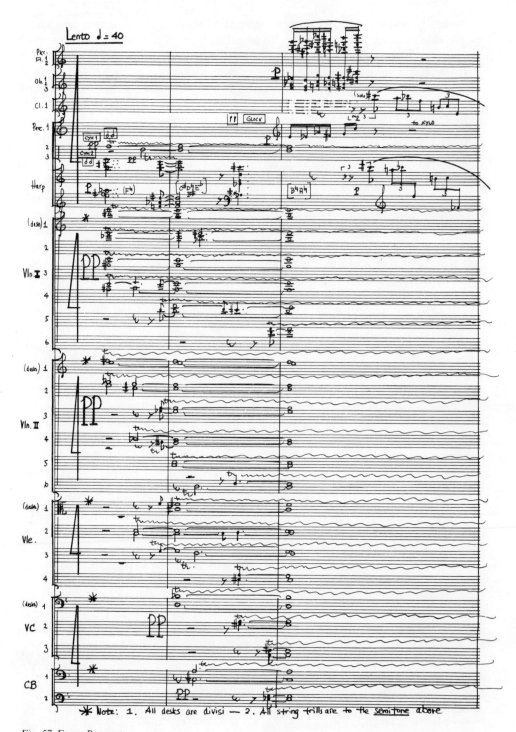

Fig. 57 From *Prospects*

Canberra School of Music. Banks talks enthusiastically about teaching programmes in electronic music and the developments taking place in this field, claiming that the invention of a new electronic instrument called the Qasar (in use at the Canberra School of Music) by the Australian designer Anthony Furse is some two years ahead of all other commercially available instruments. There is, of course, a great deal to be done in the field of electronic music and it is fortunate for Australia that a composer with Don Banks's immense gifts has returned to be in the vanguard of its development.

Notes

1. William Mann, 'The Music of Don Banks', *Musical Times*, August 1968, p. 719.

Bibliography

Strad, lxii (1952), p. 346.
Musical Times, xciii (1952), p. 179; xcv (1954), p. 382.
Musical Opinion, lxxvi (1953), p. 409.
Music Review, xiv (1953), p. 210, xvi (1955), p. 228.
Canon, x (1956), p. 193.
Feuilles Musicales, xv (1962), p. 129.
Musical Opinion, lxxxvi (1962), p. 79.
Covell, Roger. *Australia's Music: Themes of a New Society.* Sun Books, Melbourne, 1967, pp. 178–82.
Peart, Donald R. 'The Australian Avant-Garde', *Proceedings of the Royal Musical Association*, xciii (1967), pp. 1–9.
Mann, William. 'The Music of Don Banks', *Musical Times*, cix (1968), pp. 719–21.
Murdoch, James. *Australia's Contemporary Composers.* Macmillan, Melbourne, 1972, pp. 16–21.
Routh, Francis. *Contemporary British Music.* Macdonald, London, 1972.

List of Works

Publishers: Schott & Co. unless otherwise stated.

Orchestral Music
Four Pieces for orchestra (1953)
Episode for chamber orchestra (1958)
Elizabethan Miniatures for lute, viola da gamba and strings (1962)
Divisions for orchestra (1965)
Concerto for horn and orchestra (1965)
Assemblies for orchestra (1966)
Concerto for violin and orchestra (1968)
Intersections for electronic sounds and orchestra (1969)
Dramatic Music for young orchestra (1969)
Fanfare for orchestra (1970)
Meeting Place for chamber orchestra, jazz group and sound synthesizer (1970)
Music for Wind Band (1971)
Nexus for symphony orchestra and jazz quintet (1971)
Equation III for chamber group, jazz quartet and electronics (1972)
Prospects for orchestra (1974)

Chamber Music
Duo for violin and cello (1951–52)
Divertimento for flute and string trio (1951–52)
Sonata for violin and piano (1953)
Three Studies for cello and piano (1955)
Sonata da Camera for fl cl b cl v va vc pf and perc (1961)
Equation I for 12 players (1963)
Trio for horn, violin and piano (1962)
Three Episodes for flute and piano (1964)
Form X for two to ten players (1964)
Sequence for solo cello (1967)
Prelude, Night Piece and Blues for Two (clarinet and piano) (1968)
Equation II (1969)
Four Pieces for string quartet (1971)

Take Eight for string quartet and jazz quartet (1973)

Piano Music
Pezzo dramatico (1956)
Commentary for piano and 2-channel tape (1971)

Choral Music
Findings Keepings I for chorus and percussion (1968) [Novello & Co.]
Limbo cantata for three voices, eight instruments and 2-channel tape (1971)
Walkabout pieces for children's voices and percussion (1972)

Vocal Music
Psalm 70 for voice and chamber orchestra (1954)
Five North Country Folk Songs (1954)
Three North Country Folk Songs (1955)
Settings from Roget for voice and jazz quartet (1966)
Tirade triptych for soprano, harp, piano and three percussion (1968)
Three Short Songs for voice and jazz quartet (1971)
Aria from *Limbo* for voice, chamber group and tape (1972)

Electronic Music
Shadows of Space 4-track electronic music tape (1972)

Discography

Sonata for violin and piano (1953) [15'50"]. Robert Cooper (violin), Clemens Leske (piano). Schott.
ABC recording RRC/30
Four Pieces for orchestra (1953) [12'28"]. Melbourne Symphony Orchestra (Willem van Otterloo, conductor). Allan. 14 Aug. 1968.   *ABC disc RRCS/24*
Sonata da Camera (1961) [15'54"]. Members of the Western Australian Symphony Orchestra (Thomas Mayer, conductor). Schott. 26 Feb. 1970.
ABC disc RRCS/385
Trio for violin, horn and piano (1962). Brenton Langbein (violin), Barry Tuckwell (horn), Maureen Jones (piano). Schott.   *Argo disc ZRG/5474 (S)*
Elizabethan Miniatures (1962). Sinfonia of London (Doublas Gamley, conductor). Schott.
HMV disc CSD/1444
Settings from Roget (1966). Cleo Laine (vocals), Johnny Dankworth Quartet. Schott.
Fontana disc STL/5483
Assemblies for orchestra (1966) [14'00"]. Australian Youth Orchestra (John Hopkins, conductor). Schott. 13 July 1970.   *ABC recording RRCS/621*
Assemblies for orchestra [13'25"]. West Australian Symphony Orchestra (John Hopkins, conductor). Schott. 5 Mar. 1970.   *ABC recording RRCS/385*
Sequence for solo cello (1967) [13'53"]. George Isaac (cello). Schoot. 1971.   *Argo disc ZRG/695*
Violin Concerto (1968). Leonard Dommett (violin), Melbourne Symphony Orchestra (Patrick Thomas, conductor). Schott. 25 Aug. 1972.
World Record Club disc S/5264
Intersections for electronic sounds and orchestra (1969) [7'10"]. West Australian Symphony Orchestra (John Hopkins, conductor). Schott. 5 Mar. 1970.
ABC recording RRCS/385

Keith Humble

(*b.* 1927)

Laughton Harris

The recent widening horizons of activity in contemporary music in Australia, particularly in the fields of electronic music, computer applications in musical composition, music theatre and indeterminacy, owes much to the return of composers such as Keith Humble and more recently Don Banks and David Ahern, after years of active involvement in the composition and performance of new music in England and on the Continent. In Humble's case his return to the Australian musical scene in 1967 after almost fifteen years abroad, proved to be a veritable hypodermic, made all the more effective by his remarkable versatility as a conductor, pianist and teacher, as well as a composer; and by his close association with the brilliant percussionist and composer Jean-Charles François, a former student of Humble's with whom he had worked in Paris. From 1969, over a period of three years, they presented many source works of twentieth-century repertoire to Australian audiences, as well as performances of their own compositions. At the same time there came much beneficial feedback into Humble's work from one of the most advanced centres of musical creativity in the United States with his appointment to the Faculty of Music of the University of California, San Diego,—an arrangement by which he spent several months of each year working in the United States, and the balance of his time in Australia. In this way since his return to Australia Humble has provided an informed and vital contact with recent developments in new music, both in Europe and, particularly, in the United States. With his appointment to the Foundation Chair of Music at La Trobe University, Victoria, in 1974, it seems likely that Humble's creative energies will be focused more completely though no less actively in Australia than hitherto.

Keith Humble's musicianship developed on a broad front from an early age. Born in Geelong in 1927, Humble received his formal musical education at the Melbourne University Conservatorium of Music, graduating in piano and composition in 1949. His early involvement with jazz, which dated from long before he had left school, loomed as large in his life as his studies in the classical repertoire. It provided him with a useful source of income, but above all it took him to the wellspring of what he still considers to be one of the most dynamic forms of musical expression. Another important influence was that of Roy Shepherd, his lecturer in piano at the conservatorium, whom Humble now regards as a father figure in his early development. Himself a teacher of international distinction, Shepherd recognized the need for Humble to gain experience outside Australia, and took some very practical steps to launch a public appeal to make this possible.

After a year at the Royal Academy of Music in London under Howard Ferguson and Paul Steinitz, Humble moved to Paris in 1951 where he enrolled at the Ecole Normale de Musique as a piano student. His acceptance by René Leibowitz as a composition student was a turning point in his career. Leibowitz had been a pupil of Webern, and offered new and remarkable insights into the whole world of the Second Viennese school. His analysis was painstakingly rigorous, and above all he insisted that his students cultivate an acute aural sensibility: 'You must be able to *feel* the sound—like cloth!' Humble's continuing predilection for serial procedures, as well as his overall concern for precision and control in the handling of his musical material is in part attributable to Leibowitz's influence. The experience of assisting Leibowitz in the preparation and performance of works such as Schoenberg's *Gurrelieder* was also invaluable.

One of the earliest compositions Humble now acknowledges, the String Trio (1953), was completed during this period. Far from being merely a student work, the Trio already shows a secure and fluent technique in the handling of a transparent and particularly demanding medium. In true Schoenbergian tradition the row on which the work is based springs from a strong melodic gesture in the opening bars (Fig. 58), while a process of continual melodic variation pervades the overall structure which is clearly in sonata form.

Fig. 58 The opening bars of the String Trio

Similarly rooted in the serial tradition, the Piano Sonata (1959) reflects more the influence of Webern, and indeed Haydn, in its concern for small intervallic cells and textural symmetries. The all-pervasive tritone, so prominent in the row, and well in evidence in the closing bars of the first movement (Fig. 59), provides the melodic and harmonic mainspring of this work which, despite its careful argument, remains fluent and rhythmically vital.

An even greater economy of treatment is to be found in the *Fragments of War Poems* (1959) for soprano and instruments, the terse elliptical style of the words being matched by a fragmented texture through which there clearly runs a *klangfarben* vein of telling lyricism. This work was the product of a remarkably close collaboration between Harry Mathews who provided the text, and the composer. Mathews, an expatriate American in Paris and a close friend of Humble's, was also a sensitive musician. Inevitably words and music were modified as the work took shape, and a

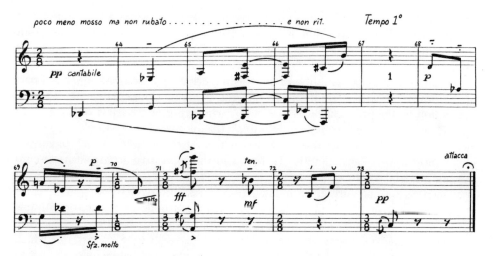

Fig. 59 Piano Sonata, first movement

concern for the musical potential of words as 'sound objects' has remained with Humble.

An earlier cycle, *Songs of Depression* (1955), in its close integration of words and music, shows a facet of Humble's musical background that is often overlooked—his involvement with the lied tradition. While in Paris he regularly accompanied soprano Ethel Semser and tenor Robert Gartside in lieder recitals, and the continuing importance of this tradition to Humble can be seen in his more recent *Trois Poèmes d'amour* (1970).

All the works mentioned so far Humble somewhat wryly labels 'monument music', a distinction which persists in his output, and which separates such works from his 'music theatre' pieces and other more occasional works which he refers to as 'furniture music'.

Briefly returning to Australia in 1956, Humble was back again in Paris by the next year working to establish a Music Centre which would provide a lively forum for the preparation, presentation and discussion of new music. Sponsored by the American Centre for Students and Artists, the Music Centre's first season opened in 1959–60, and quickly established a strong identity.

Humble then began working with Marc'O's theatre improvisation group, and in the early sixties a series of theatre pieces ensued: 'L'Entreprise' (1963), *Le Printemps* (1964), and *L'Armée des Saluts* (1965). After the closely ordered world of serialism, these projects provided a remarkable release for Humble, revealing an exciting potential for interrelating sound and gesture in new and flexible ways. The later music theatre series of *Nuniques*, many of which were presented at Monash University, Melbourne, between 1968 and 1971 after Humble's return to Australia, was an inevitable continuation of these earlier projects with Marc'O. Far from being 'neo-dada', as Australian critics were prone to claim, they were part of a continuing tradition which had its origins in futurist theatre, elements of which had been envisaged by that great original of the theatre, Edward Gordon Craig, at the turn of the century. Nor was the structure of these music theatre pieces as fortuitous as many would have liked to believe. Kirby has described the structure of the *Happening* in terms that might well have been applied to any one of the *Nuniques*: '(They are) based on the arrangement and contiguity of theatrical units that are self-contained and hermetic. No information is passed from one discrete theatrical unit—or compartment—to another. The compartments may be arranged separately or simultaneously.'[1]

The simultaneous presentation of contrasting events had been an important part of the futurist theatrical tradition, as had the breaking down of the 'fourth-wall' convention by the provocation of audience participation in a variety of ways. Both these elements featured strongly in Humble's theatre pieces with Marc'O and in the later *Nuniques*. The compartmentalized structure of these pieces, which has much in common with collage, can also be found in the successive arrangement of contrasting material in Humble's *Arcade* series, though by this time his 'discovery' of Ives and Varèse had further stimulated his interest in layered and spatial juxtapositions of diverse sound materials. But perhaps the strongest influence on Humble during his involvement with music theatre in Paris, came from a literary quarter, a *drame comique La femme pliante,* by Pierre Albert-Birot (1876–1967) in which Humble recognized a valid literary counterpart to many of the techniques he had been seeking in music.

In fact the idea of the nunique theatre itself came from Birot, and its emphasis on 'nowism' in art points to a vital aspect of Humble's philosophy: that music is above all *for now,* and that works written for posterity or performed as museum pieces are sterile by comparison. Years earlier Birot had affirmed that 'all the great philosophers, artists, poets, thinkers . . . have been, are, and will be nunists'.[2]

Birot has continued to influence Humble, who has used Birot's texts in the cantata *La Légende, Trois poèmes à crier et à danser, Trois poèmes d'amour,* as well as in *Now V* which is based on a puppet play of Birot, *Matoum et Trévibar.*

The fifties had seen the early days of *musique concrète* in Paris, but it was not until after his appointment to the Faculty of Music at the University of Melbourne that Humble seriously began to work with electronic music. Using both *concrète* and pure electronic sound sources and what now seems to be the most rudimentary equipment, he completed works for electronic media alone as well as for prepared tape in combination with other instruments. In the latter category is his *Music for Monuments* (1967), a work in open structure and for almost any combination of instruments or voices, and prepared tape. A version for bassoon and prepared tape presented at an International Society for Contemporary Music concert in Melbourne in 1967, included a collage of sounds from orchestral and *ad hoc* percussive sources, and much of the material had been derived from a 'music workshop' Humble had organized for school children, and was currently running at the Grainger Centre. Indeed Humble's early work with electronic music was always closely associated with numerous creative projects in improvisation in which music teachers, students, and children took part, using traditional and predominantly percussive instruments, as well as new instruments designed and constructed by the players themselves. Appropriately enough many of these activities took place in the Grainger Centre where gradually Humble built up a classical electronic studio, firstly with the acquisition of an EMS VCS3, and later in 1974, thanks to a generous endowment from the Gulbenkian Foundation, with the installation of an EMS Synthi 100. So from early tape music, and *musique concrète* pieces Humble moved to the use of voltage control techniques. During his annual visits to the University of California, San Diego, he has worked extensively in the field of computer-based composition, and it is in this that he plans to specialize in his newly created electronic studio at La Trobe University.

Humble has always regarded electronic media as 'just another instrument', and insists that with electronic music, as with all other music, 'all he can trust is his ears'. A remarkable consistency within his output, electronic or otherwise, shows this to be true as does the ease with which he integrates electronic sound with instruments or voices as in *La Légende*, or in *Arcade III* (b) for flute and electronics.

Both Humble's productivity as a composer and the identity of his work have notably increased in recent years. Among his most ambitious projects since his return to Australia must rank the cantata *La Légende* for solo voice, chorus, orchestra, electronic tape, and employing a variety of visual and spatial dimensions. Commissioned for the A.B.C.'s Promenade Concert series in Melbourne in 1971, the work is based on a text by Albert-Dirot in which an intensely humanistic view of creation is portrayed. Humble worked in close collaboration with the Australian artist, Noel Counihan, who completed eight paintings, the titles of which convey something of the essence of the work: the poet the father—who made the earth so beautiful; the son; the son meets his sisters dark and fair; crossing the rainbow; the search for the bride; the yearning of the virgin; the young god takes his golden maid; the death of the god. These paintings were projected in every varying sequence on to four large screens which surrounded the audience during the performance. In its breadth of conception there is little doubt that *La Légende* is a landmark in multimedia production in Australia.

The tendency for smaller works to germinate from larger works-in-progress, or works just completed, is noteworthy in Humble's output. So *Après La Légende* was an offshoot from the cantata, and *Materials for Larountala* (for 22 solo strings) from a larger project on which Humble was working at the time. Both these works provide a useful introduction to the larger (as yet unrecorded) works to which they are related. So too *Kadenz* for flute (1972) is an expanded paraphrase of the flute cadenza in *A Music for Baroque Ensemble* (1971).

Humble's inclination to group together works sharing common structural tendencies can be seen in his *Arcade* and *Statico* series. The term *Arcade* aptly suggests the presentation of a rich variety of material in collage-like succession, leaving the composer free to work within a fairly open-ended structure. The impact of the orchestral *Arcade V* depends on striking textural and timbre changes, rather than on any detailed working out of limited basic material, and the important role of timbre and dynamics as a means of structural articulation, in *Arcade III a* (Fig. 60) for flute invites comparison with Varèse's *Destiny 21.5*, though the tonal resources of the flute have been greatly extended in *Arcade III b* by the use of a prepared tape and of an extended flute technique. The *Statico* series of works, on the other hand, could be regarded as sound sculptures, in which clearly recognizable geometric shapes may be defined by the pitch spectrum, as in the orchestral *Statico III*. Throughout the *Statico* series Humble's continuing concern for systems in the articulation of a closed structure is apparent. In *Statico III* prime numbers largely determine durational patterns and, with the help of the computer, the composer has selected a row the adjacent notes of which yield a particularly rich variety of harmonic material. A further interesting feature of this work is the careful use of doublings which ensures the penetration of a strong melodic component through an immensely complex orchestral texture.

Fig. 60 From *Arcade IIIa*

The more recent and predominantly electronic *Prime* series is in a modular structure of, so far, five sections of 'panels' any one of which can be performed in its own right or in combination with any or all of the other sections. The electronic material of the *Prime* pieces was generated on a PDP 11/10 computer at the University of California, San Diego, in collaboration with Serge Terepnin, as well as on the Synthi 100 at the University of Melbourne. *Prime One* and *Prime Too* use twelve individual percussion-like sounds and nine melodic sounds respectively. *Prime One Too* consists of a synthesis of the first two sections, while *Prime Riff* is simply a version of *Prime One* for six (live) percussion instruments. The final *Prime* of the set makes use of the electronic material of the first three in combination with a percussion soloist.

Humble's increasing absorption with timbre stems from a respect for the works of both Debussy and Webern, as well as from his discovery of the works of Ives and Varèse.

In *Four Studies for 201* we see the foundations of Humble's interest in timbre: the towering figure of Webern. Within the narrow limits set by the composer for each movement, the use of subtle *klangfarben* relationships is masterly. A further example of Humble's lively exploration of timbre is *The Seasons*, a setting of seven haiku for four choirs. From the concentrated brevity of the haiku, Humble has extracted words and explored their musical potential as sound objects, building up by means of graphic notation textures both imaginative and evocative. As with many of Humble's instrumental compositions, one feels that the world of electronic sound is but a short step away. The tonal spectrum which the composer sets out to explore is enriched by the use of a variety of simple home-made or toy instruments played by each member of the choir. The effect is in fact compelling.

Humble's involvement with music has always been as completely practical as it has been uncompromising. He writes mostly with a particular performance in mind, and frequently takes part in the presentation of the work himself. Faced with the considerable practical difficulties of arranging adequate spatial disposition and quality of electronic sounds in halls that are designed more for the needs of nineteenth-century than twentieth-century music, Humble has returned not infrequently to writing 'monument music' within a closed form, the coherence of which depends on a closely worked and continuing development of the material. Such a work is *A Music for Baroque Ensemble* for oboe, flute, double bass and harpsichord, commissioned by the Astra Society of Melbourne for the Baroque Ensemble of Indiana. It is in one movement, ensemble sections separating cadenzas for each instrument, and continual development of the musical material being ensured by each ensemble section both commenting on and reacting to the cadenza just played. This piece further demonstrates Humble's remarkable capacity to use familiar timbres in an individual and entirely convincing way, but above all shows the strong melodic impulse which underlies much of his work.

Already the range of Humble's composition is as impressive as the breadth of his involvement in conducting, performance and teaching. In fact few Australian composers appear to be exploring what Salzman had referred to as 'the totality of experience' now available to the composer[3] more extensively than Humble, who remains one of the most vital and forward-looking creative energies on the Australian musical scene today. After an early and closely disciplined involvement with serialism in the fifties, he explored the many interrelationships of music and gesture in music theatre projects of the sixties and more recently his work has seen an increasing absorption in the possibilities of timbre, reflected in his firm commitment to electronic music. There is little doubt that the exciting potential of computer-based composition will continue to open up new creative possibilities for Humble's immensely fertile musical imagination.

Notes

1. M. Kirby, *Happenings*, Dutton Inc., New York, 1975, p. 13.
2. P. Albert-Birot, *SIC* [*Sons, Idées, Couleurs*], 1916.
3. E. Salzman, *Twentieth Century Music: An Introduction*, New Jersey, 1967, p. 171.

Bibliography

Covell, Roger. *Australia's Music: Themes of a New Society*. Sun Books, Melbourne, 1967, pp. 102, 233.
McCaughey, J. 'Notes on Contemporary Music', *Melbourne University Magazine*, 1970, p. 45.
McCredie, Andrew. *Musical Composition in Australia*. Australian Government Publication, 1969, p. 19.
Murdoch, James. *Australia's Contemporary Composers*. Macmillan, Melbourne, 1972, pp. 120–32.
Payne, A. 'Flair and Sensibility', *Music and Musicians*, xii, December 1963, p. 42.

List of Works

String Trio (Paris 1953). First performed Cheltenham Music Festival 1958. Published. Australian Music Fund.
Songs of Depression (Paris 1955) for soprano voice and piano.
Fragments of War Poems (Paris 1959). Words by Harry Mathews. For soprano voice and instruments. First performed Paris 1964. Published. AMF.
Piano Sonata no. 1 (Paris 1959). First performed Melbourne 1965.
Folio no. 1 for piano (three pieces) (Paris 1953–59).
Folio no. 2 for piano (three pieces) (Paris 1954).
Piece Mechamoo—I–III (1965).
Musique Limitée (1966).
A Book of Songs of Love and Death (from the Greek) (Paris 1966) for tenor voice and piano. First performed in the United States 1966.
Ainsi s'achève (Paris 1967) for three to six instruments, harp, three percussion and piano. First performed Paris 1967.
Five Pieces for violin and piano (Melbourne 1967). First performed Melbourne 1967.
Three Statements for piano (Melbourne 1967). (Allans)
Music for Monuments (Melbourne 1967) for instruments and/or voices and prepared tape. First performed Paris 1968.
Materials for Larountala (Paris 1968) for 22 solo strings. First performed Melbourne 1968.
Trois Poèmes à crier et à danser (Melbourne 1968). First performed Melbourne 1968. For choir. (Universal Edition)
Solfège I (Paris 1968). For diverse instruments, electronics ad lib. First performed San Diego 1969.
Solfège II (Melbourne 1969) for performer and electronics.
Nunique I (Paris 1968).
Nunique II (a) (Vichy 1968).
Nunique II (b) (Freiburg 1968).
Nunique III (Monash, Melbourne 1969).

Arcade I (a) (Melbourne 1969) for organ, percussion and tapes. First performed Melbourne 1969.
Arcade I (b) (Melbourne 1969) Version tape alone.
Arcade III (a) (Melbourne 1969) for flute solo. (Universal Edition)
Arcade III (b) (Melbourne 1969) for flute solo and electronics. First performed Melbourne 1970.
Arcade II (Melbourne 1969) for piano solo. First performed Melbourne 1969. (Universal Edition)
Arcade IV (Melbourne 1969) for guitar, percussion. First performed Melbourne 1970. (Universal Edition)
Arcade V (Melbourne 1969) for orchestra. First performed Melbourne 1969. (Universal Edition)
Après La Légende (Melbourne 1969) for orchestra and piano. First performed Perth 1970.
Trois Poèmes d'amour (San Diego 1970) for tenor voice and piano. First performed San Diego 1970.
La Légende cantata for solo voice, choir, electronics and instruments. Entry for Italia Prize 1970. First performed Melbourne 1971.
Statico I for organ and two synthesizers 1971. First performed Melbourne 1971. (Universal Edition)
A Music for Baroque Ensemble (1971) for harpsichord, flute, oboe, double bass. (Universal Edition)
The Seasons a setting of seven haiku for four choirs (1971). (Universal Edition)
Treatment no. 1 (For me) 1971.
Nunique VI (1971) Sydney.
Now V opera (1971). (Universal Edition)
Paraphrase in Five + Mass = Statico II (1972) Melbourne. (Universal Edition)
Kadenz for flute solo (1972) Palo edition
Statico III for orchestra (1972–73) first performed Melbourne, A.B.C. Invitation Concert Series 1974.
Electronic Pieces
(i) *Parodie:* (a) 'Time Piece' (1972)
         (b) 'Bird Songs at Even-Time' (1972)
         (c) 'Ground' (1972)
         (d) 'Mass' (1972)
(ii) *And Tomorrow* (1972) (La Jolla).
Nunique VII for Brisbane (1972) (Cardiff-by-the-sea).
Four Studies for 201 (1972) (Cardiff-by-the-sea).
In Five (1972) (La Jolla).
Sounds for/and/or cello and electronics (1972) (Queenscliff).
Sounds for/and/or bass and electronics (1973) (La Jolla). (Universal Edition)
Prime One (1974).
Prime Too (1975).
Prime One Too (a synthesis of *Prime One* and *Prime Too*).
Prime Riff for tape and six percussion instruments.
Treatments 1–20 (tape music, performers Jean-Charles Francois and Keith Humble) (La Jolla 1973–74).

Discography

Après la légende (1969) [8'37"]. Wendy Nash (piano), West Australian Symphony Orchestra (Thomas Mayer, conductor). MS. 26 Feb. 1970.
        ABC recording RRCS/386

Materials for Larountala (1967) [7'30"]. Strings of the Melbourne Symphony Orchestra (Keith Humble, conductor). MS. 1 Oct. 1968.
ABC recording RRCS/382

'Reverberations': includes Paraphrase in Five + Mass = Statico II and works by Werder, Bonighton and Nagorcka.   *'Move' MS3006*

String Trio (1953) [8'05"]. Members of the Paul Mc-Dermott String Quartet. MS. Nov. 1968.
ABC recording RRCS/382

A Music for Baroque Ensemble (1970) [10'15"]. Vernon Hill (flute), Jindrich Degan (oboe), John Mowson (double bass), Sergio di Pieri (harpsichord). 24 July 1971.   *ABC tape*

Statico No. 1 (1971) [17'00"]. Sergio di Pieri (organ), Keith Humble, Jean-Charles François (sound synthesizers). 27 July 1971.   *ABC tape*

Fantasy for Violin and Piano [7'30"]. Beryl Kimber (violin), Margaret Sutherland (piano). 1959.
ABC recording PRX/4389 (ABR only)

George Dreyfus
(*b.* 1928)

Elaine Dobson

Few composers freely and independently determine their genre of compositional activity. Rather they react to an already existing situation and become part of an evolutionary creative process. This is largely true of George Dreyfus who says

> I have *always* written music—but what composer hasn't? Some destroy or disown their early work; mine were generally unfinished. This I ascribe to the Australian musical climate of the early fifties, the time when I first started writing (I was twenty-two or three at the time). One was hardly aware of the fact that Australia had composers; there was some noise about Antill's *Corroboree*, but I was aware of little else.[1]

Dreyfus, who was born in 1928 at Wuppertal, Germany, migrated to Australia in 1939; yet much of his work reflects qualities often associated with a German musical tradition: a richness of invention, a craftsman's approach to art, an adroit sense of humour and a love of wind instruments.

In the Trio for flute, clarinet and bassoon (1956), Dreyfus creates a solid orchestral sound, reminiscent of the town bands which flourished in Germany. Repeated motives which never quite become ostinatos, movement in octaves and contrary motion and neatly placed recurrences of jaunty themes combine in this witty and energetic work. In the second of the three movements the gently shifting bassoon ostinato gives shape to the piece while the flute and clarinet move in layers above, creating a static, but inwardly moving, stream of counterpoint coloured by bell-like intonations. In the third movement verve returns and Dreyfus irreverently quotes Mendelssohn's Wedding March.

Other significant early works by Dreyfus include two song cycles: *Galgenlieder* (1957), and *Songs Comic* and *Curious* (1959), which won the Louis Lavater Prize in 1960. In each of these works parody and humour are not far from the surface. Less concerned about the style in which he was writing, Dreyfus's intent was more to set a vivid musical scene for the poems in which voice and woodwind instruments play equally important roles. *Galgenlieder* opens with an instrumental overture which displays the characteristics of the whole cycle in its sudden pauses and silences, repetitions and returns, and the mixture of surprise and predictability in the melodic and rhythmic lines.

Dreyfus sees 1961 as a year of liberation for his musical thinking. Through European musical journals and imported scores and records he had become acquainted with the works of Schoenberg, Webern and the generation represented by Boulez, Nono, Henze and Stockhausen. In the same year, Dreyfus formed and conducted the New Music Ensemble in Melbourne which permitted close contact with the problems and philosophies this contemporary music presented.

The assimilation of the serialists' techniques resulted in *Music in the Air* (1961), and *From Within Looking Out* (1962), both works displaying new formal complexity and seriousness of expression, and defined by techniques associated with dodecaphony—angularity, declamation, irregularity and neutralization of rhythms.

From Within Looking Out was selected as Australia's musical entry for the 1965 Italia Prize and it gathered considerable recognition for Dreyfus. The work is in five movements, the first of which is an instrumental introduction. This not only foreshadows the tranquil mood of the music surrounding the text (a street song from Amman), but also the use of twelve-note technique in the second movement and the cantus firmus idea of the last movement. This introductory movement is in two parts, the first led by a sustained flute melody, the second by the viola closely following the rhythm and shape of the first. The second movement is introduced by the soprano with a fully-developed twelve-note theme, later embellished by the addition of the flute and leading into the strict arch-design of the movement. Initially, the twelve-note series is heard as a sustained chord which gradually disintegrates into a horizontal organization as the number of simultaneously-sounding voice-parts decreases. At the peak of the arch the original twelve-note theme emerges as a single line divided between various instruments. The process is then reversed and the vertical structures return, concluding the movement with the twelve-note chord. It is worth noting that the second half of the arch forms a complete retrograde of the first but is compressed into half the original duration.

A more rhapsodic style characterizes the third and fourth movements. Throughout the latter, the flute is paired with the viola, the vibraphone with the celeste, each instrument moving in rhythmic unison with its partner and overlaying the whole piece with a filigree of dissonances. In the last movement structural detail returns. The long, four-bar melody on the muted viola at the beginning acts as a cantus firmus and is only interrupted for four bars in the middle of the movement. The pitch of the second half of this melody is an inversion of the first half and the rhythm varies little here or in subsequent repetitions (Fig. 61). The soprano's entrance is in strict canon with the viola, its line treated instrumentally (i.e. as a vocalise). During the third repeat of the melody the other instruments enter and gradually break the cantus firmus line in preparation for the climax, where the soprano speaks.

From Within Looking Out was followed by works in a similar vein: *The Seasons* (1963), and Wind Quintet (1965), the former taken from Dreyfus's music for a film on the Australian painter Clifton Pugh. Dreyfus has indeed acquired a sound reputation as a composer of incidental music for films and television with such works as *The Adventures of Sebastian the Fox*, and more recently *Marion* and *Rush*.

Between 1965 and 1966 Dreyfus wrote his first opera *Garni Sands*. The two acts of this work divide Frank Kellaway's libretto into a large antecedent and consequent. In the first, three situations, separated in time, represent the relationship between a squatter, his wife and daughter; four convicts who work for them; and the adversities of colonial life. It begins after a short introduction for the chamber orchestra and

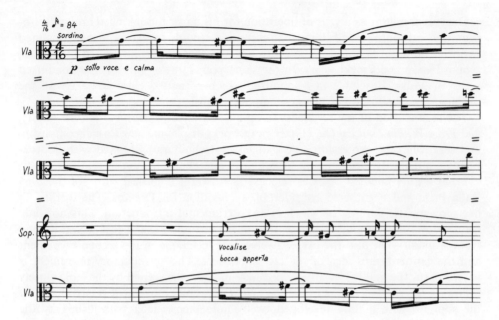

Fig. 61 *From Within Looking Out*, last movement

the Commentator who acts as narrator and observer. In the second act the three situations are drawn closer together and swept relentlessly towards the catastrophe. The dramatic and musical construction of *Garni Sands* is cohesive: particular instruments are associated with different characters highlighting their various personalities or roles, and particular instrumental timbres often define particular situations or moods; orchestral interludes occur between scenes or episodes, and, while often self-contained, they also function as transitions between time and mood. The success of *Garni Sands* in Australia and its recognition overseas represents a major breakthrough for Australian opera.[2]

In 1966 a UNESCO fellowship enable Dreyfus to visit Europe a second time. During his first visit (1954–55), he had studied bassoon at the Vienna Academy, but this time his interest lay in composition and he attended Stockhausen's course for New Music. On his return, in 1967, he became the first composer to take up a Creative Arts Fellowship at the Australian National University, Canberra, and it was during this time that another major work, the Symphony no. 1, was composed.

Whereas Dreyfus regards *Garni Sands* as a significant work in his style of the sixties, he is non-committal about his eclectic Symphony. The mere title and form suggest a repudiation of his trends immediately prior to that work. It is an assemblage of references to numerous twentieth-century European and American composers, in which the driving rhythms, ostinati, and fragmentation, found in his early pieces, reappear.

Other works for orchestra include *Jingles* (1968), *. . . and more Jingles* (1972), and *The Illusionist* (1972)—a mime drama for dancer and orchestra. The title *Jingles* arose out of a press interview given before the performance of the Symphony no. 1. Dreyfus had mentioned that the first theme of the symphony was derived from a television commercial (or jingle), for a short-lived cigarette brand, which he had composed some time previously. One high-minded critic, taking offence at the idiom of the symphony, based his negative conclusions on the fact that the composer had shamelessly used this jingle. Now it is a characteristic of Dreyfus's nature to engage public provocation 'head-on', and he therefore entitled his next work *Jingles* although, in fact, it has nothing to do with them.

Fig. 62 From *Garni Sands*

Reflections in a Glass-house: An Image of Captain James Cook (1969), is the first of a series of works written together with Melbourne author Lynne Strahan. These include *The Gilt-Edged Kid* (1970), an opera in one act; *The Grand Aurora Australis Now Show* (1973), described as 'a national anthem sing-in for young people'; and *Silver Sticks and Salt Petre*, commissioned by the A.B.C. in 1972 for its entry in the Italia Prize competition. In the latter, memories of life in the inner suburbs of Melbourne, perhaps fifty years ago, are presented through narrators, traditional children's chants, and a variety of musical ensembles. Lynne Strahan also wrote the libretto of *Proverbs for a Lalique Bird*, an opera in three acts on which Dreyfus is at present working.

Reflections in a Glass-house was written to celebrate the bicentenary of Captain Cook's discovery of Australia. Scored for speaker, children's chorus and orchestra, it omits all strings except for eight violoncelli, and includes large woodwind and percussion sections. The speaker has a dual role: the voice of both Cook and the modern Australian, for this work represents a challenge to today's Australia to reassess its national attitudes and beliefs.

In the first part the speaker reads selections from Cook's journals describing the voyage northward from Botany Bay, the music forming a backdrop against which these descriptive excerpts are set. In the second part the speaker, now representing modern Australia, challenges the spirit of Cook to admit that Australia's discovery was worthy of less casual and more visionary comments (Fig. 63). The music and dialogue offset each other here. Brittle, fracturing note-clusters accompany the speaker's impatience and resentment, and the entry of the saxophone adds mockery to his questioning. At the end the first of the children's choruses is heard.

In the third part the dialogue continues but the speaker becomes more vehement, addressing not only Cook but also the audience; bringing the author's text to a climax by re-examining the comforting assumptions by which we live: Australia the free land, the lucky country, the good life.[3] It is here that the children's chorus achieves most importance. Pitting their sweetness against the acerbity of the text, the children's voices parody the aggression of the speaker in a lilting hornpipe, countering his irony in a delicate, yet strikingly effective canon. The last song is a double-edged song of praise to Australia.

> Australia is a free land
> Free without a doubt
> If you haven't got a dinner
> You're free to go without
>
> Australia is a lucky land
> Sizzling in its wealth
> As long as you are lucky
> You needn't change yourself.
>
> Australia is a safe land
> It shall not happen here
> To keep the farms for honest men
> We'll fight our wars up there . . .

Clearly the piece possesses political overtones but this social involvement must be regarded as legitimate a technique for contemporary music as the use of twelve-note rows. In actual performance this final song is sung by a third choir (which has not previously participated), of children appearing from the back of the hall, marching

Fig. 63 From *Reflections in a Glass-house*

in procession and carrying 'mobiles, wind-charms, or similar objects, made of reflective substances' suspended from poles. They are accompanied by their own brass band while the orchestra remains on stage playing fragments from Dreyfus's other compositions. In preparation for this procession the chorale *Wachet Auf* appears as the soft accompaniment to a meditation on Cook's death. Here the image of the glass-house becomes significant, it being Cook himself who had named the Glass-house Mountains near Brisbane.

Structurally the music of the work resembles a mobile which produces an ever-changing sequence of timbres, textures, movement and motives. In the first part each section is linked by a single sustained noted like the thin wire which suspends the shapes of a Calder mobile in space.

The children's choruses in *Reflections in a Glass-house* are good examples of Dreyfus's ability to write striking music for young performers. This ability is further demonstrated in the school opera *The Takeover*, the cantata *Song of the Maypole*, *Music for Music Camp*, and the suite from *The Adventures of Sebastian the Fox*.

Whereas *Reflections in a Glass-house* was structured on a mobile, the Sextet for didjeridu and wind instruments (1971), and *Mo* (1972), are based on the technique of collage. In both works two unlikely situations are juxtaposed. *Mo* presents two disparate musical styles (music-hall songs of the twenties and thirties and a selection from movements of Vivaldi's *L'Estro Armonico*). Here the collage structure is organized by what the composer describes as a 'slide-rule principle'.

The seemingly incongruous elements in the Sextet are the primitive didjeridu and the sophisticated European wind quintet. The Sextet is the most successful synthesis of Aboriginal and Western music in an Australian composition so far. Primarily a tone-colour piece having its origins in Schoenberg's concept of *klangfarbenmelodie*, it lies within the tradition of Ligeti and Penderecki.

Only the starting and stopping points for the didjeridu are marked on the score and its part is quite improvisatory in contrast to the intricately notated parts of the quintet. The work is divided into three sections—slow, medium and excited. In the first the didjeridu merges as a 'pedal-point' in music in which there are no events or contours (in the rhythmic, melodic or harmonic sense). It is the continual meta-morphosis of tone-colour that shapes the form.

In the second section the didjeridu plays a more active part reacting to the instruments of the quintet when each takes its turn to play its rapid-moving cadenza. Each solo is linked by a static-type section. The didjeridu creates new patterns and is encouraged to use special effects, such as the 'croak', while each cadenza exploits some idiomatic aspects of the Western instruments. In the third section several lines move simultaneously at different speeds with interlocking pitches. Although basically static, the music glimmers with many refractions and reflections, the mesh of sound being broken only by powerful *sforzatissimo* chords and by the contrasting light and dark colours of high and low registers.

Fig. 64 From the Sextet

The main influences on Dreyfus's style are not difficult to discern but to describe his music within the confines of a single established school would be misleading and superficial. Dreyfus is a thoroughly professional composer in both the handling of his art and in the sense that he derives his living from composing. In 1972 he received the Henry Lawson award for outstanding service to the arts. In 1973 he received the Maggs Award for which he wrote *Old Melbourne* and was commissioned to write the *Grand Aurora Australis Now Show* for the opening of the Sydney Opera House. Such success is indicative of Dreyfus's commitment to music in Australia and is an acknowledgement of the prominent position his music holds.

Notes

1. George Dreyfus, 'George Dreyfus', *The Composers and their Work* (Australian Government, Canberra, 1969), p. 6.
2. For a detailed analysis of this opera see Kay Lucas, 'George Dreyfus's *Garni Sands*: A forward Step for Australian Opera', *Studies in Music*, 7 (1973), pp. 78–87.
3. Kay Lucas, 'Ambiguous reflections for the young', *Bulletin*, xxxxii, no. 4704 (May 1970), p. 44.

Publishers

Allans (Melbourne), Schott (London).

Bibliography

Covell, Roger. *Australia's Music: Themes of a New Society*. Sun Books, Melbourne, 1967, pp. 191–5, 266–7.

Downs, P. G. 'George Dreyfus' First Symphony', *Meanjin Quarterly*, xxvii, no. 4 (Summer 1968), 484–8.

Hoad, Brian. 'In the Wasteland', *Bulletin*, lxxxiv, no. 4811 (August 1972), 44.

Kellaway, Frank. 'Garni Sands', *Overland*, no. 60 (Autumn 1975), 28–30.

Lucas, Kay. 'Ambiguous Reflections for the Young', *Bulletin*, lxxxxii, no. 4704 (May 1970), 44.

'A Provocative Mix', *Bulletin*, lxxxiv, no. 4627 (Nov. 1968), 80.

'Australian Opera for Première in New York', *Opera Australia*, no. 6 (1975).

'Bringing the Children to the Table', *Bulletin*, lxxxxi, no. 4675 (Oct. 1969), 57–8.

'Chamber Orchestra for Local Composers', *APRA Journal*, no. 6 (Jan. 1972), 18.

'Dreyfus and the Didjeridu', *Music Maker*, xliii, no. 3 (Sept. 1972), 8–9.

'George Dreyfus', *APRA Journal*, no. 5 (Jul. 1971), 23.

'George Dreyfus's *Garni Sands*: A Forward Step for Australian Opera', *Studies in Music*, 7 (1973), 78–87.

'George Dreyfus' First Symphony', *Music Now*, i, no. 2 (1969), 26–9.

'The School Music of George Dreyfus', *The Australian Journal of Music Education*, no. 8 (Apr., 1971), 49–51.

'The Value of Communication', *Bulletin*, lxxxx, no. 4596 (Apr. 1968), 69.

'The Value of Communication', *Bulletin*, lxxxx, no. 4596 (April 1968), 69.

McCredie, Andrew D. *Catalogue of 46 Australian Composers and Selected Works*. Australian Government, Canberra, 1969, p. 5.
Musical Composition in Australia. Canberra, 1969, p. 18.
The Composers and Their Work. Canberra, 1969, p. 6.

Mintz, Donald. 'Review of Records: Australian Music', *MQ* (October 1967), 596–603.

Murdoch, James. *Australia's Contemporary Composers*. Macmillan, Melbourne, 1972, pp. 80–7.

Peart, Donald, 'The Australian Avant-Garde', *Proceedings of the Royal Musical Association*, xciii (1967), 1–9.

Symons, D. *Music and Dance*, lii (Jan. 1962), 8.

List of Works

Stage Music
Garni Sands opera in two acts (1965–66)
The Takeover school opera in one act (1969)
The Gilt-Edged Kid opera in one act (1970)
The Illusionist for solo dancer and orchestra (1972)

Orchestral Music
Symphony no. 1 (1967)
Music for Music Camp for student orchestra (1967)
Jingles (1968)
. . . and more Jingles (1972)
Reflections in a Glass-house: An Image of Captain James Cook for speaker, children's chorus, and orchestra (1969)
Mo for baritone, string orchestra and continuo (1972)
The Grand Aurora Australis Now Show (1973)
Rush (1974)

Chamber Music
Trio for fl cl bn (1956)
The Seasons for fl va perc (1963)
Quintet for wind instruments for fl ob cl hn bn (1965)
Quintet 'after the Notebook of J.-G. Noverre' for wind instruments (1968)
Sextet for didjeridu and wind instruments (1971)
Old Melbourne for bn and guit (1973)

Vocal Music
Galgenlieder for baritone fl cl bn (1957)
Songs Comic and Curious for baritone and wind quintet (1959)
Music in the Air for baritone fl va and perc (1961)
From Within Looking Out for soprano fl va cel and vib (1962)
Ned Kelly Ballads for folk singer, four horns and rhythm section (1964)

Choral Music
Song of the Maypole cantata for children's choruses (1968)
Under the Gum Trees at Sunrise anthem for two five-part choirs and four soloists (1968)
Homage to Igor Stravinsky for ten-part choir (1968)

Miscellaneous
The Adventures of Sebastian the Fox suite arranged for various ensembles (1968)
Silver Sticks and Salt Petre for radio (1972)

Discography

Symphony no. 1 (1968) [25′45″]. Melbourne Symphony Orchestra (Ladislav Slovak, conductor).

Allan. 29 Mar. 1968.   *HMV disc OASD/7547*
Jingles (1967) [13'50"]. West Australian Symphony
Orchestra (Sir Bernard Heinze, conductor). Allan.
Feb. 1969.   *Festival disc SFC 800/21*
From Within Looking Out (1962) [14'19"]. Marilyn
Richardson (soprano), Margaret Crawford (flute),
John Glickman (viola), Kay Lucas (celeste), Glen
Davies (vibraphone). MS. 5 May 1967.
                              World Record Club disc A/601
The Seasons (1963) [11'31"]. Margaret Crawford
(flute), Madeleine Dietrich (viola), Glen Davies
(percussion). MS.   *ABC recording PRX/5599*
Trio. Op. 1 (1956) [15'34"]. Neville Amadio (flute),
Donald Westlake (clarinet), John Cran (bassoon).
                              Philips disc AY/842721
Galgenlieder (1957) [17'39"]. Ronal Jackson (baritone),
Donald Hazlewood (violin); New Sydney Woodwind Quintet: Neville Amadio (flute), Guy Henderson (oboe), Donald Westlake (clarinet), John Cran
(bassoon), Clarence Mell (horn).
                              Philips disc AY/842721
Songs Comic and Curious (1959) [28'48"]. (i) Overture
—4'25"; (ii) Sonnet found in a deserted madhouse
—5'24"; (iii) Susan Simpson—1'15"; (iv) Belag-
cholly days—3'43"; (v) The bees' song—3'08";
(vi) Jabberwocky—4'53"; Brian Hansford (baritone); Adelaide Wind Quintet: David Cubbin (flute),
Jiri Tancibudek (oboe), Gabor Reeves (clarinet),
Thomas Wightman (bassoon), Patrick Brislan
(horn). Allan. 1970.   *HMV disc OASD/7558*
Sextet for didjeridu and wind quintet (1971) [16'11"].
George Winunguj (didjeridu); Adelaide Wind Quint-
et: David Cubbin (flute), Jiri Tancibudek (oboe),
Gabor Reeves (clarinet), Patrick Brislan (horn),
Thomas Wightman (bassoon). Allan. 1971.
                              HMV disc OASD/7565
Quintet 'after the Notebook of J.G. Noverre' (1968)
[19'43"]. New Sydney Woodwind Quintet: Neville
Amadio (flute); Guy Henderson (oboe), Donald
Westlake (clarinet), Clarence Mellor (horn), John
Cran (bassoon). Allan. 1971.
                              RCA Red Seal disc SL/16374

Peter Sculthorpe
(*b.* 1929)

Michael Hannan

When the history of music in twentieth-century Australia is assembled, there is little doubt that Peter Sculthorpe will emerge as the most important and influential composer, for he is certainly the first, and perhaps the only one, who seems to have established for himself a concept of what an Australian music might be, and the only one who has thought seriously of the kind of response which is appropriate to our particular social sensibility. The fact that he has pursued his vision with almost unswerving dogmatism does little to taint his achievement, for it is probably true that the lack of direction in Australian composition in this century has resulted from feelings of insecurity and inferiority about being in a country which is as far removed from the great centres of Western civilization as one could possibly imagine.

In his early years Sculthorpe realized, for a variety of reasons, that there was no future in the endless and virtually impossible quest to keep up with European developments, so he decided that his music would have to take its own course and find its own aesthetic. From a practical point of view the most contemporary scores and recordings available to a student in the 1940s with few exceptions were of Delius, Mahler and Bartók. Sculthorpe also realized that the high notions of art and philosophy which had been so important to him as a young man living in the isolation of Tasmania held no interest for his university contemporaries in Melbourne who were more concerned with everyday matters and, as far as knowledge was concerned, with facts rather than abstract ideas. Thus Peter Sculthorpe reacted against European art and philosophy as being inappropriate models for an Australian artist's response to his society.

After rejecting what little he knew about serialism and atonality he turned his attention to a few somewhat conventional composers who seemed to him to have captured a feeling which was not inappropriate to those feelings he had about Australia. He was attracted to Aaron Copland's music, for example, because he could see strong parellels between Australia and America and because Copland seemed to express a personal un-European view of his country. Similarly a love of Ernest Bloch was probably sparked off by his depiction of the Biblical wilderness which reminded Sculthorpe of the terrifying unpopulated landscapes of Australia. From these two unlikely influences sprang a music which quickly took on a life of its own, developing in strong individualistic directions, both stylistically and structurally.

Sculthorpe's initial attempt to create an Australian music contains, surprisingly enough, the bases of his mature compositional craft. Although the *Sonatina* for piano (1954) contains, not unexpectedly, stylistically embarrassing characteristics in its liberal use of bitonality and climactic gesture, it nonetheless demonstrates the composer's attraction for quick ritualistic non-melodic and non-harmonic passages and for slow, harmonically static melodies. Furthermore, whether the music is slow or quick, it is almost wholly aggregated from a family of characteristic small rhythmic structures, the uniting principle of which is simple repetition. That is, if a rhythmic pattern of two or more measures is employed, then it is repeated before any new pattern is introduced. The overall structural dislocation theoretically suggested by this manner of making a piece is cancelled out by a sameness in the rhythmic ideas used from section to section. In the quick ritual music, for example, Sculthorpe establishes a 'feel', to use a term associated with the stylistic unification which the rhythm players of jazz and rock supply to a song or improvisation. Unlike most of his contemporaries he is also prepared to employ conventional structures like ternary design and other simple returning patterns which are an elaboration of the idea of ternary design.

Fig. 65 The opening chord of the Sonatina

Although the *Sonatina* now displays a naïveté in keeping with a young composer's struggle to find a direction for his music, it is nonetheless remarkable how many of its ideas and details were retained and refined by Sculthorpe. It may be argued, for example, that the opening chord of the work represents the basis of his harmonic style (Fig. 65). It is, however, true that Sculthorpe did not encapsulate the fundamental harmonic and tonal principles of his style until the pieces for solo violin which he composed for Wilfred Lehmann in 1955. Here in looking for ways to extend the technique of the violin the composer concentrated on slow melodic lines accompanied by plucked low open strings. The open strings, naturally enough, established a static tonal basis for the melody, but in order to make the music harmonically interesting, Sculthorpe developed an elaborate melodic style using appoggiatura in as much an extensive way as Mahler did in his slow movements. Thus one finds that on a strong beat there is a tone which is dissonant to the tonal centre and on a subsequent weak beat that the tone resolves, usually by step, to a consonant tone. This procedure is continued so that there is rarely a feeling of complete resolution even though the overall shape of the melody is governed by those strict rules of rhythmic construction established in the *Sonatina*. Sculthorpe has in this way created for himself a functional harmonic system which avoids any reference to a system of chord progression such as Mahler's, but which, like Mahler's, gives the music its forward motion (Fig. 66).

Because of the non-developmental nature of highly-structured, small melodic sections, especially where no chord progressions are involved, the composer began using variational techniques in order to be able to construct larger movements and

Fig. 66 *Sonata for Violin*, third movement

pieces. Unlike the traditional air and variations form, however, Sculthorpe's characteristic single movement piece contains three or four contrasting sections, each of
which appears in several varied forms in the construction of the work, but there is
also some kind of synthesis of the different materials as a further means to achieve
a satisfactory overall shape. It has been Sculthorpe's conflicting need to deny those
complex developmental tendencies of European art-music, while still being able to
create large structures which may be judged by European standards that has led him
to achieve strikingly original results as a composer. *Irkanda IV* for solo violin, strings
and percussion (1961) is a clear example of the conflict between Sculthorpe's attraction for European gesture and expressiveness and his reluctance to allow himself to
be indulgent or to compromise his vision. Thus with the powerful expression of
grief there is also a remote restrained quality arising out of the sparseness of the
musical material, the minimal tendency towards dramatic growth and the vast
restrictions the composer places on all aspects of his craft. As well, the piece achieves
a perfection of structural completeness through its elaborate web of non-developmental variational levels.

With *Irkanda IV*, then, Sculthorpe could be said to have reached maturity as a
composer in that he had integrated his self-contained structural units into a successful larger structure. Whatever the formula of the work, however, the composer
found that subsequent attempts to recapture it were not very successful. The closest
he came in the ensuing years was with String Quartet No. 6 (1964–65) which was a
hybrid conglomeration of many of his finest sections of music salvaged from artis-
tically uneven works like *Irkanda II* (1959), *Irkanda III* (1961) and a song cycle titled
Sun (1958). Despite the excellence of large sections of *String Quartet No. 6* it does
not display the structural unification of *Irkanda IV*. Moreover, it is intensely expressionistic and thus, for Sculthorpe, too European for his liking.

One suspects that the writing of *String Quartet No. 6* made the composer realize
that no matter how much he tried to purge European qualities from his music, the
use of melody, melodic motives and a tonal approach to harmony would always
lead to a degree of expressionism. Since Sculthorpe's rhythmic style had been created
to a large extent independently from his tonal style, it is not surprising that his subsequent adoption of non-tonal musical material could be easily built into his individual small structures. It is true also that the variational techniques he had developed in *Irkanda IV* and even in the earlier solo pieces were largely founded on the
exploration of instrumental textures. *Sun Music I* (1965) was, then, an attempt by
Sculthorpe to purge expressionistic qualities from his music more completely by
substituting a language of orchestral sonorities and rhythmic textures for his tonal
language, which itself had been fashioned with the view of creating a non-expres-

sionistic style. In many ways the *Sun Music* series represents Sculthorpe's first positive step towards the formulation of an Australian style because hitherto his efforts to do so consisted of removing qualities from his music which he recognized as being essentially European. But the basis of the conception of *Sun Music* is the composer's notion that Australians, unlike Europeans, have a visual rather than an aural culture and awareness. Thus if they are to respond to an abstract music it would be to correlate the sound to an image rather than to an idea or emotional feeling, though it is likely that any image will have its particular emotional associations for the listener. The ideas and emotions which Sculthorpe specifically rejects are products of European humanism where man in his pride sees himself as the centre of the universe. They are those grand notions ranging from heroism at one extreme to despair and inner suffering at the other. Sculthorpe maintains that Australia has no knowledge of suffering and no heroes and that therefore these concepts can have no real significance for an Australian music, or indeed any other art form.

On a superficial level the actual content of the *Sun Music* style is not particularly remarkable. One suspects that the composer created the various kinds of music involved simply by trying to imagine what sonorities could best represent the power of the sun and the harsh desolation of the Australian landscape in much the same way that film music is conceived; but the straightforwardness of the material belies the subtlety with which it is joined together to form tightly structured pieces. Like *Irkanda IV* these pieces are mosaics of the particular ideas and variants of the ideas contained in them. The scant tonal material, for example, which opens *Sun Music I* is intervallically integrated into many of the following sections but with no sense of development. In the slow contrapuntal *glissando* section the largest intervals are those of the opening of the work, but the relationship between the two, although compositionally intentional, would not be obvious even to a trained listener. In *Sun Music I* another structural thread may be found in the various kinds of clusters employed throughout. These form a shapely progression, having much the same binding effect in the piece as a progression of tonal centres might in a more conventional style. The use of clusters in a structural way is further developed in *Sun Music III* (1967) where the progression involves a gradual thinning out, so that finally one is left with a chord which is recognizably from Sculthorpe's earlier tonal style.

Apart from its similarities to the musical language of *Sun Music I*, *Sun Music III* is Sculthorpe's first work to employ material derived from traditional Asian music. This was occasioned by the appearance of Colin McPhee's *Music in Bali*,[1] a study rich in transcribed musical examples. Balinese music happens to exhibit many of the qualities of rhythm and structure of Sculthorpe's music, so for this reason, together with the composer's identification with Asia as an antidote to European influences, it was natural that he attempted to incorporate it into his pieces. With *Sun Music III* and the later *Tabuh Tabuhan* for wind quintet and percussion (1968) there is an almost literal use of some of McPhee's examples of *gender wayang* music, but with subsequent works ideas are abstracted from Balinese music and that of other Asian countries, and employed in such ways as not to make their origins at all obvious. *Sun Music II* (1969) transforms the ritualistic vocal patterns of the *ketjak* into a frenetic work using amplified drum patterns and orchestral punctuations, *Music for Japan* (1970) employs textures inspired by Tibetan religious music, while in *String Quartet No. 8* (1969) the composer creates a ritual movement out of the simple rhythmic patterns of Balinese rice-pounding.

For Sculthorpe *String Quartet No. 8* is like a re-evaluation of his career, for it contains a successful synthesis of the quick and slow styles which he had been developing from the time of the *Sonatina*, and as well it incorporates several facets of the Asian music influence and the great interest in non-tonal sonorities. Movements I and V which are for solo cello, except for short instrumental imitations of bird song, are reminiscent of the style of the early solo violin pieces from a tonal and technical point of view, but they also have an oriental spaciousness similar to the non-metrical feeling of Japanese *shakuhachi* music. Movement II, the rice-pounding movement, has a slow middle section which is a refinement of the melodic style with static harmonic accompaniment, also from the early pieces (Fig. 68). This style was developed in *Sun Music III* and *Tabuh Tabuhan* on the pretext of the influence of *gamelan arja*. The only link with *arja* seems to be the freedom of the melody, since, unlike this style in the early pieces, only the accompaniment has a repetitive structure. In the central movement the unmetrical solo style and the *arja* style are synthesized in a harmonic language which has some of the expressionistic

Fig. 67 *String Quartet No. 8*, second movement

Fig. 68 Rice-pounding patterns

advanturousness of *String Quartet No. 6* but is infinitely more stylized and temporally elongated so as not to destroy its spacious feeling. A quick ritualistic movement, based on the 'feel' of the rice-pounding, but incorporating bird calls which are more rhythmic and also more recognizable harmonic elements, completes the stylistic and structural integration of the work.

String Quartet No. 8 in fact repeats the symmetrical pattern of movements established in *Tabuh Tabuhan*, and hinted at through the variational organization of works like *Irkanda IV* and *Sun Music I*. In a music where obvious developmental techniques are avoided this symmetrical pattern of movements or sections (for example A B C B_1 C_1 and A B C D C_1 B_1 A_1) is indeed an aid towards the achievement of structural efficacy but, as has been shown in the brief analysis of *String Quartet No. 8*, hardly the sole factor. Nonetheless, having settled on the pattern as being one which was very able to support his compositional procedures, Sculthorpe became increasingly aware of its adaptability. One finds that in the opera *Rites of Passage* (1972–73), by far his longest work, that he starts with a symmetrical arrangement of movements and then complicates the structure by making other connections between movements so that the symmetry is offset, but never totally destroyed.

The very forces involved in *Rites of Passage* determine its fundamental symmetrical shape. It is divided, by alternation, into what the composer terms 'chorales' for their homophonic hymn-like style and the religious nature of their Boethius text,[2] and 'rites', for the primitive ritualistic qualities of their music and text. The chorales and rites are supplied with separate groups of singers and instrumentalists although there is some involvement of rites players in the chorales and chorales players in the rites. The six chorales are separated by the four rites: 'Preparing the Ground', 'Ordeal', 'Death' and 'Rebirth'—and a central interlude. Apart from a direct correlation between 'Preparing the Ground' and 'Rebirth' and between 'Ordeal' and 'Death' the strict truth to symmetry ends here, but the idea of structural return is adhered to on many levels. The most obvious of these is the similarity of the first, third, fifth and sixth chorales, particularly between the first and fifth chorales and the third and sixth chorales; but there is much musical material in smaller sections which is incorporated in several parts of the work. The melody which is accompanied by a gamelan-like figuration in 'Preparing the Ground' and 'Rebirth' is, for example, also superimposed on the static vocal textures at the end of the 'Second Chorale', while the strict skin-drum patterns accompanying the third and sixth chorales are first heard against a different vocal style in 'Preparing the Ground'. As well as the obvious structural design outlined here there is, as with the *Sun Music* series and related pieces, an intricate mosaic of smaller musical ideas running through the entire piece so that the compositional detail is as dense as the overall shape is strong.

Rites of Passage may be considered as a culmination of all Sculthorpe's preceding music but in many ways it shows an enormous development in his craft and an expanding vision. It is, in the first place, his only very large work, and, as such, was a difficult step for a composer whose greatest gift is for miniature. The perfection of the piano pieces of 1971 is proof enough of this, but it is also true that his finest orchestral and chamber works are less than fifteen minutes in duration. Secondly, with the exception of *Sun Music for Voices* (1966) and a few minor pieces, it is Sculthorpe's first vocal work. In addition it displays a concerted attempt to develop a more complex but non-expressionistic harmonic idiom in the chorales, and also to create a new vocabulary of vocal textures. Most significantly, because it is a theatre piece, and thus deals with literary material, visual objects and spacial movement, it represents the composer's first chance to express in a more tangible form his particular philosophical standpoint.

Unlike the tradition of European grand opera there is no communication between individuals in *Rites of Passage*. Rather the work is a return to the earlier forms of theatre from which the operatic tradition sprang. It is created from a combination of speech, song, chant, cries, movement and dance, all moulded into spectacle which has much of the stylization of the Roman Mass and much of the frenzy of primitive ritual. Like all true ritual there is a spatial integration of the singers, movers and instrumentalists, and meaning is transmitted by symbol rather than realism. Sculthorpe's choice of poetry from Boethius' *Consolation of Philosophy* and from the Australian Southern Aranda tribe is not as contradictory as one might imagine, for the one springs from a pre-Renaissance world order which bridges the ancient civilizations of Greece and Rome with medieval Christianity while the other is concerned with rituals associated with man's life crises. These 'rites of passage' are manifested in all civilizations, surviving even in our own more complex Western society. Thus the work is intended to be an expression of the harmony and unity of all mankind, and it comes to a powerful conclusion in the 'Sixth Chorale' with this very idea:[3]

> O felix hominum genus
> Si vestros animos amor
> Quo caelum regitur regat.

Although *Rites of Passage* could therefore be aptly described as 'world theatre' it is still very much an Australian work in its spaciousness and terrifying sameness. Like all great works of art it expresses universal truth through the intimate regional vision of its creator. It is unlikely that Peter Sculthorpe will attempt anything as monumental as *Rites of Passage* for some time but it is also certain that his opera has opened up many paths for his future music.

Notes

1. Colin McPhee, *Music in Bali*, New Haven, Yale University Press, 1966.
2. Boethius, *De Consolatione Philosophiae*, II, viii.
3. *ibid.* lines 28–30. The following translation of these lines is usually attributed to John Thorpe (1576–1610):

   How happy mortals were,
   If that pure love did guide their minds,
   Which heavenly spheres doth guide.

Select Bibliography

Bainton, Helen. *Facing the Music*. Currawong, Sydney, 1966.
Blum, Diana. *Analysis of Music for Japan*, Master's thesis, University of Sydney, 1972.
Boyd, Anne. 'Sun Music I', *Miscellanea Musicologica*, iii (1968), 3–20.
Covell, Roger. *Australia's Music: Themes of a New Society*. Sun Books, Melbourne, 1967.
    'Music in Australia', *Current Affairs Bulletin*, 32, 8 (2 September 1963), 115–28.
Cugley, Ian. 'Peter J. Sculthorpe: An Analysis of his Music', *Arna* (1967), 49–56.
Hannan, Michael. The Piano Music of Peter Sculthorpe. Bachelor's thesis, University of Sydney, 1971.
    The Music of Peter Sculthorpe: an analytical appraisal with special reference to those social and cultural forces which have influenced the formulation of an Australian vision. Ph.D. thesis, University of Sydney, 1977.
Hannan, Michael and Peter Sculthorpe. 'Rites of Passage', *Music Now*, II, 22 (December 1974), 11–19.
Henderson, Robert. 'Peter Sculthorpe', *Musical Times* (July 1966), 594–5.
McCredie, Andrew. *Musical Composition in Australia*. Canberra, 1969.
    'Peter Sculthorpe', *Grove's Dictionary of Music and Musicians*, 6th ed., (forthcoming, 1978).
Mellers, Wilfrid. 'Antipodal', *New Statesman* (24 September 1965).
Murdoch, James. *Australia's Contemporary Composers*. Macmillan, Melbourne, 1972.
Peart, Donald. 'Some Recent Developments in Australian Composition', *Composer* (Spring 1966).
Sculthorpe, Peter. 'Rites of Passage', *Opera Australia*, 3 (July 1974), 31–3.
    'Sculthorpe on Sculthorpe', *Music Now*, I, 1 (February (1969), 7–13.

List of Works

All works are published by Faber Music Ltd unless otherwise stated.

Stage Music

Ulterior Motifs musical farce 2 pianos—SATB soloists and chorus (1956) (not available)
Sun Music ballet 3.2.2.2.–4.3.3.1.—timp 3 perc str—SATB chorus (1968) (score and parts hire)
Rites of Passage opera 2 tbas 7 piano 6 vc 4 db—double SATB chorus (1972–73) (score and parts hire)
Eliza Fraser Sings theatre piece for soprano, flute and piano (1977) (score and parts hire)

Incidental Music

Music for theatre (*Twelfth Night, Cross Section, King Lear, The Miser*, etc); documentary films (*The Splendour and the Peaks, The Troubled Mind*, etc.); feature films (*They Found a Cave, Age of Consent, Essington*, etc.); films concerned with the composer and his work (*Tabuh Tabuhan, Sun Music for Film*, etc.)

Orchestral

Irkanda IV for solo violin, strings and percussion (one player) (1961) (score FO128 parts hire)
The Fifth Continent for speaker and orchestra 0.1.0.0.–0.1.0.0.—timp 2 perc hp str (1963) (not available)
Small Town for chamber orchestra 0.1.0.0.–0.2.0.0.—timp 2 perc hp str (1963) (score and parts hire)
Sun Music I 0.0.0.0.–4.3.3.1.—timp 2 perc str (1965) (score F0052 parts hire)
Sun Music III (formerly *Anniversary Music*) 2.2.2.2.–3.2.2.0.—timp 3 perc str (1967) (score F0377 parts hire)
Sun Music IV 2.2.2.2.–4.3.3.1.—timp 2 perc str (1967) (score F0377 parts hire)
From Tabuh Tabuhan for strings and percussion (two players) (1968) (score and parts hire)
Sun Music II (formerly *Ketjak*) 2.2.2.2.–4.2.3.1.—timp 3 perc str (1969) (score F0307 parts hire)
Love 200 for rock band and orchestra 2.2.2.3.–4.3.3.1.—timp 3 perc str; winds, keyboards, bass guitar, drums and 2 singers (1970) (score and parts hire)
Music for Japan 3.3.3.3.–4.4.3.1.—timp 3 perc str (1970) (score and parts hire)
Rain 3.2.2.3.–4.2.3.1.—timp 3 perc str (1970) (score and parts hire)
Overture for a Happy Occasion 2.2.2.2.–2.2.2.1.—timp 1 perc hp str (1970) (score and parts hire)
Love 201 for rock band and chamber orchestra 2 flutes/recorders, strings and continuo; winds, keyboards, bass guitar and drums (1971) (not available)
Lament for Strings (1976) (score and parts hire)
The Stars Turn (from *Love 200*) arranged for string orchestra (1976) (score and parts hire)
Port Essington for strings (1977) (score and parts hire)

Instrumental and Chamber Music

Sonata for Violin Alone (1954) (not available)
The Loneliness of Bunjil for string trio (1954) [in preparation]
Irkanda I for violin alone (1955) [in preparation]
Three Movements for Jazz Band (1957) (not available)
Irkanda II for string quartet (1959) (not available)
Sonata for Viola and Percussion (1960) (performing score hire)
Irkanda III for piano trio (1961) (not available)
String Quartet No. 6 (1964–65) (score F0050 parts F0051)
String Quartet No. 7 (formerly *Red Landscape*) (1966) (score and parts hire)

Tabuh Tabuhan for wind quintet and percussion (two players) (1968) (score and parts hire)

String Quartet No. 8 (formerly *String Quartet Music*) (1969) (score F0513 parts hire)

Dream for any instruments and any number of performers (1970) [in preparation]

How the Stars were Made for percussion ensemble (six players) (1971) (performing score hire)

String Quartet No. 9 (1975) (score and parts hire)

Alone for solo violin (1976) [in preparation]

Sun Songs for recorders (1976–77) (published by Price Milburn)

Night Pieces for harp (1977) [in preparation]

Pianoforte

Sonatina (1954) (published by University of Sydney Music Publications/Leeds Music Pty Ltd)

Left Bank Waltz (1958) (published by Allans)

Sonata for Piano (1963) (not available)

Three Haiku (1966) [in preparation]

Night Pieces (Snow, Moon and Flowers; Night; Stars) (1971) F0367 (published separately in Australia by Allans)

Landscape for piano with tape echo and pre-recorded tape (1971) [in preparation]

Koto Music I for amplified piano and pre-recorded tape (1973) [in preparation]

Koto Music II for amplified piano and pre-recorded tape (1976) [in preparation]

Choral

Night Piece for SATB and piano strings (1966) (published by Novello)

Sun Music for Voices and Percussion (formerly *Sun Music II*) for SATB, piano and percussion (three players) (1966) (performing score F0172)

Morning Song for the Christ Child for unaccompanied SATB (1966) F0105

Sea Chant for unison voices and piano with optional parts for high instruments and percussion (1968) F0302

Autumn Song for unaccompanied SAT Bar B (1968) F0497

Ketjak for six male voices with tape echo (1972) (performing score hire)

Rain Song for unison voices and piano with optional parts for percussion (1975) [in preparation]

Sea Chant for unison voices and orchestra 2.2.2.2.–4.2.3.0.—timp 2 perc str (1975) (score and parts hire; vocal parts F0302)

Nocturne (from *Rites of Passage*) for SATB and optional bass instruments (1977) (performing score hire)

Vocal

Early Songs for soprano and piano (1945–55) [in preparation]

Twelfth Night Songs for tenor and piano (1956) [in preparation]

Sun for medium voice and piano (1958) (not available)

The Stars Turn (from *Love 200*) for high voice and piano (1970) [in preparation]

The Song of Tailitnama for soprano, 6 cellos and percussion (two players) (1974) (score and parts hire)

The Stars Turn (from *Love 200*) for high voice and strings (1976) (score and parts hire)

Discography

Orchestral

Irkanda IV (1961). Melbourne Symphony Orchestra (John Hopkins, conductor), Leonard Dommett (solo violin).

World Record Club disc R00028 Stereo Odyssey disc 32 16 0150 Stereo

The Fifth Continent (1963). Melbourne Symphony Orchestra (Thomas Matthews, conductor), Frederick Parslow (speaker).

ABC recording 0/N40493 Mono

Sun Music I (1965). Melbourne Symphony Orchestra (John Hopkins, conductor).

World Record Club disc R00028 Stereo Odyssey disc 32 16 0150 Stereo

Sun Music III (1967). Sydney Symphony Orchestra (Sir Bernard Heinze, conductor).

EMI disc OASD7547 Stereo

Sun Music III (1967). Sydney Symphony Orchestra (Sir Bernard Heinze, conductor).

World Record Club disc R03242/3 Stereo

Sun Music III (1967). Louisville Orchestra (Jorge Mester, conductor).

Louisville First Edition disc LS 735 Stereo

Sun Music IV (1967). Australian Youth Orchestra (John Hopkins, conductor).

ABC recording RRC 401 Mono

From Tabuh Tabuhan (1968). (Patrick Thomas, conductor).   *ABC recording RRC 72 Mono*

Sun Music II (1969) (known as *Ketjak* when recorded). Sydney Symphony Orchestra (John Hopkins, conductor).   *ABC recording RRCS 134 Stereo*

Love 200 (1970). Sydney Symphony Orchestra (John Hopkins, conductor) with Tully (rock band) and Jeannie Lewis (singer).

ABC recording RRCS 1466 Stereo

Music for Japan (1970). Australian Youth Orchestra (John Hopkins, conductor).

EMI disc SOELP 9271 Stereo

Instrumental and Chamber Music

Sonata for Viola and Percussion (1960). John Glickman (viola), Glen Davies (percussion).

ABC recording PRX 559 Mono

String Quartet No. 6 (1964–65). Austral String Quartet.   *World Record Club disc S 2473 Stereo*

String Quartet No. 6 (1964–65). Mari Iwamoto String Quartet.   *Victor disc VX 79 Stereo*

String Quartet No. 7 (1966) (known as *Red Landscape* when recorded). Austral String Quartet.

EMI disc OASD 7563 Stereo

Tabuh Tabuhan (1968). University of Adelaide Wind Quintet with Richard Smith and Bevan Bird (percussion).   *ABC recording RRCS 378 Stereo*

Tabuh Tabuhan (1968). The New Sydney Wind Quintet with Barry Heywood and Albert Setty (percussion).

Philips disc 6508001 Stereo

String Quartet No. 8 (1969) (known as *String Quartet
  Music* when recorded). Austral String Quartet.
                    EMI disc OASD 7563 Stereo
String Quartet No. 8 (1969) (known as *String Quartet
  Music* when recorded). Austral String Quartet.
                    ABC recording RRCS 1468 Stereo
String Quartet No. 8 (1969) (known as *String Quartet
  Music* when recorded). Allegri String Quartet.
                    Argo disc ZRG 672 Stereo
String Quartet No. 9 (1975). Sydney String Quartet.
                    Cherry Pie disc CPF 1031 Stereo

Pianoforte

Sonatina (1954). Roger Woodward (piano).
                    EMI disc OASD 7567 Stereo
Sonatina (1954). Trevor Barnard (piano).
                    Electric Records disc ELEC 4334 Stereo
Night (1970). Roger Woodward (piano strings).
                    EMI disc OASD 7567 Stereo
Snow, Moon and Flowers (1971). Roger Woodward
  (piano strings).   *EMI disc OASD 7567 Stereo*
Landscape (1971). David Bollard (piano).
                    Festival disc SFC 800 22 Stereo
Landscape (1971). Roger Woodward (piano).
                    EMI disc OASD 7567 Stereo
Koto Music I (1973) (known as *Koto Music* when
  recorded). Roger Woodward (piano).
                    RCA VRLI 0083 Stereo

Choral

Sun Music for Voices and Percussion (1966) (known as
  Sun Music II when recorded). Lyric Singers (Verdon
  Williams, conductor).
                    ABC recording RRCS 134 Stereo
Morning Song for the Christ Child (1966). Adelaide
  Singers (Patrick Thomas, conductor).
                    ABC recording RRC 65 Mono
Rites of Passage: The Chorales (1972–73). The Vic-
  torian College of the Arts Orchestra with the Mel-
  bourne Chorale Continuing Choir (John Hopkins,
  conductor).
                    World Record Club disc R 03074 Stereo

Arrangements

Theme from They Found a Cave (1961). Instrumental
  ensemble with Larry Adler (harmonica).
                    Columbia disc 7 MA 997 Mono
Morning Song (1966) (arr. Sculthorpe). Austral String
  Quartet.   *EMI disc OASD 7563 Stereo*
Morning Song (1966) (arr. Nore). King's Singers.
                    EMI disc HQS 1308 Quad
It'll Rise Again (1970) (from *Love 200*) (arr. Michael
  Carlos on *Free Fall through Featherless Flight*).
  Jeannie Lewis (singer).
                    EMI disc EMC 2505 Quad.

Malcolm Williamson
(*b.* 1931)

Brian Chatterton

Malcolm Williamson left Australia and settled in England at twenty-two years of age. The question is therefore raised as to whether a coverage of his works belongs in a book about Australian composers. The infrequency of his returns to this country since that time has done little to settle the matter, but what perhaps decides the issue beyond doubt is Williamson's readiness, not to say anxiety, to associate his music with what he calls a 'slender Australian tradition', in which he includes, among others, the music of Alfred Hill, Roy Agnew and Margaret Sutherland. His interest in a compositional ancestry is certainly more relevant to the issue than his often quoted remark, 'When I think about it, I am certain that my music is characteristically Australian although I have never tried to make it so', which adds very little of an analytical nature to the debate.

His arrival in England signalled the beginning of a compositional career pursued according to environmental influences entirely unlike those operating on his colleagues at home, despite their periodic visits to and often times lengthy sojourns in the country of his adoption. Apart from obvious issues like the constancy of the demand for Williamson's work, which is unlikely to have been equalled in Australia, no other composer from this country has been exposed to a barrage of written critical opinion of anything like comparable intensity.

From the earliest of his adult composing years, the years of the first piano sonata (1955), *Fons Amoris* (1955), the Variations for piano (1953) and *Santiago de Espada* (1957) his music has evoked responses covering a wide range of human attitudes. About the piano sonata for example, three English writers had this to say:

> It is a disappointment to see so much contrivance spent to such little effect. Not that texture is other than the thinnest of hairshirts but that the emotional impulse got lost in the expressing of it, perhaps frightened away by Stravinsky.[1]

> The contrasts unfolded in the work's three main movements, with its governing monothematic principle—and we have encountered no little transfiguration of basic motives by the time we encounter the finale—are suggestive of the sonata's rich content.[2]

> The sonata as a whole is one of the very few important pieces of really new piano writing of recent (and even not so recent) years, a fascinating and satisfying work

offering endless delight to both player and listener, on the evidence of which Williamson's might be a talent of similar order even to Britten's.[3]

The critical reaction to the piano sonata marked the beginning of a constant flow of criticism which greeted the arrival of most of his new works, some of it bitterly negative, some of it uncompromisingly eulogistic, but most of it warmly approving in a qualified kind of way and tinged with a certain puzzlement; an expectation and hope of 'sounder things to come'.

Williamson has been at the focal point of critical attention and controversy to a degree only rarely matched by his European colleagues. For him the issue of critical reaction is very much alive, and about this he holds strong views which he is not slow to express. He spoke with obvious conviction on this matter in 1965:

> To go on being what you are, musically speaking, is not always easy. Creative artists more than most people, love approbation, and to be starved of critical approbation can be painful. While knowing what asses most music critics are, composers writhe at the thought of thousands of people reading adverse notices written in haste by them.[4]

At the root of his fluctuating fortunes with English critics is the often-levelled charge that his music is excessively eclectic, and that he is constantly changing his style of composing. In any genre one is likely to hear the strictest serialism, the rhytms of jazz or Latin American music, an expansive romantic melody, or, in some very recent mini-operas, even a suspicion of aleatoricism. In the course of listening one can be irresistibly reminded of flashes of Stravinsky, Bartók and Messiaen particularly, but also Britten, Richard Rogers, Hindemith, Sibelius, Gershwin, Leonard Bernstein and Honegger.

Williamson's confessed predilection is for the luscious, the sort of music which can be fully grasped on the first hearing, but it is that which he has written in a more austere vein which has found greatest favour with the more discerning of his critics. Despite the prodigious quantity of music he writes, this however amounts to a relatively small proportion of his total output.

The First Piano Sonata was written in a strict idiom where any temptation to draw upon extended cantabile devices was avoided in favour of a tighter intellectual harnessing of the basic compositional material, particularly by way of serialism. The piece reflected the influence of his tutors and his general musical experiences to that date, and more than any other work brought him early recognition by the English musical society. His earliest training took place at the State Conservatorium in Sydney, where the Director was Eugene Goossens, but the lessons he took with Erwin Stein and Elizabeth Lutyens in England and his brief contact with the music of Boulez and Messiaen in Paris, had a rather more obvious effect on the generation of his style for this work. Its three movements are built primarily from the opening counterpoint set in $\frac{4}{4}$ with strategically interpolated bars of $\frac{3}{8}$ rendering an infectious syncopation to its already bright rhythmic character. For all its rhythmic stability and its Stravinskian tonal 'features, the work is interesting for the application of some compositional techniques commonly associated with serialism. The third movement contains examples of the so-called non-retrogradable rhythms exploited by Messiaen, and in the opening phrase of the slow movement, with exception of the off-beat A in the first bar, the bass and tenor are pitch inversions of the soprano and alto lines respectively, another device reminiscent of Messiaen (see Fig. 69).

Fig. 69 From the First Piano Sonata

After the Piano Sonata, with its success particularly deriving from the tightness of its internal structure, and the extreme density of thematic and developmental inventiveness, the direction he chose for his orchestral overture *Santiago de Espada* in 1957 must, at that time, have seemed baffling to observers of his professional development. A hearing of this piece today would raise few eyebrows, for its central feature, a slow moving, appealing melody clothed in various orchestral colours over several successive statements, is a feature we have come to recognize in much of his output, but in 1957, with the success of the Piano Sonata behind him, the adoption of this musical language constituted a marked change in compositional style and attitude.

The motives behind the shift to 'popularism' in *Santiago* can possibly never be adequately pinpointed. But two points are inescapable. First, his divergence from a strictly vanguard style was no mere flirtation, as is shown by his later output. Second, the motives may have been reflective of his conservative and detached background in Australia, or associated in some complex way with his strongly held religious beliefs, or further still, with quasi-aesthetic considerations about the accessibility and appeal of various musical styles to various audiences; but whatever their nature, his motives were stronger than any temptation to project himself as a young composer with stylistic consistency and what might superficially be regarded as 'creative honesty'.

The importance to Williamson of the so-called concession to popularism is reflected in his early willingness to risk surrendering an image of success in the strict genre, as much as in the volume of music he has subsequently produced in the popular vein.

The late fifties saw Williamson working as a night-club pianist for a living and it was by way of this experience that his attraction to popular tunes and to Cuban and jazz flavours strengthened. He turned his interests to stage musicals and of several he composed, one (*No Bed for Bacon*) was produced at the Bristol Old Vic in 1958. In the same year he also wrote his first Piano Concerto.

This work, along with the Organ Concerto (1961) and Violin Concerto (1965) and two other piano concertos (1962 and 1964), all written in the grand concerto style, strongly suggests that this is his favourite form for the concert hall. In each of them he is committed to ease of audience accessibility and achieves it with a heavy reliance on Rachmaninov-inspired bravura. Alternatively, he will feature long dreamy melodies, and contrasting animated passages based on strikingly skilful syncopation, now with a jazz inflection, now with a Latin American inflection, or as often as not with neither, but just as compelling quintessential Williamson.

No movement of any of these concertos is more typical of his output in this style than the opening of the Second Piano Concerto which is set for string accompaniment alone.[5] The movement begins in F sharp and is built upon three separate ideas. The first consists of descending triads set in continuous semiquaver motion (see Fig. 70), and are accompanied by Bartókian pizzicato string chords placed at odd points in the bar. This gives rise to a related subsidiary motive also triadically based (see Fig. 71). The second main idea, this time in D flat, is a slower moving cantabile line with a typical Williamson rhythmic quip at the end (see Fig. 72). The opening motive and the cantabile melody are used to establish an exposition of some fifty-six bars.

Fig. 70 Second Piano Concerto, first movement

Fig. 71 From the Second Piano Concerto

Fig. 72 From the Second Piano Concerto

Drawing upon the characteristic rhythmic twists of both themes, and the implied bitonality of the subsidiary idea, the composer builds a development section of similar length, beginning clearly in D flat and progressing through extended passages of tonal ambiguity back to F sharp major for the recapitulation. The first motive and the subsection which grew from it is restated with little alteration, whereas the cantabile melody returns extravagantly orchestrated in F sharp major to maintain this key for the conclusion of the movement.

Laudable as these concertos are for the immediate contact they make with an audience, and for all their undeniable inventiveness and lyricism, their reception by his critics has at best been mixed. They are often considered too facile, the selection and handling of his abundant ideas too ill-disciplined for the scale of forces and the time-span in which he chooses to work. These criticisms are most concentrated in relation to his Violin Concerto, and the Third Piano Concerto, where endless stretches of melody-dominated textures perhaps exhibit Messiaen's influence. But they lack the Frenchman's subtlety in contrasts of pitch, rhythm and colour and in the sure handling of the long time-span. Williamson may be getting in first with his defence by declaring that the concertos do not claim to be profound, but the prevalence of the criticism from many quarters can hardly be dismissed lightly.

Reaction to the second movement of the Third Piano Concerto, however, has been as uniformly positive as the reception of the whole has been mixed. Retaining the familiar Williamson lyricism and delightful rhythmic and melodic novelties, it also vies for consideration as one of the most carefully self-contained pieces of his entire output. The movement opens with a beautifully unaffected melody lying very naturally in the unusual time signature of $\frac{11}{16}$. The piano states this theme in octaves in the high treble and is accompanied by strings playing spiccato style on triadic chords tinged with a diatonic dissonance. The effect is curiously relaxed, and metreless, belying the rhythmic complexities which are only exposed upon analysis (see Fig. 73). This material, together with a section marked *ritmico e secco* based on a dotted syncopated figure in $\frac{10}{16}$, is used to set the whole movement in a kind of double binary form (A B A B).

Fig. 73 From the Third Piano Concerto, second movement

The piece is an excellent example of Williamson's reliance on what are now conservative key-systems for the basis of the tonal structures of his works. The opening is in the key of F and basically the same music is then repeated in E; the *ritmico e secco* section begins in E and travels back to F. The opening material is restated this time in B and a return of the *ritmico* material again brings the tonality back to its point of origin.

The overall tonal flavour is a curious mixture of the chromatic and almost simplistically diatonic. Bar after bar of his bass lines consist of no more than variously arpeggiated statements of the same three notes of a single primary triad, but over this solid musical superstructure he will overlay the most intricately complicated chromatic passages which defy tonal labelling. It is as if the musical substructure is the tonal antithesis of the superstructure and their junction results in an incompatability which the ear quite easily detects. The aural effect nevertheless is ultimately one of unmistaken tonality. This is further reinforced by a reliance on ostinato technique or repeating bass figures which are only minimally altered. Added to this is a high incidence of scalic passages which typically run about the distance of a hexa-chord in one key and whilst maintaining similar pitch direction, suddenly veer off at a tonal tangent, arriving at a totally unexpected destination. The same device is common in the music of Prokofiev.

A glance at the list of works shows that a very great proportion of his output is music written either for voices, or voices and organ. This includes the many pieces written in the style of a modern sacred cantata which typically feature sections for one or two soloists, some solo organ work and two or three contrasting choruses, the last of which is invariably based on a rich setting of one of Williamson's beloved popular tunes. Close in spirit to these are the many settings of traditional hymn texts. These belong somewhat to the Beaumont lineage, but their calculated popular style bears the mark of the kind of shrewd composing mind which is a comparative rarity in this (if it is not a misuse of the word) genre.

Symphony for Voices (1962) on the other hand is a much more careful proposition. The title derives from the quasi-symphonic representation of five poems by the Aus-tralian poet James McAuley. The opening poem, *Invocation*, set as a delicate monody for solo alto, meanders in metreless fashion with a signature of $\frac{6}{4}$ which has little organizational bearing on the ultimate rhythm but is there mainly to aid the eye. A rich chromaticism, and an abundance of augmented and diminished intervals renders the idiom somewhat tonally ambiguous, although the statistical frequency of the C sharp-F sharp interval, and the fact that F sharp is the precise mid-point of the C-C' twelve-note tessitura, implies that F sharp is the pitch focal point.

Of the remaining settings, *Jesus* and *Envoi* parallel in mood and sentiment the tradi-tional roles of the slow movement and scherzo in symphonic form, whilst *Terra Australia*, and *New Guinea* are more substantial settings flanking them.

The interest in four-part writing lies mostly in homophonic devices, where the simplest of procedures are put to most telling effects. Such an example is found in the setting of *The air gives ease,/There you come home (Terra Australia)* where the soprano-bass range is less than one octave and each part moves by intervals no greater than a tone or semitone. Coming as it does after one of the rarer passages relying on contrapuntal interest, this eight-note progression is pictorially very effective.

The setting of *Envoi* is a choral version of the rhythmically intriguing pieces which he writes so well in the purely instrumental medium. One notices here the secure, natural feeling he has for the setting of English words, both in the keenness of rhyth-mic syllabification and in the close marrying of musical and literary moods. Settings of these poems has involved a miniaturized application of the same skill which lies behind the success of Williamson's operas.

Apart from the concertos, the music for voices, and leaving the operas for the moment, the remaining body of Williamson's work consists of his output for organ, and little more than a handful of other pieces written for various instrumental combinations in absolute forms.

Although on the whole he seems less naturally attracted to the task of writing in these forms (he confesses openly that chamber music is for him the most difficult medium in which to compose) his achievements in this area have been, nevertheless, greeted more positively.

The second Symphony consists of a single movement 'beginning and ending just north of audibility' and is contemplative in intention. Williamson describes the work as 'polyrhythmic, polymetric, polymodal', using a form of serial writing which is not aurally evident. Moreover he is at pains to point out that the mode of construction is not relevant to listening. This piece is in a distinctly more personal vein, attempting to discover not 'what interesting thing can be produced from the mind', but to 'discern its nature'. The result is a resolutely undramatic work, absorbing in its shifts of tonal colour, in the scarcity of thematic statement and development, and in the low level of rhythmic and dynamic activity.

The Sinfonietta was commissioned by the B.B.C. for the opening of the full B.B.C. Music Programme in March 1965. The appearance in the finale (Tarantella) of a central melody which seems to verge on the banal tempts one to categorize this work, along with *Santiago de Espada* or the concertos, as one of his popular pieces, and on the face of it, any dividing line between it and them is admittedly tenuous. But the Sinfonietta has greater unity of purpose, the background textures far more complicated, sophisticated and rich with invention than one commonly finds in the concertos.

The point is further evidenced by an examination of the first two movements. The mechanistic pounding of the first theme over a bass line limited stoically to the F major triad (see Fig. 74), and its later treatment in augmentation contributes to a dark grimness of mood which is rarely encountered in Williamson's music at all, let alone sustained as it is here for an entire movement and allowed to re-emerge in a different but unmistakable guise later in the work.

Fig. 74 From the Sinfonietta, first movement

The second movement also has its own particular distinction. The tone is set in the opening strains where a sustained harmony of violin harmonics accompanies a principal melody stated in the double bass. The instrumentation gradually thickens as the melody is passed on to oboes and violins. It is interrupted then by biting, pungent wind chords which assume an ever growing ascendancy until the texture suddenly lightens once more in order for the tuba to play out the melody to conclude the movement.

Whilst hardly adhering to the B.B.C. stipulation that the work be cheery and extrovert, the Sinfonietta nevertheless served as something of an *objet de justification* for those Williamson-watchers who had long awaited some evidence of the composer's ability to grapple with sustained seriousness in the purely musical forms.

Williamson's youthful fascination for the music of Messiaen was the spur to his initial contact with the organ and its literature. He taught himself to play it, in order to discover at first hand the finer intricacies of Messiaen's writing. *Fons Amoris* was the first of a constant flow of pieces which came from his pen over the ensuing two decades. *Resurgence du Feu* (1959), *Symphony for Organ* (1961), *Vision of Christ-Phoenix* (1962), *Elegy J.F.K.* (1964), and *Epitaphs for Edith Sitwell* (1966) are the key works.

Vision of Christ-Phoenix is a set of variations on the *Coventry Carol* written for the 1962 Coventry Festival. Whilst it has probably had a more popular reception than any other of his organ works owing, one guesses, somewhat to its apocalyptic title, it is the earlier *Organ Symphony* which is his most substantial work for the solo instrument. Cast into six large movements the work has a range of styles which includes strictly serial method, passacaglia technique, isorhythm, simply-accompanied melody and, as in so much of his other music, the brilliant, nervously rhythmic idiom which makes such creative use of changing metres and the various methods of beat displacement.

Following the success of his first opera, *Our Man in Havana* (1963), Williamson has turned his musical attentions more and more to the stage. The works he has written for dramatic presentation cover as wide a cross-section of styles, both dramatically and musically, as was ever covered in his concert hall music. Here, as there, he seems to be reaching out to performers and audiences of differing musical interests and aesthetic sensibilities; to educated traditional opera audiences in the largest-scaled achievements like *Our Man in Havana*, *The Violins of Saint-Jacques*, *Lucky Peter's Journey* and the more chamber-type operas such as *English Eccentrics*, and *The Growing Castle*; to children in *Julius Caesar Jones*, and *The Happy Prince*; to non-professional performers (including children) for the staging of works like the *Red Sea* and *Dunstan and the Devil*.

His most recently devised musical dramatic form, the so-called 'cassation', is typically a short, simple sequence for one or two soloists, unison mixed chorus and piano. These miniature operas depend for their performance on more or less impromptu audience participation.

Because of the infrequency of their performance in Australia thus far, the operas as a whole are difficult to discuss, and what is more, their relevance to the contemporary Australian musical scene is at least arguable whilst they remain no more than scores in hand. The children's operas have enjoyed some local exposure, but any assessment of Williamson's operatic writing must be based on the larger works, for which one can only rely on reports of performances in England.

Our Man in Havana, set to a libretto by Sidney Gilliet based on Graham Greene's novel, was first staged at Sadler's Wells in 1963 and was sufficiently successful to earn a revival the following year. The critics received it with cautious approval, acknowledging Williamson's intuitive sensitivity to theatrical effect and praising the wealth of musical attractions in the score. These elements converged to bring about the greatest single dramatic highlight of the work, namely, a strongly convincing character portrayal of the old German doctor Hasselbacher.

The next opera, *English Eccentrics* (after the book by Dame Edith Sitwell), was a smaller-scaled work requiring, for example, no chorus and only seven orchestral players. As it lacks a continuous narrative thread, the seven scenes, each of which introduces one of Sitwell's eccentrics, assume the proportion and style of a highly sophisticated revue.

The lush musical idiom of *The Violins of Saint-Jacques* has given rise to a by now familiar criticism levelled at Williamson. The opera is set on a Caribbean island doomed to destruction by volcanic eruption and the music reverts to a romanticism, further sweetened with popular melodies and the typical musical colourings of the locale. Dramatically speaking the work is a lightweight. Little attempt is made, for example, to draw upon the submerged sexual symbolism and repressions in the story, and the appearance of some of the characters is occasionally curiously unmotivated for other than purely musical reasons.

Interestingly, Williamson explains the character of the opera in terms of conflicting external motivational pressures which operated on him at the time of receiving the commission from Sadler's Wells. The theatre, he writes, 'desire(d) . . . a comic opera which would draw the charabancs like a magnet, (whilst) . . . for many of the critical press, only something that appeared to go on where Berg's *Lulu* left off could hope for their accolade. The way out of this dilemma was to write the opera I wished to write, and this I did'.

Williamson's next opera, *The Growing Castle*, was commissioned to be performed in the small music room of the Dynevor Castle. As such it assumed musical theatrical proportions more akin to *English Eccentrics* than his 'grand' operas. The music is arranged rather modestly for only five performers one of whom is the pianist who also has an assortment of percussion instruments to handle by the keyboard. The libretto is by the composer, drawn from his own translation of Strindberg's *Dream Play*. As an attempt to portray in musico-dramatic terms the spiritual and metaphysical issues which are at the core of Strindberg's play, the venture involves Williamson on a personal level and thereby signals an approach distinctly tangential to the artistic assumptions which underlie his earlier achievements for the theatre.

Another play of August Strindberg provided the basis of the so-called opera-pantomime *Lucky Peter's Journey*. The work has received widespread and severe critical response for an alleged lack of clarity in the exposition of the story line. These critics have denied themselves the honesty of an understanding of Williamson's own views on the subject. In an article about *Lucky Peter's Journey* written for the *Musical Times* Williamson reveals himself as a serious student of Swedish letters thoroughly conversant with Strindbergian theatrical philosophy.[6] His account of the 'evolution' of *Lucky Peter's Journey* shows that this philosophy permeated the growth of the opera from the moment of its conception through the period of its composition, to its eventual staging at the Coliseum. A fair criticism of the work requires, at the very least, cognizance of Williamson's own reasoning, together with counter-argument at a comparable philosophical level. This was rarely if ever the case at the time of the staging of the work and the mature observer could only have concluded that the polemical ball had been lobbed squarely in the critics' court.

Apart from the rather special case in connection with *Lucky Peter's Journey* the question-mark hovering over the validity of the commoner criticisms levelled at Williamson remains in place, if not securely so. It is an issue which deserves resolution for it calls in to question his artistic integrity, his aesthetic sensibilities and, if some extremists are to be believed, even his possession of plain commonsense. The *sine qua non* of the criticism is basically this: Why does Williamson write on one occasion music that is tightly organized, that reflects a finely tuned control of the time dimension, and that is always inventive and resourceful in the generation, growth and mutation of musical ideas, without ever losing a distinctly personal and identifiable lyricism, and on another occasion be satisfied with an idiom which smacks of derivativeness, unashamed in its reliance on cliché and effect, and which at best is only ever likely to enjoy a short-lived appeal at the shallowest of popular levels?

The ultimate answers probably rest in the inner regions of the Williamson mind, regions that reflect his youthful musical experiences, his religious and moral convictions, and his understanding of human nature. If so, the questions will probably not be answered, and in any case, Freudian probings are hardly likely to reveal much of interest to the student of his music.

There is little doubt that Williamson possesses a shrewder, more perceptive mind than many of his detractors either know about or are prepared to admit. That he has long been aware of the common criticism is obvious. If, twenty years after beginning the practice, Williamson still continues to write in two veins, as he does, it is surprising that the critics themselves have taken so long to get the message, namely, his popularist idiom is far more important to him than relief from the critical abuse he suffers in order to continue composing it.[7]

Notes

1. Ivor Keys, 'Reviews of Music', *Music and Letters*, xxxvii, 4 (October 1956), p. 421.
2. Donald Mitchell, 'London Music', *Musical Times*, xcvii (December 1956), p. 653.
3. Colin Mason, 'Some New Music', *Musical Times*, xcvii (August 1956), p. 422.
4. Malcolm Williamson, 'A Composer's Heritage', *Composer*, xix (Spring 1966), p. 72.
5. Published as Concertino for Piano and Strings by Chappell in 1962, this was a prize-winning work in a Competition for Australian and New Zealand composers organized by the Department of Music, in the University of Western Australia.
6. Malcolm Williamson, 'Lucky Peter's Journey', *Musical Times*, cx (December 1969), p. 1227.
7. Malcolm Williamson, now living in Great Britain, was appointed in 1976 Master of the Queen's Music, the first Australian to hold this ancient office.

Select Bibliography

Covell, Roger. *Australia's Music: Themes of a New Society*. Sun Books, Melbourne, 1967.

Glennon, James. *Australian Music and Musicians*. Rigby, Adelaide, 1968.

Lang, Paul H. and Broder, Nathan (eds). *Contemporary Music in Europe*. London, 1965.

Murdoch, James. *Australia's Contemporary Composers*. Macmillan, Melbourne, 1972.

Greenfield, Edward. 'Luck Peter's Journey', *Music and Musicians*, xviii, 6 (February 1970), pp. 24–5.

'First Performances', *Tempo*, lxx (August 1964), pp. 22–4.

Mason, Colin. 'The Music of Malcolm Williamson', *Musical Times*, ciii (November 1962), pp. 757–9.

'Our Man in Havana', *Musical Times*, civ (July 1963), pp. 474–6.

Payne, Anthony. 'First Performances', *Tempo*, lxvi-vii (Autumn/Winter 1963), pp. 39–40.

'First Performances', *Tempo*, lxxiii (Summer 1965), pp. 22–3.

'First Performances', *Tempo*, lxxix (Winter 1966/67), pp. 17–18.

Plaistow, Stephen. 'First Performances', *Tempo*, lxv (Summer 1963), pp. 16–17.

Tracey, Edmund. 'Lucky Peter's Journey: Words for Music', *Opera*, xx (December 1969), pp. 1016–21.

Walda, Dorothea. 'Unser Mann in Havanna', *Musik und Gesellschaft*, xiv, 1966, pp. 476–8.

Walsh, Stephen. 'A Memory of Violins', *Opera*, xvii (November 1966), pp. 851–5.

'First Performances', *Tempo*, lxxxvi (Autumn 1968), pp. 10–12.

'Williamson the Many-Sided', *Music and Musicians*, xiii, 11 (July 1965), pp. 26–9, 55.

Waterhouse, John. 'First Performances', *Tempo*, lxxvi (Spring 1966), pp. 18–19.

Williamson, Malcolm. 'About "Julius Caesar Jones"', *Opera*, xvii (January 1966), pp. 17–20.

'"Julius Caesar Jones"' *Musical Times*, cvi (December 1965), pp. 937–8.

'"Our Man in Havana"', *Opera*, xiv (July 1963), pp. 455–6.

'"Lucky Peter's Journey"', *Musical Times*, cx (December 1969), pp. 1227–31.

'A Composer's Heritage', *Composer*, xix (Spring 1966), pp. 69–73.

List of Works

Stage Works

Our Man in Havana (opera) (1963)
English Eccentrics (chamber opera) (1964)
The Display (ballet) (1964)
The Happy Prince (children's opera) (1965)
Julius Caesar Jones (children's opera) (1966)
Sun Into Darkness (ballet) (1966)
The Violins of Saint-Jacques (1966)
Sinfonietta (ballet) 1967)
The Moonrakers (cassation) (1967)
The Stone Wall (cassation) (1967)
The Gorwing Castle (chamber opera) (1968)
The Brilliant and the Dark (operatic sequence) (1969)
Lucky Peter's Journey (opera) (1969)
Knights in Shining Armour (cassation) (1969)
The Snow Wolf (cassation) (1970)
Dunstan and the Devil (1971)
Genesis (cassation) (1971)
The Death of Cuchulain (opera) (1972)
The Red Sea (opera) (1973)

Orchestral

Santiago de Espada (1957)
Reflections on a Theme of Britten (1963)
Elevamini Symphony (1963)
Our Man in Havana (concert suite) (1963)
Sinfonia Concertante (1964)
English Eccentrics (suite) (1964)
Sinfonietta (1965)
Concerto Grosso (1965)
Symphonic Variations (1965)
Our Man in Havana (orchestral suite) (1960)
Symphony no. 2 (1969)

Orchestra and Soloist

Piano Concerto no. 1 (1958)
Concerto for Organ and Orchestra (1961)
Concerto for Piano and Strings (1962)
Concerto no. 3 for Piano and Orchestra (1964)
Concerto for Violin and Orchestra (1965)

Chamber Instrumental Music

Concerto for soprano, oboe, cor anglais, cello and organ (1957)
Variations for Cello and Piano (1964)
Concerto for Two Pianos, Eight Hands and Wind Quintet (1965)
Serenade for Flute, Piano and String Trio (1967)

Pianoforte

Variations for Piano (1953)
Sonata (1955)
Janua Coeli (Sonata no. 2) (1957)
Sonata no. 3 (1958)

Sonata no. 4
Travel Diaries (Five Volumes) (1962)
Five Preludes (1966)
Sonata for Two Pianos (1967)

Organ
Fons Amoris (1955)
Epithalamium (1957)
Variations on *Veni Creator* (1959)
Resurgence du Feu (1959)
Symphony for Organ (1961)
Vision of Christ-Phoenix (1962)
Elegy J.F.K. (1964)
Epitaphs for Edith Sitwell (1966)

Choral
Two Motets (1954)
Meditations (1957)
Mass (1957)
Adoremus (1959)
Dawn Carol (1960)
Offertory of Christ the King (1961)
Ascendit Deus (1961)
Tu es Petrus (1961)
Dignus est Agnus (1961)
Procession of Psalms (1962)
Planctus (male voices) (1962)
Symphony for Voices (1962)
Harvest Thanksgiving (1962)
Let Them Give Thanks (1962)
Easter Carol (1962)
Wrestling Jacob (1962)
Twelve Hymns (1962)
Morning of the Day of Days (1963)
Te Deum (1963)
Epiphany Carol (1963)
Agnus Dei (1963)
Australian Carol (1963)
Six Evening Hymns (1963)
Six Christmas Songs for the Young (1963)
A Young Girl (1964)
Sonnet (1964)
Mass of St Andrew (1964)
Sweet and Low (1964)
Ding! Dong! Good King Wenceslas; The Boar's Head
(1964)
A Christmas Carol (1964)

Solo Voice
Ode in Solitude (baritone) (1960)
Celebrations of Divine Love (high voice) (1964)
Three Shakespeare Songs (high voice) (1964)
North Country Songs (baritone) (1965)

Discography

The Happy Prince (1965). The prince—Pauline Stevens
(contralto), the swallow—April Cantelo (soprano),
the author—Maureen Lehane (mezzo-soprano),
Guildhall Chamber Choir, String Quintet and Percussion, Malcolm Williamson, Richard Rodney
Bennett (piano duet), Marcus Dods (conductor).
Weinberger. Mar. 1966.   *Argo disc ZRG/2800*

Julius Caesar Jones (1965). April Cantelo (soprano),
Norma Proctor (contralto), Finchley Children's
Music Group (John Andrews, conductor). Wein-
berger. Sept. 1967.   *Argo disc ZRG/529*
Violin Concerto (1965). Yehudi Menuhin (violin),
London Philharmonic Orchestra (Sir Adian Boult,
conductor). Weinberger. Feb. 1972.
HMV disc ASD/2729
Violin Concerto (1965) [26'03"]. Ronald Thomas
(violin), West Australian Symphony Orchestra (Tho-
mas Mayer, conductor). Weinberger. 16 May 1969.
World Record Club disc S/4930
Piano Concerto no. 1 (1958) [17'46"]. Igor Hmelnitsky
(piano), Sydney Symphony Orchestra (Nicolai
Malko, conductor). Boosey & Hawkes.
ABC recording PRX/4716
Harvest Thanksgiving (1962) [6'50"]. Cathey Webber
(soprano), Adelaide Singers, James Thiele (organ),
Patrick Thomas (conductor). Weinberger. 6 Feb.
1968.   *ABC recording RRCS/400*
Dignus est Agnus (1961) [1'15"]. Genty Stevens (so-
prano), Adelaide Singers, David Merchant (organ),
Patrick Thomas (conductor). Aschenberg. 2 Oct.
1970.   *ABC tape*
Christmas Cantata: Adoremus (1959) [7'53"]. Norma
Hunter (contralto), Neville Hicks (tenor), Adelaide
Singers, David Merchant (organ), Patrick Thomas
(conductor). Boosey & Hawkes. 2 Oct. 1970.
ABC tape
I Will Lift up Mine Eyes (1970). Choir of St Stephen's
Church, Sydney. Chappell. Royal Visit. 3 May 1970.
HMV disc OXLP/7526
From a Child's Garden (1967–1968). April Cantelo
(soprano), Malcolm Williamson (piano). 1971.
Argo disc ZRG/682
Arrangements of 'While Shepherds Watched Their
Flocks', 'Angels from the Realms of Glory', 'In
Dulci Jubilo', 'O sanctissima'. Ambrosian Singers;
London Symphony Orchestra (Erich Leinsdorf, con-
ductor).   *CBS disc*
Piano Concerto no. 2 (1961) [14'35"]. Malcolm
Williamson (piano), Strings of the Melbourne Sym-
phony Orchestra (Patrick Thomas, conductor).
Chappell. 20 Sept. 1967. *ABC recording RRCS/127*
Piano Concerto no. 3 (1962) [28'20"]. John Ogden
(piano), Sydney Symphony Orchestra (Joseph Post,
conductor). Weinberger. June 1964.
ABC recording PRX/5584
Concert Suite from the Ballet *The Display* [24'25"].
Sydney Symphony Orchestra (John Hopkins, con-
ductor). Weinberger. 27 July 1971.
World Record Club disc S/5264
Sinfonia Concertante (1964) [16'45"]. Mervyn Simpson
(trumpet), John Schmidli (trumpet), George Dobson
(trumpet), Melbourne Symphony Orchestra (Pat-
rick Thomas, conductor). Boosey & Hawkes, 20
Sept. 1967.   *ABC recording RRCS/127*
Santiago de Espada (1958) [6'32"]. Sydney Symphony
Orchestra (John Hopkins, conductor). Boosey &
Hawkes. 30 Jan. 1970.   *ABC recording RRCS/384*
Quintet for piano and strings (1967–68). Malcolm
Williamson (piano), Gabrieli String Quartet. Wein-
berger. 1971.   *Argo disc ZRG/682*

Pas de Quatre (1967). The Nash Ensemble. 1971.
Argo disc ZRG/682
Variations for cello and piano (1964) [12'11"]. Jennifer
Ward-Clarke (cello), Ian Lake (piano). Weinberger.
Tower disc BLM/1002
Travel Diaries (1961). Michael Mann (piano).
ABC recording 2XS-2935
Piano Sonata (1957) [11'04"]. Peter Cooper (piano).
Boosey & Hawkes. Oct. 1968.
Pye disc GSGC/14110
Five Preludes for Piano (1966). (i) Ships; (ii) Towers;
(iii) Domes; (iv) Theatres; (v) Temples. Malcolm
Williamson (piano). 1971.   *Argo disc ZRG/682*
Epitaphs for Edith Sitwell (1966). Allan Wicks (organ).
Weinberger. Apr. 1969.   *HMV disc CSD/3657*
Symphony for Voices (1960). Pauline Stevens (con-
tralto), John Alldis Choir (John Alldis, conductor).
HMV disc released in Australia by World Record
Club.   *Record Society S/6/90*
Symphony for Voices (1960) [15'28"]. Norma Hunter
(contralto), Adelaide Singers (Patrick Thomas, con-
ductor). Weinberger.   *ABC recording RRCS/384*
Four Settings of Elizabethan Love Songs. Owen
Brannigan (bass), Elizabethan Singers (Louis Hal-
sey, conductor).   *Argo disc ZRG/496*
Canon (1968) [1'18"]. Adelaide Singers (Leonard
Burtenshaw, conductor). Weinberger. 4 June 1968.
ABC recording RRC/68
A Young Girl (1964) [3'51"]. Adelaide Singers (Patrick
Thomas, conductor). Weinberger. 2 Oct. 1970.
ABC tape
Mass of Saint Andrew (1964)
Process of Palms (1962)
Three Hymns (1962). (i) 'Jesu, lover of my soul';
(ii) 'Ye choirs of New Jerusalem'; 'Agnus Dei'.
Elizabethan Singers, John Alldis Choir, William
Davis (organ), Louis Halsey (conductor). Wein-
berger. Aug. 1966.   *Pye disc CSCL/4005*

Richard Meale

(*b.* 1932)

Elizabeth Wood

In Sydney in the fifties, when Richard Meale was writing his first works and studying at the State Conservatorium of Music, there was no contemporary music being performed and little knowledge of post-war European music even in tertiary musical education. He was fortunate to study pianoforte with the late Winifred Burston, whose eagerness to extend his repertoire and, later, to follow his discoveries of the piano works of composers such as Messiaen and Boulez encouraged in her students the kind of insight and impetus needed to break the old slavery to transplanted nineteenth-century traditions among Australian musicians. Yet as a composer Meale followed an individual and radical course: individual because he launched himself into the musical present by importing scores, recordings and books and, apart from some formal tuition in traditional music theory with Dr Alex Burnard, he taught himself; radical because his was a restless questioning of conventions and exploration of new forms of expression. As fast as he absorbed what he had learnt he repeatedly astonished his colleagues, critics and audience by his apparently divergent style and interests which so outgrew the Australian musical experience that many felt uncertain about his path and potential. His periodic withdrawal or disinterest in previous works denotes a persistent determination to discard what became outmoded or irrelevant through this process of assimilation, and a personal struggle with creativity in a conservative cultural context.

An illustration of the nature of this struggle is contained in the Spanish poet García Lorca's illumination of the *duende* or creative spirit as expressed in the bullfight, as both a fight with death and destruction and with 'geometry, the fundamental basic measure of the spectacle':

> To help us seek the *duende* there is neither map nor discipline. All one knows is that it burns the blood like powdered glass, that it exhausts, that it rejects all the sweet geometry one has learned, that it breaks with all styles ... The appearance of the *duende* always presupposes a radical change of all forms based on old structures. It gives a sensation of freshness wholly unknown, having the quality of a newly-created rose ... [1]

In 1960, at a turning point in his career, Meale rejected all his earlier solo piano works, chamber music for one instrument and piano, songs, ballets and theatre pieces, broken with past influences progressing from Bax, Bartók, Stravinsky and Messiaen, and followed his own *duende*. An important contribution to this new direction was the award of a Ford Foundation Scholarship which took him to the Institute of Ethnomusicology at the University of California at Los Angeles. Here he devoted himself to practical and theoretical studies of Asian music, particularly Indonesian and Japanese, with Asian musicians and the West Coast group who included the composers Colin McPhee and Henry Cowell. He was also able to visit Europe and spent some time in France and Spain. These experiences gave strong stimulus to his compositions from 1960 to 1969, and may be found indirectly in the Spanish-influenced works such as *Las Alboradas* (1963), *Homage to García Lorca* (1964) and 'Very High Kings' from *The Mystical Voyage of Christopher Columbus* (1968) and in the Asian-influenced works *Clouds now and then, Soon it will die* (both 1969) and more directly in *Images (Nagauta)* of 1966. During the sixties his main preoccupation was with orchestral works, often with large forces and on a large scale, of which *Nocturnes* is the outstanding example (1967).

These finished works were often slow in production, appearing after a long intellectual gestation. Meale's creative process involves a thorough working-out of form and structure during an intense literary-philosophical experience, but once the 'culture' has fully formed, the actual writing takes place quite rapidly and the initial experience or stimulus is left behind like scaffolding. The late C.M. Prerauer wrote of *Nocturnes*:

> Meale worked almost three years at this score and achieved with musical self-discipline a perfect translucence . . . Once again a concrete programme has turned into abstract music in the composer's hands—a procedure which goes like a fine thread through all his works.[2]

The title, 'programme' or context of a work often plays a poetic role in providing an outer symbol, but is more usually an impulse, a springboard to invention, or an acknowledgement of a rich personal experience. This is so in *Homage to García Lorca* where the lyric *casida* and gypsy *cante jondo* transmitted through Lorca's poetry, his imagery, the sonorous role of his lines, are realized by Meale in purely musical terms, and acknowledged in quotations to the Prologue and Postlude from the 'Casida del Herido por el Agua' and from the great four-movement elegy 'Llanto por Ignacio Sanchez Mejías'. The title of 'Very High Kings' is the salutation of Columbus to Ferdinand and Isabella in a letter setting out his desire to 'enquire into the secrets of the world' and in whom the composer has found symbolic material for a cycle seeking to treat 'the actual experience of artistic creative endeavour as well as the adventure of living'.[3] In tribute to another poet, Arthur Rimbaud, in *Incredible Floridas* (1971) each of the six movements is headed with the title of a poem; the title itself is from 'Le Bateau Ivre' (The Drunken Boat): 'I have struck, do you realize, incredible Floridas, where mingle with flowers the eyes of panthers in human skins! Rainbows stretched like bridles under the seas' horizon to glaucous herds!'.[4] Like Lorca, Rimbaud knew that inventions from the unknown demand new forms and stretch out explosively towards the future. The 'Saison en Enfers' is also the 'seasons' of alchemy, and Meale has reflected in strict serial procedures in the Interlude movement headed by three poems from 'Les Illuminations' the alchemical formulae and magic sophisms of Rimbaud's 'Délires II: Alchimie du Verbe' in which the hallucination of words, disordering of the senses and the pursuit of 'philosophic gold' are means by which the poet becomes seer and god-like. The mysterious connection of sounds and colours which have emerged from the black stage of dissolution (for example, 'Voyelles') is approximated in Meale's work in magical musical imagery.

Formal as well as symbolic interest attaches to the titles. In *Nocturnes* the astrological and poetic symbolism of the movement of heavenly bodies, here concentrating on the movement of the moon, provides relationships which Meale uses to control the form of the long six-movement work. The literal meanings of the movements are: I Aphelion (the greatest distance of sun from earth), II Perigee, the first Nocturne (the point in the moon's orbit nearest to earth), III Zenith (the highest culminating point directly overhead), IV Eclipse, the second Nocturne (the interception of the moon's light by intervention, obscuration, the absence of light), V Nadir (the point directly underneath, the lowest place and time of degradation) and VI Apogee, the third Nocturne (the point in the moon's orbit where it is farthest from earth, the climax). From these meanings, Meale has drawn a symmetrical structure linking I-III-VI, II-VI, III-V pivoting on IV, the Eclipse and silence. In the two completed works of the triptych based on the delicate seventeenth-century Japanese 'haiku' of Matsuo Bashō, *Clouds now and then* and *Soon it will die*, there are also links between structure and poetic symbolism; for example, the measured syllabic structure of the poems finds correspondence in the proportionate number of time periods, experienced in time, which are regular, tightly-balanced subsections to the major or higher sections of *Clouds*. The most direct application of an external form is found in the orchestral work *Images (Nagauta)*, prompted by Meale's love of the ancient court music of Japan, the 'Gagaku', on which the composer has written:

> Although this was not meant to imitate Japanese music, the formal structure of the Nagauta play gave me strict formal patterns to consider by taking the first seven sections of its traditional shape.[5]

The seven sections of the Nagauta are presented in two movements: I: Oshirabe, an introductory piece, and Shidai, a song of the secondary Kabuki actor, and II: Michiyuki, the entrance of the principal actor; Issei, his song; Mondo, a recitative-like furthering of the plot by questions and answers; Kuri, a short revelation of the emotional climax of the plot, and finally Kuse, a dance revealing the essence of the principal actor. The intensity of expression in the drama in its highly stylized setting is reflected in the rather static instrumental patterns and the rhythmic continuity within each brief section.[6]

Whilst these examples show that the context of a work can charge it with poetic meaning and give strength and authority to its structure, the real importance is in its heightening of the composer's personal experience, not as information to the listener. He says: 'Mine is a formal symbolism of relationship of experience' and 'My endeavour is to provide a rich experience'.[7] It is through form, strong abstract structural design, that this experience is conveyed, and without any loss of intensity or immediacy. No matter with what numerical, psycho-physiological or literary-philosophical symbols he begins, he 'invents musical systems founded on exclusively musical criteria'.[8] The sense that each of Richard Meale's works is complete, exactly planned, and controlled is due to the balance between his inventiveness of sound and form and great technical mastery, and his keen self-disciplined intellect. It is particularly evident in the more refined, abstract chamber music since 1970, written since his appointment as Senior Lecturer in Music at Adelaide University, in works including the two wind quintets, the string quartet, *Interiors/Exteriors*, *Evocations* and *Coruscations*, his first work for solo piano since *Orenda* (1959).

The interaction of intuition and logic can be demonstrated in *Coruscations*, a major work which is receiving increasing acclaim since its first performance by Roger Woodward in London in April 1971, with subsequent recordings and international performances by Woodward and Yuji Takahashi. Once again literary, personal and scientific references are contained in the title, alluding to the series of quivering, vibrating flashes of light of the Aurora Borealis, and to ingenious, concise and epigrammatic dialogue. The following description of Meale's compositional process deduced from his working papers to this piece may seem at first reading difficult and technical. Yet it may serve to show the listener that, even as the sounds are heard to effervesce in seemingly random keyboard patterns, they actually emanate from a highly predetermined and strictly logical structure. The architecture involves number systems, set and group theories, serialism and permutation as useful means by which to control some facets of the music and to give rise to combinations of sounds which might not have occurred otherwise to the composer's intuition. While the application of mathematical systems and procedures in the 'precomposition' stage has allowed the composer to work with his materials in a purely logical way, free from the usual aural connotations, yet, in the final intuitive interpretation, Richard Meale has achieved a lyricism and a spaciousness of musical texture which permit an exceptional aural quality of spontaneity.

The work is created from an arbitrary set of possibilities presented at the outset in ten sonorities (A-J), each with all transpositions. These were then subjected by the composer to permutational computations. Firstly, he formed five terminal groups each with six series of the ten sonorities with their transpositions, occurring five times through successive overlapping pairings, for example, in Group I (A-J) from A1   B2   C3   D4   E5   F6   G7   H8   I9   J10 he derived the

second series: A11   C12   E1   G2   I3   B4   D5   F6$_2$ H7   J8 and

so on. This process, itself involving inversion and retrogression, forms isomorphic symmetrical figures (Groups 1–5) which may be shown graphically as [1]A-J, [2]B-I, [3]C-F, [4]E-H, [5]G-D:

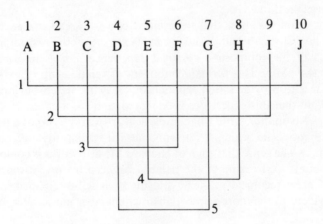

and from which both symmetrical (1, 2) and asymmetrical (3, 4, 5) group structures form, and through which certain axis (A, J) and nexus points (F) subsequently arise.

Secondly, by parallel series-selection, these terminal groups yield six networks of five series each of the ten sonorities and their transpositions, thus subjecting the initial set A-J to a total 300 sonorities. The first of these networks is shown here:

A1	B2	C3	D4	E5	F6	G7	H8	I9	J10
B1	A2	D3	C4	F5	E6	H7	G8	J9	I10
C1	E2	B3	D4²	A5	H6	J7	G8²	I9²	F10
E1	B2²	D3²	A4	C5	J6	G7²	I8	F9	H10
G1	I2	C3²	E4	A5²	F6	J7²	B8	H9	D10

[reproduced by permission of the composer, from his MS. papers]

Each network builds sequences initiating from A-J, B-I, C-F, E-H, G-D with parallel numbering series on (i) 1–10; (ii) 11–8; (iii) 9–6; (iv) 7–4; (v) 5–2; (vi) 3–12, arriving logically at the terminal point D12.

The ten sonorities (A-J) are themselves arrived at by a process of multiplication or additive-enrichment. From an original series 1 → 5:

Fig. 75 From MS. papers

and its inversion, the following vertical sonorities are derived:

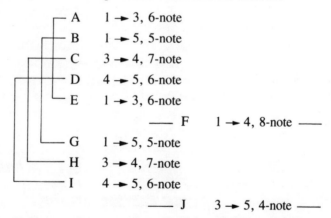

These display further symmetries. The intrinsic intervallic symmetry of F and J is especially significant in the articulation of the musical structure.

An example of an enriched sonority achieved by multiplication is seen in the formation of E1. In this process, each note of the original series figure ③ (see Fig. 75) is used as a basis for the transposition of the first figure ① , the sum of which retains its generative intervals and becomes the first position of the mode E:

Fig. 76 From MS. papers

As there are for the character E 1–12 alone 120 × 10 × possibilities, clearly there are almost endless combinations of possibilities in permutations, inversions and transpositions from which to select, which demonstrates, as Boulez suggests, 'the absolute necessity for a logically organised consciousness at the outset',[9] as exemplified in the stages of ordering here. The depiction of the autonomous sonorities in all transpositions has provided an order of succeeding sequences 1–12 which, within the logic of permutational computation, reach an intrinsic closure when the limits of the numerical network are reached at the 300th sonority.

There are many examples of tight formal control in Meale's works, for example, the palindrome in the second movement of *Las Alboradas* in which a seventeen-bar middle section pivots on whole-bar silences at the centre of the arch. But there are few examples of indeterminacy such as found in the two concluding sections to this same early work, though even here 'free' interpretation is sculpted by the conductor and terminated by a written-out coda, just as the oboist and conductor 'control' the thunderous punctuation of basses, harp, bassoons, horns and piano during the coda to *Evocations*, which appears at 6–10 second intervals yet remains unrelated to the rhythm of the solo oboe:

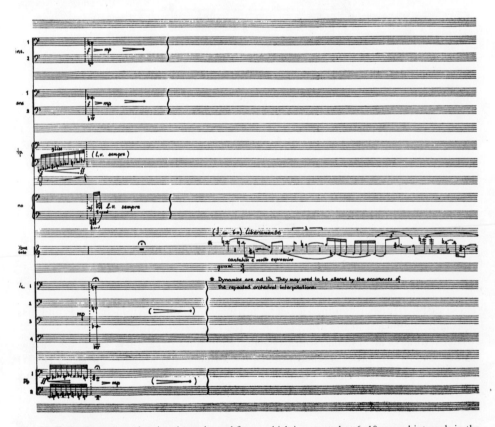

Fig. 77   From *Evocations*, showing the orchestral figure which is repeated at 6–10 second intervals in the ensuing oboe section

This is rather an example of 'free play' which occurs in his works and is very related to Asian rhythmic schemes and to Meale's concept of time as a variable, of measuring points between which things, impossible to notate exactly, can occur.

Another important aspect of his music is the handling of initial materials and the *modus operandi* of the introductions and beginnings to pieces, which frequently contain the embryo of the whole, and from which structural unity is derived. Examples include the flute motive announcing *Las Alboradas* I and III:

Fig. 78 The flute motive

and the short Prelude to *Homage to García Lorca*, in which, in the first seven bars, a basic intervallic series gradually accumulates through sustained bowed sonorities marked off by pizzicato sforzando entries until all twelve tones have appeared, and from whose harmonic aggregations resulting from the distribution of entries among the twenty string parts all subsequent melodic, harmonic and rhythmic materials are derived.[10] In the Postlude to the work, five sections (described by Meale as 'plateaux') relate back to the opening bars, reunifying preceding materials in 15, 5, 5, 10 and 15-bar sections in a gradual decrescendo towards a final accumulative sonority of the twelve tones built up over a bass pedal in the final seven bars. Just as symmetry orders the larger shape, internal, often interlocking symmetries are unifying factors: this example from *Clouds now and then* shows a simultaneous interlocking of the cellular intervals which control the horizontal and vertical aspects of the piece:

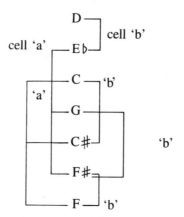

The cells themselves comprise (a) a perfect fourth with minor second, (b) four adjacent half-tones, and (c) a perfect fifth with major second; (a) and (c) also appearing in transposed form (see Fig. 80). As in *Homage*, they are fully formed in the opening bars (see Fig. 78).

Interlocking is mainly achieved through shared, or paired, common notes: this example, from bar 14, shows the clarinet part with interlocking pitches from (a) and (b) cells; accompanying it are trumpets with (b) and bass clarinet with (a):

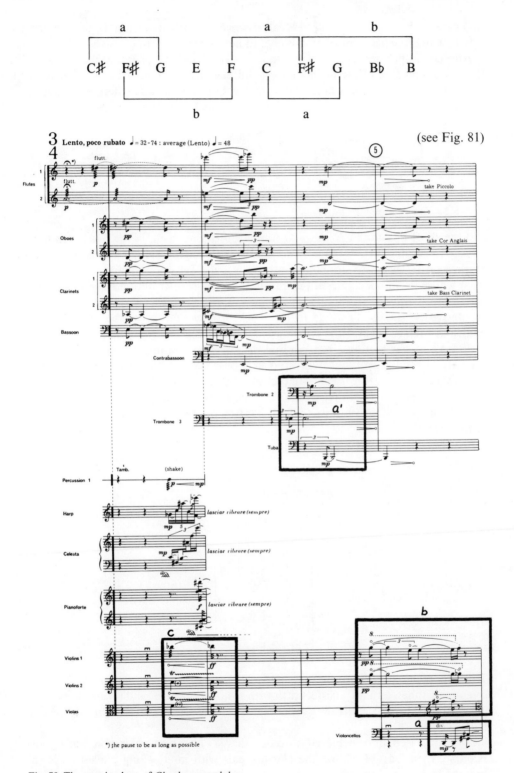

Fig. 79 The opening bars of *Clouds now and then*

Fig. 80 From *Clouds now and then*

Fig. 81 From *Clouds now and then*

From *Coruscations*, the following shows how an occurrence of common notes through the sequence I3-E4-D5-H6-G7 can acquire a sustaining quality through E flat E G flat G D flat D. In this example, the preceding mobile staccato formation shows the selected functioning of shared notes from the sequence C11-B12-A1-J2, where, for example, the G flat of B12 is omitted because F sharp has appeared in C11, and the E is omitted from A1 in anticipation of its undesirable reference to the sustained E in common to I3, E4, D5 and H6:

Fig. 82 From *Coruscations*

An interesting feature of *Coruscations* is its modal ambit in a serial usage, and the way in which the *sequence* of sonorities, (individually differing, like modes, in their intervallic series and capable of tranposition) also has a fixed compass serving as a kind of 'final'. The horizontalization of the sonorities produces a spacious texture with predominantly uplifting tessitura, but when presented vertically or as simultaneities, points of initiation or brief termination help to articulate the sound. In a structure which is highly logical and predetermined, qualities which are intuitive such as articulation, tessitura, duration and dynamics are very important. In *Coruscations* the tessitura is inextricably linked to pianism, yet maintains and sustains a direct organic relationship to the modal compass of the sonorities. Meale has provided meticulous directions and identifications in this score to maintain hand distribution, points of articulation, internal rhythmic groupings and accentuation, but, without in any way interfering with the architecture, there is scope for modification of the tempo, dynamics and accents at the performer's discretion.

Sound textures and densities are also generated by structure, although it is through their instrumental distribution that they vibrate and explode with colour. Meale's procedures vary: in *Homage* density is built on sustained pianissimo chords; in *Evocations* use is made of anticipatory tones and note-passing within a sustained sound from one instrument to another while foreign notes to the sustained string sonority eject from the more percussive harp or piano. In the coda (bar 83) to *Clouds now and then*, a dispersal of density is heard on the three trombones (Fig. 83).

Staggered entries, canonic in *Homage*, are effective in *Evocations* at bar 129 H through the slight attack given in the production of each note (Fig. 84).

Glissandi, clusters, pedals and silence are also features of the density-formations in *Nocturnes*, fourth movement.

Fig. 83 From *Clouds now and then*

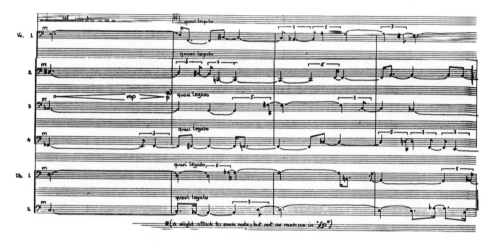

Fig. 84 From *Evocations*

Density is also explored through spatial distributions. Antiphonal divisions and pairings of dissonant intervals, melodic note distribution (such as that found in the overlapping trumpet section Issei of *Images* on page 20 of the full score)

Fig. 85 From *Images*

and the passing of an interval from one orchestra to another (in *Homage*) or one instrument to another, give added spatial dimensions to the sound. Meale also employs physical spatial placements of his players in, for example, the separated 'sound communities' for *Soon it will die*, where eight string trios are seated four on either side of the conductor and between them, to the rear, are three woodwind quartets with a back row of horns and trombones. In *Interiors/Exteriors* the two pianos are widely spaced between the three percussion players, and in 'Very High Kings' the central organ, like the harp in *Soon it will die*, plays an important commentary role, fanfares emanate from rear-positioned trumpets and the amplification for the two pianos is placed in the ceiling. Antiphonal effects and physical exhilaration result. In these examples spatial placement is also a structural device which projects dramatic contrasts between single musical entities and massive densities.

Richard Meale has written no specifically dramatic works since his pre-recorded music for the Old Tote stage production by Robin Lovejoy of *King Lear* (Sydney 1968) in which he manipulated three levels of percussive sound to reveal symbolism, to depict characters in the drama and to underline the structure of the text. Yet he has expressed a continuing desire to write an opera. He is indeed a natural dramatic composer. He has produced vivid contrasts and dialogue in, for example, the second section of *Evocations* where piano and harp interject with oboe and violin obligato and then reverse roles before a tranquil wind quintet. In his handling of *tutti* and solo passages, in the extraordinary rhythmic tension he creates, not only through a profuse variety of rhythmic possibilities within barlines but through the pull between notes and the activations of inner dynamics, he has succeeded in producing many varieties of energy in his musical textures. These qualities of dramatic energy, of lyricism, of virtuoso instrumental writing, coupled with the sense of flow in his music which obscures the discrete sections, all combine in an impression upon the listener —and the performer—of power, stature and conviction rare in Australian music.

His inventiveness and constantly variating technique and intellectual clarity have often been admired[11] but the critical attention paid to his technical and intellectual gifts, especially to his preoccupations with abstractions, ideas, systems, has at times appeared unresponsive to the sheer physical impact of his sounds or to the beauty realized in form which is poised, precise and logical. Some critics have implied that the 'intellectual process' of writing music may lead to stagnation or even silence, as if logic were potentially damaging to imagination, or the intellect were somehow divisible from emotion and intuition. Meale has never taken expression and feeling out of music.

The prominent place Richard Meale holds in Australian music today is as composer, pianist and teacher. He has continued to be the 'rallying figure' of new music inaugurated by his activation and promotion of the first Australian branch of the I.S.C.M. in Sydney revived during the late fifties, which introduced for the first time in Australia performances of works by such seminal composers as Messiaen, Boulez, Stockhausen, Webern, Schoenberg, Berio, Maderna, and younger American composers. He also performed and promoted new composers in Australia such as George Tibbits, Ross Edwards, Alison Bauld and Anne Boyd, and among his pupils in composition have been Ross Edwards, Martin Wesley-Smith, Peter Brideoake, Bozidar Kos, David Ahern and Ian Farr. He has been a catalyst also in keyboard performances with artists such as Marilyn Richardson and the late Peter Richardson. Recent performances of his music by Roger Woodward, Yuji Takahashi, Heinz Holliger, the Fires of London, the Collegium Musicum of Zurich under Dr Paul Sacher, have brought his words to increasing international notice. This platform was first provided through the UNESCO International Rostrum of Composers which presented *Homage to García Lorca* in 1964, *Images (Nagauta)* in 1966, *Nocturnes* in 1967, *Clouds now and then* in 1969, *Interiors/Exteriors* in 1972 and *Coruscations* in 1974. His early Flute Sonata was the first Australian work performed at the I.S.C.M. World Festival in Amsterdam (1960) other than the *Concertino da Camera* by the then expatriate Australian Peggy Glanville-Hicks in 1948. It was followed by *Incredible Floridas* at the I.S.C.M. London Festival in June 1971. Important Australian premières of his work have been promoted through the Australian Broadcasting Commission, Musica Viva, Project New Music, the I.S.C.M. and the Adelaide Festival of Arts, and his music has been performed in many countries.

Whilst an international reputation is important both personally and to Australian music, he has reversed the custom among Australian composers to travel and live abroad whilst establishing their careers, by remaining in Australia to compose and teach and also play an influential public role in musical organizations. His broadcasts in the sixties of new music whilst employed by the Australian Broadcasting Commission were the first of their kind; his lectures at Adelaide University since 1969 have been provocative and stimulating and his classes in analysis and composition have generated a focal group among younger composers. Richard Meale's outstanding place in Australian music is indisputable.

Notes

1. Lorca's lecture, 'The Theory and Function of the *Duende*' given in Cuba in 1930, is reproduced in J.L. Gili (ed.), *Lorca*, London, 1960; see pp. 127–9, 131, 137.
2. *Nation*, 8 April 1967, p. 17.
3. Composer's programme note to the recording, WRC S/4930.
4. O. Bernard (ed.), *Rimbaud*, London, 1962, pp. 165–71, 171–2, 326–30.
5. *The Composers and Their Works*, a booklet accompanying *Music by Australian Composers— Survey No. I* (Canberra, Advisory Board, Commonwealth Assistance to Australian Composers, 1969), p. 15.
6. Further comments by the composer are quoted in J. Murdoch, *Australia's Contemporary Composers*, Melbourne, 1972, pp. 143–5.
7. *ibid.*, pp. 148, 149.
8. S. Bradshaw and R.R. Bennett (trans.), *Boulez on Music Today*, London, 1971, pp. 30–1.
9. *ibid.*, p. 33; see also pp. 38–40, 78–80.
10. For a detailed analysis of these bars see A. Boyd, 'Homage to García Lorca' in *Music Now* I, i (Feb. 1969), pp. 18–23; see also S. Walsh, 'Richard Meale's *Homage to García Lorca*' in *Tempo* LXXV (1965–66), pp. 17–20.
11. See, e.g. C.M. Prerauer, *Nation*, 25 March 1967, p. 18; 8 April 1967, p. 17; see also R. Covell, *Australia's Music: Themes of a New Society*, Melbourne, 1967, pp. 211–24; A.D. McCredie, *Musical Composition in Australia,* Canberra, 1969, pp. 22–3; D. Peart, 'Some Recent Developments in Australian Music' in *Composer* XIX (1966), pp. 73–8; 'The Australian Avant-Garde' in *Proceedings*, R.M.A. XCIII (1966–67), pp. 1–10; 'Richard Meale' in *Music Now* I, i (1969), pp. 25–8; and L. Sitsky, 'New Music' in *Current Affairs Bulletin*, 46, 3 (29 June, 1970), pp. 42–3.

List of Works

The List of Works comprises the major works acknowledged by the composer. Previous lists are published in A.D. McCredie, *Catalogue of 46 Australian Composers and Selected Works*, Canberra 1969, p. 15, and J. Murdoch, *Australia's Contemporary Composers*, Melbourne 1972, pp. 154–6.

1959 *Orenda* solo pf. Universal Edition, 1977.
1963 *Las Alboradas* fl vn hn pf. Boosey & Hawkes, 1970.
1964 *Homage to García Lorca* double str orch: (i) 6, 9, 3, 3, 1; (ii) 21, 19, 7, 7, 2, or of 20 solo players (i) and (ii) 5, 2, 2, 1. Boosey & Hawkes, 1966.
1966 *Images (Nagauta)* 2 fl 2 ob 2 cl 2 bn; 4 hn 3 tpt 3 trbn perc (2) str. Boosey & Hawkes, 1968.
1967 *Nocturnes* solo cel vib hp; 3 fl 3 ob 3 cl 3 bn 4 hn 3 tpt 3 trbn tuba perc (2) str. Universal Edition, 1971.
1968 'Very High Kings' from *The Mystical Voyage of Christopher Columbus* 2 amplified pf org 6 tpt full orch. Universal Edition, 1972.

1969 *Clouds now and then* 2 fl 2 ob 2 cl 2 bn 4 hn 2 tpt 3 trbn tuba timp perc (2) hp cel pf str. Universal Edition, 1975.
1969 *Soon it will die* 3 fl 3 ob 3 cl 3 bn 4 hn 3 trbn hp str (8, 6, 6, 4). Universal Edition, 1975.
1970 *Interiors/Exteriors* 2 pf 3 perc. Universal Edition, 1975.
1970 *Variations for Orchestra* 2 fl 2 ob 2 cl 2 bn 2 hn 2 tpt 3 trbn perc (1) str. Universal Edition, 1975.
1970 *Quintet for Winds* fl ob cl hn bn. Universal Edition, 1975.
1971 *Coruscations* solo pf. Universal Edition, 1975.
1971 *Incredible Floridas* (Homage to Arthur Rimbaud) fl cl vn vc pf perc. Universal Edition, 1977.
1971 *Plateau* fl ob cl hn bn. Universal Edition, 1975.
1973/4 *Evocations* solo ob vn obbligato chb orch: fl ob 2 bn 2 hn hp pf 7 vn 4 va 4 vc 2 db. Universal Edition (in prep.)
1974/5 String Quartet. Universal Edition (in prep.)

Discography

Las Alboradas. Ronald Ryder (violin), Peter Richardson (flute), Douglas Trengove (horn), Nigel Butterley (piano), R. Meale (conductor).   *WRC-S/2472*
Homage to García Lorca. West Australian Symphony Orchestra (John Hopkins, conductor).
   Festival SFC 80021
Clouds now and then. West Australian Symphony Orchestra (John Hopkins, conductor).
   Festival SFC 80021
Nocturnes. Sydney Symphony Orchestra (John Hopkins, conductor).   *WRC S/5656*
Soon it will die. South Australian Symphony Orchestra (Patrick Thomas, conductor).   *WRC S/5656*
Coruscations. R. Woodward (piano).
   HMV-OASD 7567 also VRL 1–0083
'Very High Kings'. Sydney Symphony Orchestra (Joseph Post, conductor).   *WRC S/4930*
Plateau. University of Adelaide Wind Quintet.
   HMV-OASD 7565
Quintet for Winds. University of Adelaide Wind Quintet.   *HMV-ASD 7558*
Orenda. R. Woodward (piano).   *VRL 1–0083*
Evocations. Holliger/Langbein/Collegium Musicum, Zurich (Sacher, conductor).   *ABC 1026*

Colin Brumby

(*b.* 1933)

Philip Bracanin

The most significant works of Colin Brumby's output date from the time that he settled in Queensland in 1959. At that stage in his creative development he took it upon himself to make a thorough study of the twelve-note method as employed by Schoenberg and Berg, and as a result composed a small number of dodecaphonic works. The first substantial work of this type was *Partite* for clarinet and strings (1961). Schoenberg's, and more particularly Berg's, influence on this work extends beyond the mere application of the twelve-note method, for *Partite* is strongly expressionistic and cast within the mould of the baroque suite. This temporary adoption of dodecaphonic processes however, did not constitute a radical departure from Brumby's general approach to composition, as the twelve-note method relies, at its most fundamental level, on the kind of motivic procedures commonly employed by him. Besides this, tonal implications are apparent in *Partite* through: use of chords with octave doublings (as in the opening bars of the first movement); repetition (at the same pitch) of passages within each of the four movements; the final movement's recapitulation of the opening ideas of the first. Further reference to tonal thinking is evident in the organization of the series. In the first movement, for example, the same sequence of series (original, inverted, retrograde, retrograde inverted) in the clarinet part is transposed up an augmented fourth and repeated. In fact, this procedure determines the length of the movement. Although the piece seems at times a little contrived, the clarinet is treated throughout with masterly skill, and especially impressive are the passages in the third movement during which it is accompanied by the strings in harmonics.

Brumby's dodecaphonic trend was strengthened by his period of study with Alexander Goehr during 1962–64. The most significant works written during this period include the *Fibonacci Variations* for orchestra (1963) and the Quintet for wind instruments (1964). These works are strongly rhetorical and their declamatory rhythmic character is embodied in a consistently polyphonic texture. The same features are encountered in the works following this period but they are tempered by a marked re-emergence of tonality and a more spontaneous lyricism. Brumby's ideas on musical articulation at the time were published in a monograph entitled *The Art of Prolonging the Musical Tone* (O.U.P.; 1968). From this the reader is informed of the

Fig. 86 From *Partite*

importance that Brumby places on the relationship between the analysis of relevant works and the composition process. Central to all his thinking is the concept that tonality, however simple or complex, in one form or another, underlies all musical articulation. These facets of his style are clearly revealed in the *Stabat Mater Speciosa* (1965).

The text of the *Stabat Mater Speciosa*, a vivid depiction of the Manger story, dates from the last decade of the fifteenth century. Brumby set the original version by Ozanam rather than any of the later nineteenth-century revisions, as its authenticity, particularly the occasional metric irregularities, evoked for him an archaic atmosphere. This he reproduces in the score by employing small forces to give the appropriate lightness of texture associated with its traditional pastoral setting. The work is based on the opening clarinet motive of the Sinfonia (an upward semitone and a downward tone) and proceeds largely by continuous variation. The opening chorus, 'Stabat Mater Speciosa' is a processional with tonal overtones beginning in F major-minor. 'Pro Peccatis', the third movement, has a tenor incantation leading into a choral recitative and concluding with a duet for mezzo soprano and baritone in which the opening motive reappears. 'Sancta Mater' is chant-like in effect, reminiscent of passages from Stravinsky's *Symphony of Psalms*, but still retaining the distinctive Brumby fingerprint. The fifth movement, 'Carol', calls to mind a medieval round-dance during which references are made to material from previous movements. The sixth movement forms the climax to the entire work. Here Brumby makes use of double canon by inversion to which the soloists are added in augmentation.

The work ends, as it began, ritualistically, with the choir restating the processional melody of the opening and the piece concludes in B flat major.

Fig. 87 From *Stabat Mater Speciosa*

(cont.)

(Fig. 87 cont.)

From the time of writing the *Stabat Mater Speciosa* until his second period of study overseas in 1972 Brumby extended his output with a large number of works in almost every media, particularly choral and orchestral music, and opera. Especially noteworthy in the years 1968–71 were his contributions to the highly specialized field of children's opera in which he collaborated with his wife, soprano Marisa Brumby who was both the producer and a performer with the company. During this period a number of extra-musical themes recur in Brumby's works and these form the kernel of his creative stimulus. Paramount amongst them is the picture of innocence and, more particularly, outraged innocence. This is central to such works as *Bring out Your Christmas Masks* (1969), the climax of which depicts The Slaughter of the Innocents, and *A Ballade for St Cecilia* (1971) in which St Cecilia, who is martyred in ancient Rome for her Christian beliefs, is the 'innocent'. Another important theme is that of cynicism resulting from an inability to resolve inner conflicts. This is mirrored in the composer's own text for the cantata *Charlie Bubbles' Book of Hours* (commissioned for the First National Conference of the Australian Society for Music Education and the UNESCO Seminar on Music in Tertiary Education held in Brisbane, August 1969, and included in the series of Australian works recorded by Festival in 1972), and that spoken by Everyman, the principal protagonist in his opera *The Seven Deadly Sins* (premiered in Brisbane in 1970). The culminating point towards the end of the period prior to his study overseas is the work *Litanies of the Sun* (1970–71).

Litanies of the Sun was commissioned by the Australian Broadcasting Commission for the Australian Youth Orchestra to whom it is dedicated. It is a symphonic suite in four movements inspired by Paul Hamlyn's book *Egyptian Mythology*. Each movement depicts an aspect of the Egyptian sun god. In the first movement 'Ra-

Atum', the reposed sun god, rises 'by an effort of will from the abyss [the primordial ocean] and appears in glittered splendour...'[1] The entire movement is based on a mosaic-like variation of the segments making up the nine bars following the solo flute introduction. Essential melodic and harmonic material for these nine bars is heard during the opening three bars of the solo flute introduction, and Brumby's predilection for chords based on the perfect and augmented fourth is clearly evident from the outset of this work, being first heard here in their melodic guise. 'Ra-Atum', the most economic of the four movements, probably more than the others, gains much of its effectiveness from the skill with which the orchestra is handled. In fact, all four movements ('Ra-Atum', 'The Phoenix', 'Holy Child in the Lotus Flower', and 'Ra-Haratke') are economic in their use of material and are vividly orchestrated. *Litanies of the Sun* is pure Brumby without any obvious traces of the influence of other composers.

Fig. 88 'Ra-Atum', introduction

A situation recalling that of the composition of *Partite* for clarinet and strings occurred in 1972 with the appearance of two new Brumby works, *Doubles* for piano, and *Player Chooses* for keyboard and three other instruments. As in 1961 these works were, for Brumby, departures from the mainstream of his output. *Doubles* was written for the young Australian pianist Geoffrey Saba who premiered the work at his Wigmore début in London in 1972. In *Doubles* the barline is dispensed with, giving the performer a degree of rhythmic latitude. Although the piece gives the impression that it is rhapsodic in overall design, its flamboyant character conceals a fairly strict variation form incorporating an intervallic procedure which makes use of interval combinations (such as the major seventh and major third in the opening of the piece) which function both melodically and harmonically. In fact, such a procedure is a more thorough application of that used in *Litanies*. *Player Chooses*, commissioned by the Organ Institute of New South Wales, was an exercise in closed form and free structure undertaken while Brumby was studying in Rome with Franco Evangelisti. The pitch parameter of the piece is predetermined according to a 'tritone clock' consisting of d (12 o'clock), e flat, g flat, f (3 o'clock), e, g, a flat (6 o'clock), a, c, b (9 o'clock), b flat, c sharp; but the players are given a limited number of choices regarding the octave position of the notes, their dynamics, mode of attack, and duration. Because of this, and the fact that the players proceed throughout

Fig. 89 From *Player Chooses*

independently of each other, the piece will change considerably with each performance, as can be seen in the following directions from the composer's score:

Duration: to be determined by incidence (in preceding pitch series) of following quatrads:—

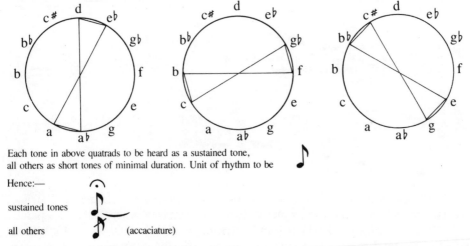

Each tone in above quatrads to be heard as a sustained tone, all others as short tones of minimal duration. Unit of rhythm to be ♪

Hence:—

sustained tones

all others   (accaciature)

Three versions of pitch-duration relationships therefore as follows (to be heard simultaneously, i.e., polyphonically, but independently of each other)

Tempi: Independently of each other.

Fig. 90 From *Player Chooses*

An extension of the principles involved in *Player Chooses* were employed in the composition of *Sonnets and Sonetti* for ten flutes and prepared tape (commissioned by the Queensland Flute Guild in 1973). The same 'tri-tone clock' forms the basis of each part over which the players lay a transparent sheet consisting of various designs, the points of which indicate the fragments to be played. All the parts relate to a prepared tape which determines the overall form of the piece.

Almost as a reaction, however, to the stylistic divergencies that these works represented, Brumby swung back to tonality more strongly than ever before in response to a commission from Musica Viva for a work to be included in the Australian tour of the Academy of St Martin-in-the-Fields in 1974. This resulted in *The Phoenix and the Turtle* in which the composer once again responds to the catalystic image of the Phoenix already encountered in *Litanies of the Sun*.

The idea of regeneration is at the core of Brumby's personal philosophy, and translates readily in a musical context into the concept (already noted) of continuous development in which the new continually arises, Phoenix-like, from the old. *The Phoenix and the Turtle* does not attempt a musical parallel of Shakespeare's poem (even if such a thing were possible); rather it is a free fantasia stimulated by the experience of the poem. In few other works does Brumby respond with such spontaneity to his lyrical impulse, nor employ such simple means to express it.

Although many of the works discussed here seemed at the time of composition to be departures from his underlying aesthetic, such apparent divergences have served to reinforce and enrich Brumby's continuing development and have helped to place him amongst the foremost of Australian composers.

Fig. 91 From *The Phoenix and the Turtle*

(cont.)

(Fig. 91 cont.)

Note

1. Paul Hamlyn, *Egyptian Mythology* (Paul Hamlyn, London, 1965), p. 45.

Select List of Works

Opera
The Seven Deadly Sins (two acts) for four sopranos, tenor, baritone, dancers and tape (1970)

Operettas for Children
Rita and Dita (1968)
The Wise Shoemaker (1968)
The Prince Who Couldn't Laugh (1969)
Rita and Dita and the Pirate (1969)
The Two Suitors (1969)
Rita and Dita in Toyland (1970)
The Marriage Machine (1971)
Rita and Dita and the Jolly Swagman (1971)

Orchestral
Partite for clarinet and string orchestra (1961)
Fibonacci Variations (1963)
Five Days Lost for speaker and orchestra (1969)
Violin Concerto (1970)
Litanies of the Sun symphonic suite (1971)
The Phoenix and the Turtle for string orchestra and harpsichord (1973)

Chamber Music
Quintet for wind instruments (fl ob cl hn bn) (1964)
String Quartet (1968)
Player Chooses three instruments and keyboard (1972)

Piano
Doubles (1972)

Chorus and Orchestra
Stabat Mater Speciosa Christmas cantata (1965)
Bring out Your Christmas Masks (1969)
Charlie Bubbles' Book of Hours (1969)
A Ballade for St Cecilia (1971)
Celebrations and Lamentations (1971)
This is the Vine

Vocal
Three Italian Songs for high voice and string quartet (1964)
Bess Songs for soprano, flute, guitar and prepared tape

Children's Works
Songs and Signs (1961)
A Windy Beach (1970)

Discography

Aegean Suite (1961) [11′32″]. Patrick Thomas (flute), Strings of the Queensland Symphony Orchestra (Rudolf Pekarek, conductor). MS. 1961.
ABC recording 2XS/2378
Partite (1962) [8′03″]. Jack Harrison (clarinet), strings of the West Australian Symphony Orchestra

(Thomas Mayer, conductor). MS. Oct. 1966.
ABC recording RRC/72
Fibonacci Variations (1963) [12′25″]. South Australian Symphony Orchestra (Patrick Thomas, conductor). MS.
ABC recording RRC/28
Antipodea (1965) [13′18″]. South Australian Symphony Orchestra (Patrick Thomas, conductor). MS.
ABC recording RRC/28
Entradas (1968) [2′30″]. Tasmanian Orchestra (Patrick Thomas, conductor). MS. 2 May 1968.
ABC recording RRC/72
Charlie Bubbles' Book of Hours (1969) [17′35″]. Genty Stevens (soprano), Norma Hunter (mezzo soprano), Neville Hicks (tenor), Robert Dawe (baritone); Adelaide Singers; South Australian Symphony Orchestra (Patrick Thomas, conductor). Albert. Sept. 1970.
Festival disc SFC 800/21
Five Days Lost (1969) [10′00″]. Barry J. Gordon (speaker), West Australian Symphony Orchestra (Verdon Williams, conductor). Albert. 12 Feb. 1970.
ABC recording RRCS/386
Gilgamesh (1967) [7′40″]. Jack Hume (speaker), Adelaide Singers, brass and percussion of South Australian Symphony Orchestra (Patrick Thomas, conductor). MS. 22 Nov. 1967.
ABC recording RRC/72
Christmas cantata: *Stabat Mater Speciosa* (1965) [18′43″]. Joan Gill (soprano), Norma Hunter (mezzo soprano), Malcolm Potter (tenor), Robert Dawe (baritone); Adelaide Singers, instrumental ensemble (Patrick Thomas, conductor). MS.
ABC recording PRX/5586
Twelve Bagatelles [13′45″]. Malcolm Potter (tenor), Adelaide Singers (Patrick Thomas, conductor). Albert. 11 Mar. 1971.
ABC tape
Three Italian Songs (1964) [8′15″]. Molly McGurk (soprano), Oriel String Quartet. Albert. Feb. 1971.
Festival disc SFC800/24
The Cloths of Heaven [1′25″]. Noreen Stokes (piano), female voices of the Adelaide Singers (Patrick Thomas, conductor). MS. Nov. 1967.
ABC recording RRC/67
Various songs for male voices [6′06″]. (i) 'It's No Go the Merry-go-Round' (1961)—0′48″; (ii) 'Once I Loved a Maiden Fair' (1961)—1′52″; (iii) 'Roman Walls Blues' (copyright unavailable)—1′01″; (iv) 'How Sleep the Brave' (1961)—1′52″; (v) 'Will There Never Come a Season?' (1961)—0′33″. Male voices of the Adelaide Singers (Patrick Thomas, conductor). MS. Nov. 1967. *ABC recording RRC/67*
Various works for SATB chorus. (i) 'I Will Lift Up Mine Eyes' (1961)—1′36″; (ii) '*Christus resurgens*' (1961)—1′42″; (iii) '*Ave Maria*'—1′39″; (iv) 'How Joyful 'tis to Sing' (1967)—3′44″. David Merchant (organ in 'How Joyful 'tis to Sing' only); Adelaide Singers (Patrick Thomas, conductor). MS. 1967/68.
ABC recording RRC/65
Various works for SATB chorus. (i) 'Our Andy's Gone with the Cattle' (1965)—1′57″; (ii) 'Three Kings in Great Glory (1964)—1′40″; (iii) '*Tantum ergo*' (1967)—2′33″; (iv) 'Jesu, that dost in Mary Dwell' (1962)—1′48″; (v) '*Dormi Jesu*' (1965)—2′02″. Adelaide Singers (Patrick Thomas, conductor). MS. 1967/68.
ABC recording PRX/5600

John Exton
(*b.* 1933)

Roger Smalley

How to account for the presence of an Englishman in a book on Australian composers? The first answer must be biographical. John Exton was born at Wolverton, Buckinghamshire, in 1933. He learned the violin from the age of eleven although, he says, 'I composed long before I could read music'. Whilst at school he joined the National Youth Orchestra, of which he later became leader. He still remains active as a performer, especially of chamber music, although in recent years he has concentrated increasingly on the viola. Study at King's College, Cambridge (begun in 1951, continued as a research student in 1954, and later as a College Fellow from 1957), was interrupted by National Service, spent working in an acoustics laboratory attached to the medical branch of the R.A.F. The work he did there—analysis and measurement of noise and tests on hearing—was later to prove useful when he began to set up an electronic studio at the University of Western Australia. He returned to Cambridge to complete his Fellowship, having written a thesis entitled The Nature of Tonality, and taking his Mus.D. in 1963. This research provided the theoretical foundation for the immensely practical general composition course which he now leads with his students in Perth. His first acknowledged compositions and performances date from these Cambridge years and his twin vocations, of composer and teacher, were decided.

Whilst still a research student at King's he had spent one year (1956–57, on a Mendelssohn scholarship) studying with Luigi Dallapiccola in Italy. When he finally left Cambridge he could clearly have entered the professional metropolis as an orchestral player but chose instead to take the post of Director of Music at Bedales, a progressive co-educational school in Hampshire. The enlightened music policy of Bedales provided a stimulating environment in which he wrote several works for school performance. The Orchestral Variations on the name BEDALES which were written for the school orchestra (and have been recorded by the West Australian Symphony Orchestra on O/N 40566) shows what an exceptionally high standard must have been reached. During this period the first fully professional performances of his music took place. The Partita for string quartet, composed whilst he was studying with Dallapiccola, was played by the Amici Quartet at the 1962 I.S.C.M.

Festival in London and, together with the earlier Three Pieces for oboe solo (1955), was published by J. & W. Chester.

In 1966 he joined the Music Department of the University of Western Australia in Perth, where he is now an associate professor. It is impossible to categorize John Exton in relation to any particular compositional 'movement' or 'school' of composers. Never a great enthusiast for Festival-trotting and other peripherals of the composer's world he has always preferred to work slowly and steadily and alone. The calmer—but far from isolated—world of Perth seems ideally suited to his temperament, and he shows no inclination to leave it. In this sense, then, he could be said to have become an 'Australian composer'—and it is perhaps no accident (although obviously dependent on other factors as well) that all his best music has been written since he came to Perth.

To approach the opening question from another point of view we must first consider whether there can actually be such an animal as the 'Australian composer' and, if so, is John Exton therefore an English composer living in Australia? But this question presupposes another—namely, when he was still living in England was Exton an 'English' composer? This, at least, can be answered with an unequivocal negative. There is no trace of that quintessential 'Englishness' in any of his music— and if I add, thankfully, then I am merely expressing a personal prejudice. His early works exhibit a variety of influences, none of them English and all of them European. Because he was a chamber music player we can particularly detect his inside knowledge of Bartók's string quartets, Berg's *Lyric Suite* and the later chamber music of Webern. At this time these diverse influences had not yet become fully assimilated. It was a period of stylistic experimentation, and the gradual attainment of technical mastery. Works vary disconcertingly from the prolixity of the Second String Quartet (on the Berg/Bartók axis) to the almost academic dryness of the Piano Variations and Concertante for piano and five instruments (both of which employ a Webernian twelve-note technique).

Of all his early works the Partita for string quartet (1957) represents the most successful synthesis of these various influences, a fact perhaps attributable—at least in part—to the guidance of Dallapiccola's refined sensibility. Although the music shows, not unexpectedly, its indebtedness to that of Dallapiccola this remains, nevertheless, a very personal work. The Bergian emotional world is more restrained. Bartókian repeated figures and rhythms are employed sparingly, the twelve-note technique is used with greater subtlety and a burgeoning lyricism.

Fig. 92 The BACH motive

The Partita is based on a twelve-note set (Fig. 92) which begins with the familiar BACH motive. In Webern's String Quartet Op. 28 (whose set begins with the same notes) this motive is pervasive but in the Exton it predominates only in the first and last of the Partita's seven brief movements. Whereas Webern completes his set with two further transformations of the same four-note motive, Exton's set is really made up of four three-note segments, each consisting of a minor second plus a major third. The second hexachord of the set is a retrograde of the first, transposed a tritone lower. The large number of possibilities which this gives rise to, of combining different forms and transpositions of the set which contain the same groups of pitches, are exploited with considerable compositional resource and finesse.

The opening bars, for example (see Fig. 93), superimpose four-note segments of the basic set and its inversion a semitone lower (P_0 and I_{11}) in a series of four six-part chords. The BACH motto is in the first violin and the chords are laid out so that the second two are a retrograde of the first two transposed by a tritone (thus reflecting the linear structure of the set itself) and, in addition, the viola and cello parts are an inversion of the two violin parts. In bar 3 the BACH motive sets out in crotchets on the cello (later passing to viola and second violin), like a *cantus firmus*. The other instruments weave counterpoints, emphasizing the three-note minor second/major third cell, metrically displaced against these equal crotchets (the texture here is particularly reminiscent of Dallapiccola).

Fig. 93 From the Partita, opening bars

The tiny canon by inversion which opens and (with *dux* and *comes* interchanged) closes the third movement is also very ingeniously constructed, and emphasizes two-note groups in the set (Fig. 94). Each of the sets used (P_5 and I_{10}) contain the same six dyads, but in I_{10} they occur in the reverse order to that of P_5. Thus the first quintuplet of Fig. 94 belongs to P_5, the third to I_{10} and the second (at the central point of the canon) simultaneously to both sets.

These two examples, which can be amplified by a study of the entire score, show that Exton had absorbed principally European models and techniques. Since he came to Australia his musical language has broadened considerably. Although it might be tempting (and would certainly fit in with some current notions about the 'Australization' of the indigenous music) to see the calmer, more expansive vistas of his recent work in terms of the vastness and bleakness of the Australian landscape this interpretation is not borne out by the observable and stated influences, which are American (via the philosophy of John Cage) and oriental (the use of the I-Ching, and a Japanese rock-garden in Kyoto).

The final answer to my initial question can only be, I believe, that John Exton is simply a composer who happens to live in Australia. One cannot be an outsider to

Fig. 94 From the Partita, third movement

a tradition which barely exists. The most important consequence for Exton's development was not so much that he came to Australia but that he left Europe. His comparative isolation from the continuing European tradition has allowed his music to develop in ways I don't think it otherwise would have. In retrospect the Third String Quartet (1969)—one of the first works composed in Australia—could almost be seen as an elegiac leave-taking of various aspects of the European tradition. Uniquely for Exton it quotes existing music—the hymn *Veni Creator Spiritus* and the third of Webern's Four Pieces for violin and piano Op. 7.

His present preoccupations are already adumbrated in a lecture given in 1967 called 'Forward to First Principles' (and significantly subtitled 'An Article of Faith'): 'Recently there have been two developments in music which may fairly be described as being essentially new: electronic music and indeterminacy'. He has explored both of these paths in his work since 1970. Electronic music is, of course, only a medium but one whose vocabulary is, as he remarks, 'far more suitable for indeterminate "treatment" than the old, familiar, vocabulary of instrumental and vocal sounds'. In his electronic pieces *A Thousand Feet in the Life of . . .* and *Breathing Space* he has allowed the basic sound-material and its subsequent electronic treatment to interact in a random way.

The implications of indeterminacy go much deeper. In the article he draws attention to the fact that 'we commonly recognise that one listener's reaction to or experience of the communication of a particular work will not necessarily—not even probably—be the same as any other listener's' and asks 'When we hear a piece of traditional music which is apparently making sense, are we really sharing or communicating with the composer's musical experience, or are we very largely generating our own?' He continues: 'The idea of indeterminacy simply questions, and makes capital of this very instability in the hope of any definite communication between composer and listener', and concludes that 'however hard or skilfully the composer tries, he still cannot guarantee, or even hope to channel the listener's musical experience in the slightest degree. Why not therefore simply let him hear any old (or new) noises in any old (or new) order? He will still have his valid experience, if he is going to have one at all!'[1]

Exton's most recent group of works (String Quartets IV–VI, *Ryoanji*, and some of the tape pieces) represent a very interesting and thought-provoking attempt— and a successful one I would say—to put this theory into practice, to show that a valid and meaningful musical communication can take place without every facet of the musical structure being under the conscious control of the composer.

In order to distance himself from the structural process Exton has turned, as did John Cage in the early fifties, to the sixty-four hexagrams of the I-Ching, the ancient Chinese Book of Changes. There are, however, fundamental differences in the way the two composers have used the I-Ching, and Exton's music bears no resemblances to that of Cage. In Cage's music the basic musical material which is fed into the forming process controlled by the I-Ching is itself generated by chance means, or is left totally free (so that every performance will sound different). Looking at Exton's String Quartet V on the other hand (his first work to be composed using this technique), we can see that this material is both limited and carefully selected, comprising the following categories:

1. 12 chromatic pitches
2. 6 timbres (*con sord.*, *pizzicato*, *sul pont.*, *sul tasto*, *col legno*, *naturale*)
3. 3 dynamic regions (loud, *mezzo*, soft) with tendencies (*crescendo*, *diminuendo*)
4. 3 tempi (slow, medium, fast) with tendencies (*accel.*, *rit.*)
5. 4 durations (long, medium, short *fermata*)
6. 3 registers (high, middle, low)
7. 3 textures (monody, heterophony, homophony)

Furthermore, whilst Cage uses the I-Ching itself in a random way Exton exploits the structural potential of the totality of sixty-four hexagrams. He has arranged them in an 8×8 square by combining, vertically and horizontally, all the eight possible upper and lower trigrams (units of three lines). The hexagrams are then numbered according to their position in the book. Quartets V and VI both have sixty-four sections corresponding to the hexagrams in the sequence 1 to 64. Because the numbering of the hexagrams in the I-Ching is without any apparent system[2], this means that the most diverse structural types are brought into juxtaposition.

Within this overall formal structure the basic material is distributed as follows. For each of the categories listed above the I-Ching is asked 'In which of the sixty-four sections does this parameter (for example: C sharp, *sul tasto*, *crescendo* etc.) appear?'. By throwing three coins six times each question is answered by one hexagram. Each question need only be asked once because the single hexagram so obtained can be transformed into two, four, eight, sixteen or thirty-two other hexagrams according to the principle of 'moving lines'.[3] In this way a network of cross-relationships is set up between the sixty-four sections, with the same limited number of elements constantly reappearing and interacting in different contexts and combinations. The final shaping of the material is still very much in the hands of the composer who says that during the process of composition 'some categories may be negated or at least discouraged by the answers to other questions. Quartet V became almost entirely what I thought of as monodic because that was largely the way I felt it emerging. Note that some questions are more specific than others—i.e. the twelve pitch values may be quite precise, but ideas such as 'homophonic' or '*fermata*' may be interpreted in many ways.'

In that they were not composed linearly but by distributing a limited number of basic elements in a fixed form Exton's Quartets V and VI are related to Stockhausen's concept of 'Moment-form'. Unlike several of Stockhausen's own works in Moment-form (notably *Momente* itself) the sixty-four sections of Exton's Quartets are not mobile (although there is no reason why they should not be, since they are *conceptually* mobile). Each Quartet represents only one possible arrangement of the material, which is thus heard from only one of the potentially infinite number of viewpoints.

In two other recent works—String Quartet IV and *Ryoanji* for forty strings and three percussions—this idea of multiple viewpoints is explored within a single work. The following description relates specifically to *Ryoanji*, although Quartet IV is based upon essentially the same principles. The I-Ching is again used, this time to generate not the form but the basic pitch material of the work. The sequence of numbers obtained by reading the columns of the 8 × 8 I-Ching table both vertically and horizontally is used to select pitches from the gamut of sixty-four semitones extending upwards from the first C natural below the bass stave to the second E flat above the treble stave. These pitches are then grouped into a series of fifteen chords containing between six and fifteen pitches. Each of these chords stands for one of the fifteen stones, laid on a bed of raked white gravel, which constitute the sixteenth-century rock-garden in the grounds of the Ryoanji Temple in Kyoto.

The paradox of this garden is that no matter where an observer stands it is impossible for him to see all fifteen stones simultaneously. Every shift of position brings them into a new set of relationships. In his work Exton has composed-out these relationships as seen from fifteen different positions spaced equidistantly around a 360-degree circle. The size of each rock is represented by the duration of the chord and its distance from the observer by dynamics (near to far being equated with loud to soft). For each of the fifteen positions these measurements were made with a fair degree of accuracy, by placing a transparent grid over a scale drawing of the garden (aerial view). The three percussionists play a completely independent structure of rubbed, scraped and tapped sounds which form an aural equivalent to the moss surrounding each stone and the gravel which separates them. (In String Quartet IV these are represented by electronic ring-modulation and reverberation, which produces a halo around each chord.) The resulting sound-panorama of dense, fluctuating sound-masses and quiet imperturbable percussive clicks and scrapes arises from a unique combination of chance and control.

The composer has written:

> The score does not in any way set out to be an emotional impression of the atmosphere of the garden (however impressive that may be). It is a transcription. But in following the essential forms and proportions of the garden, it may be that something of its essence is conveyed or recreated.

The future of Exton's work is rich in possibilities. A series of no less than twenty-one string quartets has been projected, containing between them a total of (not surprisingly) sixty-four movements, each quartet having between one and five movements. There can be no doubt that as the series progresses new extensions and applications of the I-Ching system will reveal themselves. In the electronic field the continuing expansion of the studio in Perth (soon to include computer control) will open up further possibilities in another direction. I do not wish to conclude by attempting to place John Exton's work in the general context of music today; that would be much too premature, and at this stage in musical history it may not even be useful to do so. Perhaps the most we can do is to evaluate music according to the aims and intentions of its individual composers. At an age when many composers are settling down to the unthinking repetition of an already established style, John Exton is opening up whole new areas of discovery for himself. We can, therefore, look forward to his forthcoming works with an entirely justifiable enthusiasm.

Notes

1. The complete article can be found in *Studies in Music*, no. 1, 1967, The University of Western Australia Press, pp. 89–97. In selectively quoting from a long article I have, of course, greatly oversimplified its complex argument.
2. The composer comments: 'This is contestable, whether or not it constitutes a factual error. Indeed the arrangement of the hexagrams is one of the more fascinating aspects of the book; it is perhaps this that my quartets are *about*!'
3. Full details of the workings of the I-Ching can be found in the introduction to any edition of the book. In his article 'The *I-Ching* and Structure: A note on the composition of my String Quartet V' (*Studies in Music*, no. 7, 1973, p. 77) the composer recommends the Wilhelm translation, which has a foreword by C.G. Jung (English version by C.F. Baynes, 3rd edn, Routledge & Kegan Paul, London, 1968).

Discography

Movements for Orchestra (1963) [11′27″]. West Australian Symphony Orchestra (Thomas Mayer, conductor). MS. 7 Mar. 1968.

ABC recording RRCS/124

String Quartet no. 3 (1969). Oriel String Quartet. Albert. Feb. 1971. *Festival disc SFC 800/25*

List of (Acknowledged) Compositions

Three Pieces for oboe solo (Cambridge, 1955, revised 1961)—publ. Chester
Dialogues for two violins (Cambridge, 1957)
Partita for string quartet (Florence, 1957)—publ. Chester—also arranged as: *Variations for Small Orchestra* (Cambridge, 1961)
Three Simple Pieces for piano (Cambridge, 1961)
String Trio (Cambridge, 1961)
Variations for piano, Concertante for piano and five instruments (Cambridge, 1961)
Six Caprices for violin solo (Cambridge, 1961)
Fantasy for violin and piano (Cambridge, 1961)
String quartet no. 2 (Cambridge, 1961)
Movements for Orchestra—Fanfares and Diversion on the name B-E-D-A-*-Es (Hampshire, 1963–64)
The Story of Christ's Nativity according to St Luke, for speakers, singers and instruments (Hampshire, 1965)
Two Psalms and a Homily, for double choir and organ (Perth, W.A., 1966)
Quintet for flute, oboe, clarinet, horn and bassoon (W.A., 1967)
String Quartet III (W.A., 1969)
Electronic Jazz (i.e. tape works, generated by fully- or semi-automated analog processes):
   i. *Fantasia among One Note*
   ii. *One-way Ping Pong*
   iii. *Go Boil your Head in E-flat*
   iv. *A Thousand Feet in the Life of...*
Breathing Space (tape) (Guildford/Cardiff, 1972)
   i. *Musaic* ii. Aria (tape) (Cardiff, 1972)
String Quartet IV (with electronics) (Somerset, 1972)
String Quartet V (Kent/Somerset, 1972)—publ. University of Western Australia Press
Ryoanji for 40 strings and percussion (U.K./W.A., 1972–73)
String Quartet VI (W.A., 1973–74)
String Quartet VII (W.A., 1975)

Larry Sitsky
(*b.* 1934)

Donald Thornton

It cannot be claimed, in the mid-seventies, that Larry Sitsky belongs to the Australian avant-garde. Yet Sitsky, with the determination and enthusiasm which are paramount in his character, continues to produce a steady stream of works that are stimulating, challenging, and even provocative; works which show a growing maturity, and which are slowly and steadily building for the composer an enviable reputation shown, for example, by the impressive number of commissions offered to Sitsky in recent years from a wide variety of sources. An appreciation of this composer's style necessitates some knowledge of his unique background.

Born in 1934 in Tientsin (China) of Russian Jewish parents, Sitsky's linguistic achievements include a working knowledge of Chinese, together with fluency in Russian and English. His lively intelligence has delved deeply into the unusual range of literature thus open to him. Yet, he had little contact with the Western European languages more normally linked with the English-speaking world and, on his own admission, he lacks first-hand contact with Western European culture, even though his music derives basically from European style.

Sitsky is a pianist of uncommon ability. His virtuosic octave and chord technique, allied to a tremendous physical power at the keyboard, make him an ideal interpreter of the late Romantic and early twentieth-century composers. He is superb in the grand gestures of Liszt, Tchaikovsky, Bloch and Barber, in the red-blooded excitement of Bartók and early Stravinsky, and in the intellectual semi-sterility of late Busoni. Yet the intimate and more subtle romanticism of Chopin, Schumann and Ravel frequently eludes him in performance. His playing is masterly in gesture and rhetoric, if lacking in intimacy.

As in music, so in literature. He delights in the grand romanticism and philosophical undertones of such disparate writers as Büchner, Kafka, Poe, Dostoyevsky and Thomas Wolfe, He is drawn to the symbolism found in many of the above writers, but less so to the elusive symbolic quality of Mallarmé and Maeterlinck. He is interested in the philosophies that developed in Russia early in the century, and in the mysticism of the Orient. Indeed, his approach to religion is intellectual and philosophical rather than emotional.

All of this personal background can be related to Sitsky's music. Paramount in his style is the intellectual control of musical material, the interrelationships and development of motifs, all clearly derived from traditional European music. Often there is a philosophical or extra-musical link with this material reminiscent of late Scriabin; for example, in the work notes of his Violin Concerto (1971) (which the composer considers his 'finest purely orchestral work') we come across a cluster of notes designated 'mystic chord', with the clarification, 'only at this pitch'.

The second obvious characteristic of Sitsky's music is its peculiar brand of romanticism. It is a warning to all performers of this music that behind those often terrifying avalanches of notes there is usually a colourful idea which may be little more than a rhetorical gesture. Indeed, after a study of the score it can be something of a revelation to hear Sitsky perform his own piano music. One cannot help but be impressed by the logic, the shaping and rhythmic freedom, the colourful masses of sound, and the musical inevitability of passages which sometimes look awkward on paper. In the works of this composer the printed notes are often merely an approximation to the aural effect; a creative musical sensibility is needed to bring the music to life.

Beneath these basic qualities of Sitsky's music we can often discern the pianistic styles of the performer: the opulent, massive sonorities of much of his instrumental writing clearly relate to Busoni and Liszt; the use of extreme technical virtuosity to create excitement and a sense of climax derives from his own performances.

All these examples can be seen in the *Fantasia in Memory of Egon Petri* (1962), a piano work employing a wide range of sonorities illustrated in Figs 95–98. The opening of the work (Fig. 95) is shrouded in mystery, and rhythmically so free that

Fig. 95 From the *Fantasia in Memory of Egon Petri*, opening bars

time signature and barlines have been deemed unnecessary; indeed, much of this work dispenses with the conventions of rhythmic notation. Sitsky's approach to pianistic technical virtuosity is demonstrated in Fig. 96. Here the clusters can be traced to Bartók, but the texture, consisting of a simple melodic line over a rumbling surge of bass sonority is a favourite of the composer. Marked *quasi chorale* Fig. 97 derives from Busoni, and especially from that composer's indebtedness to Bach, but Sitsky takes Busoni's harmonic freedom a step further, and again dispenses with barlines so as to place all rhythmical emphasis on the shape of the phrase. The final extract (Fig. 98) to be played in octaves, is typical of Sitsky's own keyboard ability, but presents formidable difficulties for the unwary; it is typical of Sitsky's constructional logic that this passage is merely a contrapuntal inversion of a passage heard in the rarified texture of the opening page.

The *Fantasia in Memory of Egon Petri*, although a fairly early work, shows Sitsky's personal approach to romanticism, a style which remains typical of his piano music, though considerably developed in the seventies. 1973 saw the production of two

Fig. 96 The clusters in *Egon Petri*

Fig. 97 From *Egon Petri*

Fig. 98 The final extract from *Egon Petri*

important works for piano: *Bagatelles* and *Twelve Mystical Preludes*. The former, representing Sitsky's most serious approach to piano works of a didactic nature, is a highly imaginative group of miniatures exploiting new keyboard techniques in a simple way. The latter, commissioned for the opening of the Sydney Opera House, again exploit new piano techniques, including the third (middle) pedal in a way that is reminiscent of Berio and Stockhausen.

One of Sitsky's finest and most successful works to date is Concerto for Wind Quintet and Orchestra (1971), a work which exploits the virtuosity of flute, oboe, clarinet, bassoon and French horn in a texture of colourful brilliance, and which also serves as an excellent example of the composer's structural logic. The entire work is based on a set of linear and chordal material, shown in Figs 99 and 100. Looking at first glance like a 'classical' tone-row, Fig. 99 reveals on closer inspection eighteen instead of twelve notes, but as in those of Schoenberg the prime consideration here is clearly melodic, for it is the basis of all melodic shapes in the work. As in elementary serial technique, the melodic shape undergoes a number of precompositional processes, including inversion of the intervals, and simple transposition of the resulting shapes to every available pitch. Sitsky also includes in his melodic materials the retrograde versions, and several different partitionings[1] of the row.

Fig. 99 From the Concerto for Wind Quintet and Orchestra

Fig. 100 Linear and chordal material in the Concerto for Wind Quintet

The chord materials shown in Fig. 105 bear no precompositional relation to the melodic row. The chords are more than Schoenberg's 'simultaneities', the texture, spacing and even the exact pitch being structural properties. Again, as with the melodic material, Sitsky transposes the entire chord progression to every available pitch, and the resulting progressions form the basis of the whole work. Theoreticians may query the unity of this practice in comparison with the theory behind classical serial technique, but to Sitsky's mind the melodic and chord materials form a contrapuntal unity based purely on sound, without the need for theoretical justification. This structural principal is the basis of all Sitsky's mature works.

The Concerto for Wind Quintet begins with a cadenza for the flute, based clearly on the linear material shown in Fig. 96, and accompanied very subtly by percussion; the mood is atmospheric and rhythm free, giving the impression that the work emerges from almost nothing. As other instruments enter the structure achieves more definition, wind instruments building an ever more complex polyphony based on the linear material, over slow string chords which prove to be a statement of the chordal material of Fig. 97. In its use of textural and rhythmic devices the rising intensity of this movement shows the skill of a fully mature composer. The clarinet cadenza which follows is again accompanied by percussion instruments, the natural agility of the clarinet leading logically into a fast brilliant movement. It is in such movements that Sitsky is most aggressively modern, and here the complexity of the texture and assymetrical rhythmic groupings are such as to almost defy aural analysis. The ensuing slow movement, with its predominant horn solo, is an interesting study of orchestral colours and sonorities; it leads directly into the climax of the work, an elaborate cadenza for the wind quintet, again later accompanied by percussion. The rhythmic complexity and excitement of this cadenza require virtuosity of the highest order from the percussion players as well as the soloists; indeed the percussion gradually becomes more predominant as the cadenza proceeds, moving in a series of waves to its climax.

The Concerto for Wind Quintet and Orchestra succeeds brilliantly due to the masterly, idiomatic writing for the solo instruments and percussion, together with the natural contrasts of colour and character of the instruments. Less can be said for the Concerto for Two Solo Pianos (1967). The similarities between these two concertos are to be clearly seen in the type of material used and its development, in the exploitation of instrumental virtuosity, and especially in the structural importance of the cadenza. No critic could deny that the canons and rhythmical canons are ingeniously constructed, but many of the rhythmic ideas are so complex as to be difficult to comprehend aurally, and the resulting effect is often arid and academic. In fairness it must be said that this criticism cannot be levelled at the fully developed fugue, which gathers momentum in an almost hysterical way.

Perhaps the most significant landmark in Sitsky's creative development was his unexpected diversion into operatic writing in 1965 when he produced *The Fall of the House of Usher*, a one-act work to an excellent libretto by Gwen Harwood, after the story by Edgar Allan Poe. Its performance at the Hobart Festival of Australian Opera in that year stands as the first successful presentation of an opera by an Australian composer, a success which has since been eclipsed by the outstanding production of Sitsky's second venture into this field, *Lenz*, at the Sydney Opera House in 1974. These two works have placed Sitsky's name in the forefront of Australian opera composition.

The success of *The Fall of the House of Usher* was at once both unexpected, yet predictable. Up to that time Sitsky had concentrated on instrumental writing, a fact which explains some of the shortcomings of his first opera; yet his literary interests and especially his extraordinary fascination with the macabre made him an ideal interpreter of Poe's chilling story. The fact that Debussy had thought seriously of setting the same story probably meant little to Sitsky, for their approaches to theatre are quite opposed, Sitsky revelling in surrealism which Debussy would almost certainly have considered vulgar. It must be admitted that the success of *The Fall of the House of Usher* is largely attributable to the dramatic qualities of the instrumental writing, and the imaginative sound spectrum of the instrumentation and prepared tape at the dénouement. Solo vocal writing was a new world to Sitsky at the time, and it is clear that he tried to make the voice an important medium of emotional expression, yet there is an undeniable rhythmic inflexibility in the vocal writing.

The overture is a masterpiece of the macabre. It consists of a long and elaborate harpsichord solo, aided by a solo flute and a prepared tape. The extensive use of the harpsichord throughout the opera is one of Sitsky's most original inspirations, and the percussive, virtuosic approach to it is set in this overture. Percussion note clusters, rapid repeated notes, and black-note *glissandi* alternate with textures such as that in Fig. 101, which could derive from Falla's Harpsichord Concerto. The flute unfolds its ideas almost independently of the harpsichord, with only a cue and an approximate tempo given for each section; much of the flute part is melodically related to vocal melodies to follow later, while other sections are brilliant and incisive. The prepared tape for the overture is striking in its simplicity, consisting merely of a short passage of two-part unaccompanied singing for soprano and alto, played at double the original speed; the high *tessitura* of the soprano part creates a series of blood-curdling screams, which contrast brilliantly with the metallic clangour of the harpsichord, suitably amplified.

Fig. 101 From the overture to *The Fall of the House of Usher*

The opera then proceeds in a series of separate sections, the names of which are almost sufficient to tell the story: Narrator's aria, Usher's first aria, Madeline's arietta, Narrator greets Usher, Usher's aria with mimed death of Madeline, Storm scene (orchestral interlude with interpolations by Narrator and Usher), Reading scene, Usher's monologue, and Death of Usher. Each of these sections is accompanied by a different group of instruments, allowing for strongest contrasts of mood.

This unfolding of the opera is accompanied by a gradual progression from the idea of 'innocence' (or 'good') to 'evil', or at least the knowledge of evil by the main characters. Sitsky represents this dramatic progression in musical terms by a corresponding progression from melodic singing to speech, or the nearly equivalent *sprechstimme*. This progression from lyricism, representing innocence, to a more declamatory style, representing evil, can be seen in microcosm in Madeline's arietta. Compare Fig. 102, Madeline's opening phrase, with Fig. 103, which is her final statement in the arietta. In the case of the Narrator, the movement to speech is complete

Fig. 102 Madeline's opening phrase

Fig. 103 Madeline's final statement in the arietta

in the Reading scene; in the earliest version of the opera, Usher's monologue was also spoken, but the revised version raises the dramatic temperature by using *sprech-stimme*, the end of which is to 'be shrieked,with no attempt at pitch at all'.

Underneath this dramatic structure there is a more subtle musical structure, connecting the thematic material of the different sections. Compare the themes set out in Fig. 104: (a) is the basis of the flute theme in the overture, (b) the vocal line of the Narrator's aria, (c) from Usher's first aria, (d) from Madeline's arietta, and (e) from the Reading scene. A cursory inspection of these themes reveals some basic similarities of shape, while closer study makes clear the importance of certain notes which keep recurring, namely, B. A, and C sharp. Also, the beginnings of (a) and (e) are related by inversion. Fig. 105 shows further melodic material taken from Usher's first aria, where the relationships are much more precise. (b) is derived from (a) by using every second note; (c) uses every third note of (a), while (d) derives from every second note of (c).

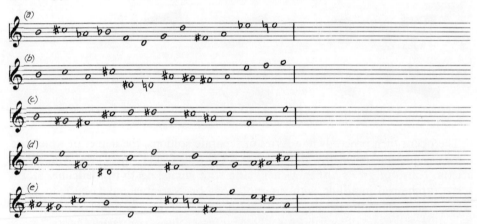

Fig. 104 A comparison of themes in *The Fall of the House of Usher*

Fig. 105 From Usher's first aria

When the themes of Fig. 105 are compared with those of Fig. 104 it becomes clear that Sitsky has invented a mass of interconnected thematic material, which is partly responsible for the admirable unity of the entire opera. It should be pointed out that the formal processes of Sitsky's music are rather more subtle than the foregoing explanation might suggest, but it is important to understand some of the principles of his thinking.

The first performance of Sitsky's second one-act opera, *Lenz*, proved one of the triumphs of his career. Produced in a double billing with Felix Werder's *The Affair* at the Sydney Opera House in March 1974, the auspicious occasion was the first serious attempt to present Australian opera to the public by the country's national opera company.

The story of the psychological breakdown of Jakob Lenz, a demented poet of the eighteenth century, is told in a short novel by Georg Büchner. Büchner (1813–37), himself something of a tormented soul, produced in his short life a series of psychological dramas, the impact of which has been felt only since the rise of Expressionist ideals in the twentieth century. Wozzeck was his creation, and the influence of Berg's music is clearly acknowledged in Sitsky's score for *Lenz*. The librettist, Gwen Harwood, has produced a tightly knit work, in which the dramatic tension rises in a continuous line to a climax of shattering intensity, resulting in an opera free of the static passages that were evident in *The Fall of the House of Usher*. The titles of the sections indicate the extraordinary line of development of the drama:

> Prologue: Lenz enters the village of Waldbach
> I: Lenz and Frederike in the village square (The loss of spiritual love)
> II: Oberlin's aria (The mystical experience)
> III: Lenz's sermon (Almost a parody of II)
> IV: Lenz and Frederike in the graveyard (The loss of physical love)
> V: Kaufmann visits Lenz (The rejection of men)
> VI: Lenz and the sick child (The rejection of God)
> VII: Lenz attempts suicide (The rejection of self)
> Epilogue: Lenz is taken away.

Much of the orchestral writing in *Lenz* derives from an earlier work, which is included in the opera score as a prelude, but which 'is only to be used if there is some strong dramatic reason. The music to *Lenz* is complete without this prelude; on no account is it to be played with the curtain down, in the traditional overture fashion.' The mere fact that the fabric of this earlier orchestral work could be developed into such a tense, extended drama testifies to the emotional and pictorial basis of Sitsky's instrumental writing. Already in the prelude can be seen a clear tendency to treat the traditional sections of the orchestra as blocks of sound colour, which are sometimes fairly static within themselves. Hence the opening passage of the prelude, for strings, serves in the Suicide scene, and elsewhere, for Lenz's incipient madness; the related passage in harmonics sets the scene in the graveyard; the staccato, 'chatter-like' woodwind music serves excellently to paint the characters of Kaufmann and his wife; and the wild *portamenti* over the strings, together with the *tutti 'presto ad lib.'* music represents the hysteria of Lenz's attempt to revive the sick child. Important additions in the orchestral writing to the music from the prelude include a chaconne bass which, reminiscent of Bach, underlines the devotional attitude of the crowd in the Prologue, and stressing of the note B in passages pertaining to death. This latter device is clearly a reference to Berg's *Wozzeck*, as it culminates with a crescendo on a unison B at the point of Lenz's attempted suicide, which relates to the music in the murder scene of *Wozzeck*.

The vocal parts of *Lenz* are structured in Sitsky's usual manner, from a linear series for each major character, each series undergoing the Schoenbergian precompositional devices which create a wealth of melodic material. In this work the composer has been particularly careful about the preservation of natural speech rhythms, and the rare melisma on a single syllable is reserved for words of special importance.

In *Lenz* Larry Sitsky and Gwen Harwood have achieved what is probably the most perfect mating of libretto and music in Australian opera to date. Nevertheless, the range of characters and emotions presented is severely limited by the nature of the work, and the time is ripe for Sitsky to develop his fine dramatic gifts into a full-scale opera, in which a wider spectrum of life could be portrayed. There are strong indications that we may not have to wait too long for such a work. Recent commissions include a full-length opera (for the Australian Opera) which is to be based on the fifteenth-century legends of the Golem from the Prague ghettos. Furthermore, a different aspect of Sitsky's musical personality should be shown in a projected short comic opera to be based on *The Miller's Tale*, after Chaucer and Boccaccio. Whatever the future for Larry Sitsky, it seems certain that opera will remain an important *genre* among his work.

List of Works

Operas

The Fall of the House of Usher (1965). G. Ricordi & Co. Commissioned by the 2nd National Conference of Australian Composers.

Lenz (1970). G. Ricordi & Co. Commissioned by the Australian Opera.

The Fiery Tales (1975), after Chaucer and Boccaccio; libretto by Gwen Harwood. Commissioned by New Opera South Australia.

Ballet

The Dark Refuge for T.V. (1964).

Orchestral Works

Sinfonia for Ten Players (1964)

Four orchestral pieces (which can be played separately, or as a cycle):
1. *Prelude for Orchestra* (1968)
2. *Apparitions* (1966) Boosey & Hawkes. Commissioned by the Queensland Youth Orchestra.
3. *Symphonic Elegy* (1962/1973)
4. *Song of Love* (1974). Commissioned by the Queensland Youth Orchestra.

Concerto for Woodwind Quintet and Orchestra (1971). G. Ricordi & Co. Commissioned by the A.B.C.

Concerto for Violin, Orchestra and Female Voices (ad lib.) (1971). Commissioned by University of Melbourne for the A.H. Maggs Award (subtitled *Mysterium Cosmographicum*, after the writings of Johannes Kepler).

Chamber Music

Burlesque for flute, oboe and piano

Sonatina for violin and piano (1962). G. Ricordi & Co.

Sonatina for oboe and piano (1962)

Woodwind Quartet (1963). Boosey & Hawkes. Commissioned by the First National Conference of Australian Composers.

String Quartet (1969). Commissioned by Musica Viva for the Alfred Hill Award.

Narayana for piano trio (1975). Commissioned by the Melbourne Trio.

Atman: A Song of Serenity (1975) for cello, violin and piano. Commissioned by the London Trio.

Variations on *Waltzing Matilda* (1975) for flute, guitar and cello. Commissioned by the Sydney Concert Trio.

Solo Pieces

Sonata for violin solo (1959)

Sonata for flute solo (1959). Albert & Son.

Improvisation and Cadenza for solo viola or cello (1963)

Improvisation for Harpsichord (1965)

Seven Meditations on Symbolist Art for organ (1974)

Bardo Chodol Sonata for flute solo no. 2 (1975). Commissioned by the National Flute Convention.

Guitar Music

Israeli Dances (1968). G. Ricordi & Co.

Diversions for David (1973). G. Ricordi & Co.

Sonata for solo guitar ('The Five Elements') (1974)

Sonata for two guitars (1968)

Piano Music

Little Suite (1958). Allans Music.

Sonatina Formalis (1959). Allans Music.

Fantasia in Memory of Egon Petri (1962). G. Ricordi & Co.

Seven Statements for piano (1964).

Petra (1971). Commissioned and published by the Victorian Music Teachers Association.

Bagatelles for Petra (1973). G. Ricordi & Co.

Twelve Mystical Preludes after the Nuctemeron of Appollonius of Tyana (1973). Commissioned by the A.B.C.

Beginner Pieces for Young Pianists (1974). Commissioned and published by the A.M.E.B.

Dimensions for piano and two tape recorders (1964)

Concerto for two solo pianos (1967). Boosey & Hawkes. Commissioned by A.P.R.A.

Choral Music

Five Improvisations for SATB and piano (1961). Walton Music Corporation.

The Ten Sephiroth of the Kabbalah for SATB and percussion (1974). Walton Music Corporation.

Vocal Music

Four Settings from Tagore (1955–56) for soprano and piano

Footprints in the Snow (1955) for soprano and piano

Encore for soprano, flute and piano (1958)

Five Songs for high voice and piano (1960)

Eight Oriental Love Songs for high voice and piano (1960)

Concert Aria for low voice, clarinet, horn, cello, piano, organ, percussion, tapes and synthesizer (1972). Commissioned by the Australian National University.

A Whitman Cycle for low voice and piano (1972). Commissioned by the Beecroft Music Club.

Eight Settings After Li-Po for low voice, flute, cello and piano (1974). Commissioned by the New Music Society.

Five Orchestral Songs for low voice (1972/74)

Miscellaneous

Eleven Abstractions on Paganini's 'La Campanella' (1974) for carillon

The Legions of Asmodeus for four theremins. Commissioned by the Australia '75 Festival of Arts.

Fiery Tales, one-act comic opera commissioned by New Opera South Australia. Premiered at the 1976 Adelaide Festival.

Works in Progress

The Golem, full length opera commissioned by the Australian Opera Company. Libretto by Gwen Harwood, after a legend from 16th century Prague.

Concerto for piano and orchestra ('The 22 Paths of the Tarot'). Commissioned for the opening of the new Canberra School of Music.

Century: a series of 150 pieces for beginner pianists

Voices in Limbo, radiophonic work commissioned by the ABC for FM radio. Libretto by Gwen Harwood.

Trakl Songs for soprano and chamber ensemble. Commissioned by the Goethe Institut. Scheduled for première at the 1978 Adelaide Festival. Text by Trakl in the translation by James McAuley.

Discography

Apparitions (1966) [8'00"]. West Australian Symphony Orchestra (Patrick Thomas, conductor). Boosey & Hawkes. 22 February 1968.
                                     ABC recording RRCS/125
Prelude for orchestra (1968) [3'34"]. Tasmanian Orchestra (Patrick Thomas, conductor). MS. 2 May 1968.   *ABC recording PRC/72*
Concerto for woodwind quintet and orchestra (1971) [27'00"]. New Sydney Wind Quintet: Neville Amadio (flute), Guy Henderson (oboe), Donald Westlake (clarinet), Clarence Mellor (horn), John Cran (bassoon); Sydney Symphony Orchestra (Charles Mackerras, conductor). 25 April 1971. Ricordi.
                                                  ABC tape
Usher's Aria from *The Fall of the House of Usher* (1965) [3'25"]. Brian Hansford (baritone), flute, oboe, trumpet from West Australian Symphony Orchestra (Hans-Hubert Schonzeler, conductor). Ricordi. February 1971.   *Festival disc SFC 800/24*
Five Improvisations (1960) [15'18"]. (i) 'Hymn to the Sun'—3'41"; (ii) 'Footprints in the Snow'—3'39"; (iii) 'They Loved Each Other'—1'40"; (iv) 'Shakespeare, from Love's Labours Lost'—1'51"; (v) 'Walt Whitman, from Civil War poems'—4'05". Norma Hunter (contralto), Adelaide Singers, Trixie Shepherd (piano), (Patrick Thomas, conductor). MS. 2 Oct. 1970.   *ABC tape*
Dimensions (1964) for piano and two-track tape [8'30"]. Donald Hollier (piano). MS. 15 April 1968.
                                     ABC recording RRCS/126
Sonata for solo flute (1959). Patrick Thomas (flute). Albert.   *Brolga disc BZM-21*
Sonata for solo flute (1959) [14'45"]. Margaret Crawford (flute). Albert. 20 February 1971.
                                     Festival disc SFC 800/22
String quartet (1969).
    ABC recording AC1017, Australian Composers
                                     Series/*WRC*
Concerto for two solo pianos.   *WRC*
Concerto for violin, orchestra and female voices
    (Mysterium Cosmographicum).   *WRC*
A Whitman Cycle.   *WRC*

Writings on Music

'The Emergence of New Music in Australia', *Perspectives of New Music*, iv, I, p. 76.
'Australia', essay in *Dictionary of Contemporary Music*, (ed. E.P. Dutton), 1974.
'Busoni', essay in above; this Dictionary is issued in the Commonwealth by Thames and Hudson as the *Dictionary of 20th Century Music*.
'The Six Sonatinas of Ferruccio Busoni', *Studi Musicali*, Accademia Nazionale di Santa Cecilia, Anno II —1973, N. 1.
'Busoni and the New Music', *Quadrant*, Jan.–Feb. 1965.

'Debunking Stockhausen and Co.', *Quadrant*, May–June 1965.
'Transcriptions and the Eunuch', *Quadrant*, Sept.–Oct. 1966.
'The Young Pianist and the Twentieth Century Idiom', *Aust. Journal of Music Education*, Oct. 1968.
'Modern Music in Australia', *Asian Pacific Quarterly*, Autumn 1971.
'Sitsky on Sitsky', *Music Now*, April 1971.
'Quo Vadis, Music Criticism?', *Quadrant*, Sept.–Oct. 1971.
'Ferruccio Busoni's "Attempt at an Organic Notation for the Pianoforte", and a Practical Adaptation of It', *The Music Review*, Feb. 1968.
'The Six Sonatinas for Piano of Ferruccio Busoni', *Studies in Music*, University of Western Australia, no. 2, 1968.
'New Music', *Current Affairs Bulletin*, University of Sydney, 29 June 1970.
'New Music in Australia', *Hemisphere*, Nov. 1969.
'Music at the Tempo of Life', *Hemisphere*, April 1974.
'An International Approach to Music', essay in 'Australia—This Land—These People', *Readers Digest*, 1971.
'Summary Notes for a Study on Alkan', *Studies in Music*, University of Western Australia, no. 8, 1974.
'An Impression of a Quarter Century of Musical Life in Australia', *A.P.R.A. Journal*, 50th Anniversary issue, 1975.

A book on Busoni entitled *Busoni and the Piano: The Music, the Writings, the Recordings: A Complete Survey* is to be published by Leo S. Olschki, publisher of the St Cecilia Academy, in the series *Historiae Musicae Cultores*, Florence.

Nigel Butterley
(*b.* 1935)

David Swale

In the music of Nigel Butterley, Australian music gains an individual voice. Though his name may be associated by the public with contemporaries such as Sculthorpe and Meale, his work has little in common with theirs.

Butterley was born and brought up in Sydney. There is no marked reaction against traditional values in his work, no sign of protest, only of a continual advancement—not always spectacular—along a chosen path of personal discovery. The first significant landmark on this road was the work for eight instruments called *Laudes* which was first heard at the Adelaide Festival of 1964. It marks the end of a stylistic struggle which in his early works led him to sample various tonal styles. The style which emerges in *Laudes* is a fairly neutral serialistic one, enabling the composer to concentrate on what is to be said without the suggestion of reminiscence. It came about through the impact of Butterley's first acquaintance with Europe and the Middle East, and the exciting discovery of the possibilities which recent styles of music offered, a discovery promoted by his studies with Priaulx Rainier. This journey began at the end of 1961, and it was in Ravenna that the revelation came to him of the embodiment of all this experience in a work of praise.

Its four movements are meditations prompted by the spiritual qualities of four churches—the Basilica of Sant' Apollinare Nuovo at Ravenna, with its beautiful mosaics, the Norman Apse of Norwich Cathedral in England, the Chapel of King's College, Cambridge, and the modern Church of the Reconciliation of the Community of Taizé in Burgundy. In general *Laudes* is an austere and impressive work. In relation to Butterley's output it contains much, both in its ideas and its techniques, which show the germs of things to come. The fragmented, mosaic style of the first movement was new to Butterley's music, and it finds a place in most of his works (Fig. 106). Other mosaic elements in this movement are the splashes of colour created by the organization of chord formations within instrumental groups, and the gentle bell-sounds of the piano high up against a dialogue of trumpet and clarinet. The Gregorian Te Deum penetrates the texture at many points. Where this first movement tends to treat the instruments in concertante groups, the Norwich piece is much more dense in texture. The sectional division between instrumental groups is broken down

Fig. 106 The first movement of *Laudes*

and all the instruments tend to contribute to a general massive texture in which there are strong dynamic conflicts culminating in a searing crescendo in the last seven bars. This sense of conclusion is interesting. In the first movement a culminating was achieved quite differently by massing the three divisions into opposed chordal groups. Consistent with its subject, the King's movement has predominantly gentle lines—in the first movement they tend to be upward moving, in the second angular. The instruments play independently of one another, so that the total effect is of a shimmering interplay of flickering sounds above which, in isolation, but comparable delicacy, the trumpet plays its distant Te Deum. In the Taizé movement, the tough chordal opening for the piano shows the new virtuosic spirit of this last movement. The entry of the instruments is a sheen of single notes which at bar 21 changes to a unity—a single melodic line changing in tone colour. Later there is a return to the concertante chordal structures of the first movement and a hint of the Te Deum melody, but it is with the unity of the single melodic line that the work ends (Fig. 107).

All these musical features—the use of opposing, clearly-defined instrumental groups, the use of fragmented figures of widely disparate rhythm, and the capacity for long unbroken lines—have a bearing on the music which was to follow. The skilful control of melodic lines had in fact long been one of Butterley's skills. Earlier pieces, such as the *Arioso* for the piano (1960) and the still impressive *Canticle of David* for string orchestra (1959) show his capacity for writing flexible, extended lines which are beautifully poised (Fig. 108).

If *Laudes* established Butterley's reputation as a composer, it also less fortunately supplied him with a label. He became regarded as a man who lived, to use his own words, 'in the rosy glow of light diffused through stained glass', perhaps with the further suggestion that this is an un-Australian attitude. It is true that many of his best works have a mystical basis, but on a broader view it will be seen that they are also very much concerned with people, both with the composer's personal relations with people, and with practical music-making. They are not usually the meditations of a recluse.

Most, if not all, of Butterley's mature works have used some form of serial technique. *Laudes* uses small note-cells, but in the works which follow twelve-note rows appear, often arranged in diatonic groupings, as in *Canticle of the Sun* and *The White-throated Warbler* (both of 1965). *Canticle of the Sun* was written for amateur groups, and its treatment of two large groups of players offset by an improvising group of soloists is rather heavy-handed. On the other hand, *The White-throated Warbler* for sopranino recorder and harpsichord is one of the most successful of Australian miniatures.

Since most contemporary music seems to be written in response to specific commissions, the output of Australian composers has been coloured quite considerably by the demand for certain kinds of music. For instance, wind quintets figure in the lists of most of them in one form or another, largely because Sydney and Adelaide both have such groups for which the repertoire is limited. Demand may also have something to do with the large number of Australian string quartets, Butterley's contribution to the medium being a notable one. In form and content this, his first string quartet (1965), derives from a mystical poem by Henry Vaughan called 'The Revival'. It contains the words:

Unfold, unfold! Take in his light
Who makes thy cares more short than night.

The two movements are complementary, and the work has to do with kinds of musical growth. The opening expands in the palpitating manner of something about to burst into leaf. The chordal passages in both movements seem to open and close according to their increasing or retracting note-values. The second movement begins with a great flourish—not a forward movement, but an arrival, a blossoming. It is an extension of the Stravinskian technique of multiple *ostinato* figures, each part independent except in relation to the cello. The time-values of the chordal passages in this movement show a recession and then irregularity. The movement is arranged

Fig. 107 From *Laudes*, the conclusion

in accordance with four set recurring tempos. This is a rewarding and original work, very characteristic of its composer.

In the following year (1966) Butterley composed the work by which he is best known—*In the Head the Fire*. It was commissioned by the Australian Broadcasting Commission, and won the Italia Prize for a composition designed exclusively for radio. In this work Butterley was able to turn to artistic advantage his experience

Fig. 108 From *Arioso*

of broadcasting techniques, and in so doing to start a new line of investigation in his own music. *In the Head the Fire* is one of Butterley's longer works, and its creation involved performers up and down Australia and a large number of individual recordings had to be made and collated to produce the final tape which was to be the definitive performance of the work. The words come from a wide variety of sources —the Dead Sea Scrolls, the Mass, Latin, Irish and Hebrew texts. Music for separate groups of instruments and vocal ensembles is recorded and superimposed. Certain sounds are not naturally obtainable—for instance the sound of handbells without their attack, and in *The War of the Sons of Light and Darkness*, a section for three trumpets is recorded three times and the recordings are superimposed. One impressive feature of this work is its assurance. With all the vast possibilities which such a medium offers, there is never any suggestion of loss of control or diffusion of effort. It marks the beginning in Butterley's work of an interest in collage techniques which as yet shows no signs of exhaustion. The central part of the work is *The War of the Sons of Light and Darkness*, which is full of apocalyptic splendours (including the terrifying sounds of the Jewish shofar) showing an unexpected animation and violence quite new to the composer's music. *In the Head the Fire* is the nearest thing to a great oratorio that Australian music has to offer.

There are a few minor but interesting ventures in the immediate wake of *In the Head the Fire*. One was the Variations for wind quintet, piano and recorded piano, a rather bleak work in fifteen short movements which are commentaries on an exposition rather than variations on a theme. Each section has its own instrumentation, and the recorded piano is used in various ways. At its first appearance it plays an *ostinato*, elsewhere it has chords which are played backwards at half-speed; and flourishes for the recorded piano are set against flourishes for the live piano. The 'Four Latin Poems of Spring' entitled *Carmina* for mezzo soprano and wind quintet reflect the composer's delight in medieval music, and also no doubt in twentieth-century neo-medievalists. The songs each have their distinctive techniques which we have seen at work in other contexts. The first and last movements are related; there is some vigorous and graphic writing in the second song ('The Little Dog'), while the third ('The Salmon') has a strongly declaimed chant-like line with the instruments proceeding for the most part in independent flourishes.

But the major work of 1968 had been planned for some time, and as Butterley's first major orchestral work it occupies a very special place in his output. This is the *Meditations of Thomas Traherne*. Each of its five movements contains a quotation from Traherne's prose work, *Centuries of Meditation*. Nigel Butterley says of this writer: 'Thomas Traherne's particular attribute is his ability to see childhood in a fresh sort of way, to experience afresh the idea of a child coming into the world and seeing everything new'.[1] The movements are continuous, but the repeated notes with which the first movement starts form, one way and another, an introduction to each of the five movements. The tendency towards slow, tentative starts may almost seem a mannerism of Butterley's but here at least it is fully justified by the interest which is to be awakened. Throughout the work the orchestra tends to be divided into concertante choruses playing frequently as individual groups. A special feature of the scoring here is the use of an exquisitely shrill chorus of recorders, which had shown their effectiveness in an earlier work, *Music for Sunrise* (1967). From time to time the work contains short instrumental solos which are of a strikingly tonal caste, though here the various elements of style are convincingly assimilated.

This is particularly evident in a string phrase in the second movement, 'The corn was orient and immortal wheat which never should be reaped nor was ever sown', where it has an element of timelessness which is very precise. Features which appeared fragmented in the first movement take on a new and glowing richness in this movement, while the massive *fortissimo* with metallic percussion figurations is one of the major climaxes of the work. In the third movement, 'The world is a mirror of infinite beauty, yet no man sees it', similar techniques prevail, but at first the textures are veiled, the melodic lines as empty as the cor anglais solo in *Tristan*. The element of recapitulation in this movement emphasizes its central position and its 'mirror' quality. The fourth movement is massive and exciting. Many of the melodic phrases which have appeared in the previous movements reappear here, and Butterley's skill in devising long, strong lines comes into play again. The orchestra divides itself into masses of sound moving independently of other masses and combining in a tumult of energy. The movement bears the quotation: 'You never enjoy the world aright till the sea itself floweth in your veins, till you are clothed with the heavens and crowned with the stars'. The satisfying intensity of this movement marks it as a great achievement for its composer. After this the last movement, on the theme of eternity, is very simply stated.

1968 also saw the creation of a short and interesting work for a large wind and brass ensemble called *Pentad*. Five clearly-defined themes are stated, and each is repeated five times. The order of the statements, however, varies each time and their behaviour also varies. While one theme remains fairly constant in its length and character, another progressively expands, while another steadily contracts; the other two vary particularly in their last statements, which is in one case shorter, in the other longer. Both the idea and its execution are satisfying and readily comprehensible. *Refractions* (1969) for wind quintet and 28 stringed instruments is another work built to an abstract design. The strings play in blocks of sound throughout and the wind instruments filter through them like the patterns of light seen through a prism. The idea is imaginative, the musical results somewhat limited.

Explorations for piano and orchestra was written for the Captain Cook Bi-Centenary Celebrations in 1970, and uses a tone-row derived from Ian Farr's Cello Sonata. There are fifteen continuous movements, the first three of which may be regarded as points of departure for the rest of the work. They are plainly discernible areas—the first characterized by the massive movement of sustained wind sounds broken up by percussion, the rest by a huge span of subtly inflected piano chords. Then comes a much more fragmented section and from here the various explorations branch out. Among these the listener will readily recall the solo passage for timpani and the wonderful haze of sound created by the divided strings in the thirteenth section. At the very end, the piano is given a statement in two isolated lines, related to its earlier chordal sections and stretching out seemingly to eternity.

Two works which may be considered together are the piano piece, *Letter from Hardy's Bay* (1971), and the recent orchestral work, *Fire in the Heavens* (1973). In the piano work (its title being a place closely associated for Butterley with his compositions) the instrument is 'prepared' by the insertion of metal bolts between the strings to produce a special sonority from a gong-like chord which plays an obsessive, structural role in the piece. The writing is not virtuosic, but is concerned with a structure based on certain sonorities: an extension of the tonal possibilities of the piano as we are used to it. The piece employs a very direct and simple form of notation.

The use of note-heads and spatial indication of time-values together with a wide degree of dynamic variation gives a very direct visual form to the passages in single notes, which stand out against passages of sharp chords or tone-clusters or bravura passages. This is a very personal work with a great range of emotion (Fig. 109).

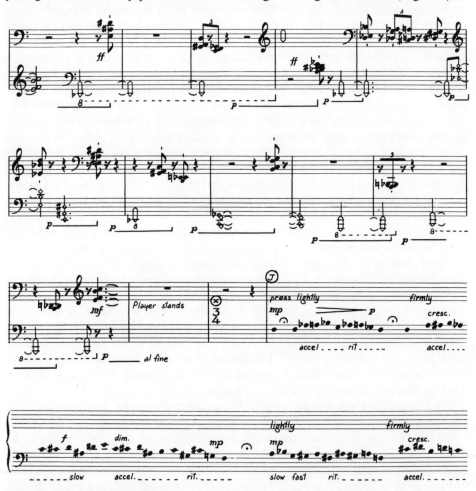

Fig. 109 From *Letter from Hardy's Bay*

Butterley himself suggests that *Fire in the Heavens* is an extrovert companion-piece to *Letter from Hardy's Bay*. It is a work of comparable length, but this time for a large orchestra. Composed to celebrate the opening of the Sydney Opera House, it is an exuberant work which revels in the rich tone-qualities of a virtuoso symphony orchestra. The first performance was given by the Cleveland Orchestra under the direction of Lorin Maazel. The disposition of the music is rather more classical than one might expect. Themes are proposed, developed and recapitulated. The piece begins vigorously and has a dynamic and abrupt ending. This in itself creates the strong impression that its approximately nine-minute duration is packed with incident. And this is assisted by memorable splashes of colour, such as the brass flourishes early on, and the luscious passage for the divided strings towards the end. Such elements of symmetry and sound make for comfortable listening.

Between these two companion-pieces are two others which, though diverse and even surprising in character, are evidence of Butterley's continuing interest in collage techniques. One is the witty and ingenious melange of light classical music for Barry Humphrey's *First Day Covers*, and a more serious application of the same idea in a work entitled *The Four Elements*, now in process of revision, in which each of the four movements borrows music from an ancient source: *Earth* employs the Sanctus from the *Missa cum jubilo*, *Air* uses six love songs, *Fire* is based on 'L'homme armé', and *Water* on the Volga Boat Song.

The key-works of Butterley's output up to the present and after *Laudes* must be regarded as *In the Head the Fire*, *The Meditations of Thomas Traherne* and *Explorations*. Indeed, they may well be regarded as a trilogy. Alongside these we can set some shorter works which are more like intimate communications—the First String Quartet, the *Letter from Hardy's Bay* and *Fire in the Heavens*. Whatever may follow we may be sure that in Butterley Australia has found one of its most distinct voices.

Note

1. 'Butterley on Butterley', *Music Now*, i, 1, (Feb. 1969).

Publishers

J. Albert & Son

Bibliography

Covell, Roger. *Australia's Music: Themes of a New Society*. Sun Books, Melbourne, 1967, pp. 224–32.
Peart, Donald R. 'Some Recent Developments in Australian Composition', *Composer*, xix (1966), p. 73f.
'The Australian Avant-Garde', *Proceedings of the Royal Musical Association*, xciii (1967), pp. 1–9.
Music Now, i (1969), p. 29f.
Murdoch, James. *Australia's Contemporary Composers*. Macmillan, Melbourne, 1972.

List of Works

Ballet Music
The Tell-tale Heart (1964)

For Radio
In the Head the Fire tableau for broadcasting for narrator, soloists, chor wind ensemble perc pf org and electronic tapes (1966) [Interaction music with painter (1967)]

Orchestral Music
Canticle of David for str orch (1959)
Canticle of the Sun for wind ensemble (1965)
Meditations of Thomas Traherne (1968)
Violin Concerto (1968)
Pentad for 17 wind instruments (1968)
Explorations for piano and orchestra (1970)
First Day Covers for orchestra and speakers [with Barry Humphries] (1972)
The Four Elements for massed school orchestras (1971) [also for normal orchestra 1974]
Fire in the Heavens for orchestra (1973)

Chamber Music
Sonatina for oboe and piano
Diversion for brass quintet (1958)
Laudes for fl (a-fl) cl (bass cl) tpt hn v va vc and pf (1963)
String Quartet (1965)
The White-throated Warbler for rec and hchd (1965)
Variations for fl ob cl bn hn pf and recorded pf (1967)
Carmina—Four Latin Poems of Spring for voice and wind quintet (1968)
Mini-music for ob hn and db bass (1969)
Refractions for wind quintet and 28 stringed instruments (1969)
Voices for wind quintet (1971)
Second String Quartet (1975)
Sometimes with One I Love song cycle for sop bar speaker and six instruments (1975)

Water-shore for four speaking voices, flute, percussion and piano (1976)

Keyboard Music
Arioso, Toccata (1960)
Comment on a Popular Song (1960)
Sonorities for carillon (1962)
Piano Games (1970)
Letter from Hardy's Bay for piano (1971)

Vocal Music
Six Blake Songs (1955/6)
Child in Nature for sop and pf (1957)
Joseph and Mary carol for sop and fl (1959)
Christus petra for unacc. ten (1962)
Carmina for voice and wind quintet (1968)
Music for Man of Mode two solo songs, words by Etheridge (1971)

Choral Music
Anthem for a Dedication SATB (1960)
Prayer during Sickness SATB (1960)
Psalm 100 SATB (1961)
What Shall I Render to the Lord SATB (1965)

School Music
Music for Sunrise rec and perc (1967)

Discography

Five Blake Songs (1955). James Christiansen (baritone), Nigel Butterley (piano).
Brolga disc BXM-09
Laudes (1963) [15′42″]. (i) 'The Basilica of Sant' Apollinare Nuovo, Ravenna'—5′35″; (ii) 'The Apse, Norwich Cathedral'—2′37″; (iii) 'King's College Chapel, Cambridge'—3′54″; (iv) 'The Church of Reconciliation, Burgundy'—3′42″. William Frater (piccolo/flute/alto flute), Anne Menzies (clarinet/bass clarinet), John Robertson (trumpet), Douglas Trengove (horn), Donald Hazlewood (violin), Ronald Cragg (viola), Gregory Elmaloglou (cello), Richard Meale (piano), Nigel Butterley (conductor). Albert. 19 May 1965.
World Record Club disc A/602
The White-throated Warbler (1965). Carl Dolmetsch (sopranino recorder), Joseph Saxby (harpsichord). Albert. 7 Apr. 1965.   *ABC tape*
String Quartet (1965) [12′59″]. Austral String Quartet: Donald Hazlewood, Ronald Ryder (violins), Ronald Cragg (viola), Gregory Elmaloglou (cello). 15 Dec. 1968.   *ABC recording RRCS/126*
Prayer During Sickness (1966) [2′42″]. Adelaide Singers (Patrick Thomas, conductor). Albert. 1967/68.
ABC recording RRC/65
In the Head the Fire (1966) [28′22″]. Alexander Archdale (speaker), John Brosnan (baritone), David Galliver (tenor). Michael Deutsch (cantor and shofar); Adelaide Singers, members of Sydney and South Australian Symphony Orchestras (John Hopkins, conductor). Albert. 1966.
World Record Club disc S/2495

Music for Sunrise (1967) [5'15"]. Students from Methodist Ladies College, Perth (Verdon Williams, conductor). Albert. 12 Feb. 1970.

ABC recording RRCS/382

Meditations of Thomas Traherne (1968) [18'22"]. Beecroft Children's Recorder Group, Sydney Symphony Orchestra (Moshe Atzmon, conductor). Albert. 10 July 1968.   *ABC recording RRCS/135*

Pentad (1969) [9'15"]. Woodwind and brass of Sydney Symphony Orchestra (Moshe Atzmon, conductor). Albert. 29 Mar. 1969.   *ABC disc RRCS/135*

Refractions (1969) [9'35"]. Sydney Symphony Orchestra (John Hopkins, conductor). Albert. 20 Jan. 1970.   *ABC recording RRCS/382*

Variations (1969) [20'40"]. Joyce Hutchinson (piano), Neville Amadio (flute), Guy Henderson (oboe), Donald Westlake (clarinet), Clarence Mellor (horn), John Cran (bassoon), Nigel Butterley (recorded piano). Albert. 4 June 1969.

Philips disc 6508001

Explorations for piano and orchestra (1970) [26'30"]. Ian Farr (piano), Sydney Symphony Orchestra (Moshe Atzmon, conductor). Albert. 22 May 1970.

Festival disc SFC 800/19

Letter from Hardy's Bay (1971) [12'50"]. David Bollard (piano). Albert. 16 July 1971.

Festival disc SFC 800/25

Voices (1971) [12'29"]. Adelaide Wind Quintet: David Cubbin (flute), Jiri Tancibudek (oboe), Gabor Reeves (clarinet), Patrick Brislan (horn), Thomas Wightman (bassoon). Albert. 1971.

HMV disc OASD/7565

First Day Covers: A Philharmonic Philatelia (1972). Barry Humphries as Mrs Edna Everedge; Sydney Symphony Orchestra (John Hopkins, conductor). Albert. Mar. 1972.   *Phonogram disc*

Barry Conyngham

(*b*. 1944)

David Symons

Barry Conyngham is a significant representative of the youngest generation of composers considered in this book. Born in Sydney in 1944, Conyngham's early musical interest was in the field of jazz. He had begun piano lessons early: during his secondary and university undergraduate years he gained professional engagements as a jazz pianist and leader of his own group. His academic training in music began relatively late—in 1965 at the University of Sydney, where Peter Sculthorpe was his composition teacher. He also studied composition privately with Raymond Hanson and Richard Meale during this period.

Conyngham has withdrawn his earliest compositions, written up to 1967. These consist of piano and chamber works in a neo-tonal idiom, some reflecting his early interest in jazz. The first work he now acknowledges is the unaccompanied choral piece *Farben*, completed while he was still a student, early in 1968. *Farben* ('Colours') is written for two choruses which are directed to be placed as far apart on stage as possible. The text consists simply of the German words for various colours: its discontinuous, non-narrative quality, as well as the choice of a foreign language, emphasize the fact that the composer was interested in the words from a musical, rather than a literary, standpoint. The various colours have their musical parallel in the work's seven sections of differing tempi and textures.

In *Farben* the general direction that Conyngham's style has taken, at any rate up to the time of writing this chapter, is firmly indicated. Some basic features of this style may now perhaps be enumerated.

Firstly, it combined both tonal/melodic material and the various elements of the 'music of textures' of European composers such as Ligeti, Xenakis and the 'Polish school' of the sixties: tone clusters and bands of varying densities, unusual timbres and a wide range of indefinite pitched sounds. Although Conyngham's music has shown an increasingly individual absorption of these technical and stylistic sources (and also incorporated others as we shall see later), it is probable that the most immediate influence at the outset was the music of his teacher Sculthorpe who, working at different times in either a tonal/melodic or a 'texture music' idiom, was also combining these elements in works such as *Sun Music IV* written shortly before Conyngham's first acknowledged pieces.

Secondly, the music is based on essentially clear, mostly sectional, forms (another quality he shares with Sculthorpe). He has so far avoided both the extremes of serial or stochastic methods and—notwithstanding the frequent use of 'ad lib.' and improvisatory passages, and occasional experiments with open forms—total indeterminacy. Formal simplicity and clarity are, however, linked to an increasing subtlety and sensitivity in the interrelating of material and the linking of sections. In nearly every work the form is connected to an extramusical idea inherent in the title or associated programme. Although there are specifically literary associations in a few works, Conyngham has, except for the theatre avoided the setting of a conventional text and has mostly confined himself to instrumental media and occasionally to an instrumental treatment of voices.

Finally, most works involve multiple groups of instruments or voices, spatially separated and/or texturally contrasted, while a number of pieces contain concertante elements.

The first blossoming of the composer's musical personality is seen in three instrumental pieces: *Crisis: Thoughts in a City* (1968) for two string orchestras and percussion; *Five Windows* (1969) for orchestra; and *Three* (1969) for string quartet and two percussionists. In *Crisis*, a fairly short single movement piece, the basic idea is the confrontation of material representing the sounds of a city with those representing the thoughts of an individual. The explosive clusters and melodic fragments in the first orchestra and a pianissimo polyphony of long notes in the second, respectively express these two elements, while the percussion adds a third strand of ideas which the composer has described as a 'stimulant' to the other two. The opening gesture— an arresting figure made up of chromatically adjacent notes—acts as a *ritornello*— or obsessively recurring thought—throughout. The contrasting material of the two orchestras and percussion is varied and gradually blended into a unity, so that the dramatic progress of the work is very clearly that from confrontation to reconciliation. The form is lucid, if perhaps at this stage somewhat lacking in sophistication.

The idea behind *Crisis* implies development: that underlying *Five Windows*, Conyngham's first major work, is much more static and frankly impressionist in character. The title refers in the first instance to William Blake's poem *Europe— A Prophecy*:

Five Windows light the cavern'd Man; thro' one he breathes the air;
Thro' one hears music of the spheres; thro' one the Eternal Vine
Flourishes that he may receive the grapes; thro' one can look
And see small portions of the Eternal World that ever groweth;
Thro' one himself pass out what time he please, but he will not.

The inspiration for Conyngham, however, was the misquoting of this poem by Gully Jimson, the chief character in Joyce Cary's novel *The Horse's Mouth*, who, the composer says, 'has his own mad way of interpreting literature'. Jimson omits the third and the fifth of the 'windows' in his quotation:[1] however, Conyngham uses the 'five' of the title as the basis for a work in five sections, although there is no direct programmatic link between any particular section and any particular part of the poem. We are left, therefore, with a work which operates according to its own formal logic, but reflects the composer's personal response to the poem's imagery —via the vibrantly human, if eccentric, spirit of Jimson rather than the more austere, mystic Blake. The overall form, as in *Crisis*, is basically clear and has quite traditional qualities, especially the fairly obvious recapitulation of material in the closing stages of both works. The sections of *Five Windows* are separated by low piano clusters or gong strokes. The orchestral writing is colourful, and although greater subtlety in the handling of both form and orchestration has been achieved in subsequent works, *Five Windows* still stands as a notable success and is a work of considerable beauty and sensitivity.

Three, Conyngham's next work, is the first of a number of pieces with a purely numerical title and association, in which the number refers directly to formal elements, both spatial and temporal. Here there are three instrumental groups: a string quartet placed on stage, and two percussionists performing on groups of instruments respectively placed in the left and right hand corners of the hall, behind the audience. The piece is dedicated to Peter Sculthorpe: however, although there are fairly direct Sculthorpian associations in the writing for the string quartet (sometimes recalling that composer's own quartets and *Irkanda* pieces), the percussion writing seems more purely characteristic of Conyngham, and its sophistication and virtuosity may reflect indirectly the composer's early jazz associations.

Also belonging to this first period in style is the theatre piece *Edward John Eyre*, the plot of which deals with the tragic journey by the explorer across the Nullarbor Plain in 1841. The work has existed in various versions and, while the final one was not completed until 1973, much of its composition took place in 1969 and firmly links it stylistically to the works already considered. Inspired by Geoffrey Dutton's book *The Hero as Murderer*, it began as the setting of a series of poems by Meredith Oakes for alto voice and orchestra. For its première as a theatre work in 1971, a chorus and mimed action was included. In the revised (1973) version, a narrator's part has been added, quoting extracts from Eyre's journal. The original poems are sung in this version by soprano (called 'the Society Lady'), also ('the Observer') and tenor (Eyre). Despite the fact that *Eyre* is Conyngham's first extended work— and his first for theatre—it should not, perhaps, be singled out as one of his best achievements, despite many effective passages. The polyglot juxtaposition of narration, action, lyrical vocal writing and mainly textural material for chorus and orchestra seems not to have formed a compelling unity—which may be due, in part, to the work's piecemeal composition.

Late in 1969 Conyngham received a Churchill Fellowship for six months study with the Japanese composer Toru Takemitsu in Tokyo. Apart from music commissioned earlier for a film called *Horizon*, shown at the Australian pavilion of Expo '70 in Osaka, two works are products of this period: *Ice Carving* (1970) for amplified solo violin and four string orchestras; and *Water . . . Footsteps . . . Time . . .* (1970–71) for amplified solo instruments (piano, harp, electric guitar and tam tam) and orchestra (divided into two smaller orchestras).

Ice Carving recalls Conyngham's structural methods in *Crisis* in that a programmatic idea is directly—and graphically—realized in the work's overall shape. The inspiration was the activity of people fashioning various figures from blocks of ice brought for the purpose (during summer!) to the gardens of the Imperial Palace in Tokyo. The solo violin part, aggressive at first, parallels the chipping or carving action of these amateur sculptors, while the material for the four string groups, initially block-like and immobile, may be thought of as reflecting the character of ice. Gradually motivic life emerges in the string groups and rises to a maximum of polyphonic density, illustrating the completed shapes fashioned out of the ice. The next stage is reached when the violin solo part ceases, and the string orchestra shapes gradually decay into *glissandi* and sounds of indefinite pitch, just as the ice sculptures melt in the afternoon sun. Finally, after a cadenza, the solo violin lyrically and nostalgically reminisces on the material of the central section, perhaps suggesting the memories of the sculptors in the face of their melted creations (the strings are now almost totally static and cloudlike in texture). This work is one of considerable sensuous beauty as well as structural firmness. In addition, there is a new melodic and textural sensitivity and elegant gentleness in places which already reveals the response of the composer to the qualities of Japanese music and the influence of Takemitsu in particular.

Such influence is more pronounced in the major work of this period, *Water . . . Footsteps . . . Time . . .* Here the music springs once again from an essentially static impressionist inspiration: compared with *Five Windows*, however, the work shows a considerable advance in subtlety and sophistication, both in the deployment of material and the handling of orchestral colour. There are four main sections—dominated respectively by the solo piano, harp, guitar and tam tam—and separated by brief *ritornello*-like orchestral episodes. Conyngham has described this work as 'a personal reflection on Japan' but has denied any specific programme. The title simply refers to images in the Japanese environment which stimulated the composer's imagination. This work is strongly reminiscent of Takemitsu's *November Steps* in which the traditional Japanese biwa (a lute) and shakuhachi (an end blown flute) provide relatively dynamic concertante figuration against a delicately textured orchestral accompaniment. Conyngham's treatment of soloists and orchestra is basically similar—indeed the guitar and harp writing in particular seem to evoke the sounds of the Japanese koto and biwa or shamisen—but there is no charge of blatant imitation implied here. As with the pervading influence of Sculthorpe (less obvious in later works) Conyngham has managed to make these new elements essentially his own, and this work is undoubtedly one of his major achievements so far.

A minor by-product of *Water . . . Footsteps . . . Time . . .* was the piano piece *Ends* (1970) based on fragments from the larger piece, organized in an open form manner somewhat akin to Stockhausen's *Klavierstück XI*.

The period following Conyngham's return to Australia saw the composition of two more works with numerical titles: *Five* (1971) for wind quintet; and *Six* (1971) for six solo percussionists (playing at various times, a total of eleven instruments or groups of instruments) accompanied in one version by orchestral wind and percussion and in another by string orchestra in six parts. The titles of these pieces refer not only to the number of performers but also to the sectional structures. Of the two works *Six* appears to be the more solid musical achievement, but the most noticeable innovation in both is the visual aspect of performers changing position for different sections of the works—in the case of *Five*, these positions are arranged throughout the concert hall. In addition, *Five* contains the highest degree of performance freedom and improvisation so far found in Conyngham's music: however, it is not an open-form piece like *Ends*, but has a firm, clear and even symmetrical overall arrangement of material in its five movements.

It is possible to characterize the period after 1971 as one relatively dominated by technical experimentation. One work, however, refers back to earlier programmatic pieces—namely *Voss* (1972), a large, six-movement composition for solo female voice (textless), piano, six other solo instruments and percussion (all amplified), choir (textless) and orchestra (again divided into two smaller orchestras). This is Conyngham's longest and biggest orchestral work so far and is extremely rich and complex both in its instrumentation and structural details. However, its overall organization is clear and, once again, directly springs from a programme—in this case based on Patrick White's novel of the same name. It is the relationship between the chief characters—Voss, the German explorer (a fictional version of Ludwig Leichhardt) and Laura Trevelyan, the product of fashionable Sydney colonial society which provides the major theme of the novel and is mirrored in the basic structure of Conyngham's work. The solo piano and female voice represent Voss and Laura respectively, each part being associated with accompanying textures suggestive of the characters' respective emotional and/or physical environments. The first movement reflects the early meeting of Voss and Laura, their initial lack of rapport and even antipathy—and is musically an exposition of the work's basic material. The inner movements are symmetrically arranged: the second and fifth, associated with Voss and the desert crossing, are relatively densely scored, predominantly 'texture' movements; while the third and fourth (from which Conyngham has extracted a chamber work entitled *From Voss*) are sparser movements of both lyrical and dramatic intensity, reflecting Laura's emotional development in her totally alien physical environment to that of Voss. In the final movement there is a blending together of material from previous movements, representing the spiritual unity between Voss and Laura at the end of the novel. Musically, the development of material from a state of confrontation and contrast to eventual blending and unity is a procedure which Conyngham has explored before: in *Voss* it is handled with great subtlety and poetry. The work stands as perhaps the major landmark in this period of Conyngham's career, summing up and synthesizing many essential features of earlier works.

Late in 1972 Conyngham took up a Harkness Fellowship for two years study in the United States. During 1973 he produced two works which have shown a particular interest in relatively technological procedures. *Playback* is written for solo double bass with four-channel sound mixer and tape recorder. The piece is conceived quadrophonically (although a stereophonic version is also available). Despite the electronic ramifications, the form remains clear and simple. There are four sections of material for the soloist, recorded during performance. In the second, third and fourth sections this is combined, via tape playback, with the material heard in the previous section(s) so that in the final one the material of the entire piece is superimposed. At the end of each section the tape is rewound audibly (to prepare for recording the next section). Here is the *ritornello* device noted in a number of earlier works: but it is further integrated thematically, as the sound is mimicked by the soloist at various points throughout the work.

The second piece composed in the United States, *Snowflake*, is formally much more complex. It is written for one performer playing piano, harpsichord, celeste and electric piano. The piece consists of 144 fragments (36 per instrument) arranged in a crystalline or 'snowflake' pattern on each page. Conyngham has made use of a computer to decide the arrangement of these fragments according to their quality of 'melting in' with adjacent fragments. A performance may consist of all or some of the fragments. It may begin with any fragment, after which the sequence is determined by the player's choice of one of the two or three possible directions from each fragment to an adjacent one (including what the composer calls 'jump fragments', through which the performer may move from instrument to instrument). The formal focus is thus upon the continuity of related material rather than on an overall sectional scheme (although a free one is built in to every realization of the score in performance). This is only the second time Conyngham has employed an open form (albeit a very controlled one here): the seeds of his approach to it, however, are apparent in other works where there has been increasing attention to this 'melting in' factor in the linking of sections.

Thus concludes this necessarily brief account of Barry Conyngham's work up to the end of 1973[2]—a period which, although without (yet) the wisdom of hindsight, one may label the composer's early maturity. His work during this time has been full of interest and evidence of an intensely sensitive musical mind. His study, in the United States, of electronic music and, more especially, computer techniques in composition[3] have already suggested significant new directions for his own musical development—the later fruits of which will no doubt be the subject of critical comment in future articles and surveys of Australian musical composition.

Notes

1. Jimson's version reads: 'Five Windows light the cavern'd Man; thro' one he breathes the air; Thro' one hears music of the spheres; thro' one can look And see small portions of the Eternal World that ever groweth'.
2. Since the writing of this chapter, Conyngham has completed further compositions, notably the orchestral work *Without Gesture* (1973) and the music theatre piece *Ned Mark II* (1975–76) which is yet another variation on the 'opera-within-an-opera' idea, in this case involving an android as the 'actor/singer' who plays the part of Ned (Kelly). Both these works may be said to combine certain of the methods and approaches of the pieces written in the U.S.A. with those of the earlier orchestral compositions.
3. Conyngham subsequently spent a year (from August 1974) studying with a group specializing in computer techniques at Marseilles. He then returned to Australia to take up a lectureship in composition at the University of Melbourne at the beginning of 1976.

List of Works

Farben for double chorus unaccompanied (1968)
Crisis: Thoughts in a City for two string orchestras and percussion (1968)
Five Windows for orchestra (1969)
Three for string quartet and two percussionists (1969)
Music for Expo '70 film *Horizon*—multi-track tape collage (1970)
Ice Carving for violin (preferably amplified) and four string orchestras (1970)
Water ... Footsteps ... Time ... for piano, harp, electric guitar, tam tam (all amplified) and orchestra (1970–71)
Ends for piano (1970)
Edward John Eyre—theatre piece (1969–71; revised version 1973)
Five for wind quintet (1971)
Six for six solo percussionists with orchestral wind and percussion (version I) or strings (version II) (1971)
Voss for vocal and instrumental soli (amplified), choir and orchestra (1972)
From Voss for female voice, harp and percussion (1972)
Playback for solo double bass with 4-track mixer and 4-track tape (1973)
Snowflake for keyboard solo (piano, harpsichord, celeste and electric piano) (1973)
Without Gesture for orchestra (1973)
Mirror Images for four actors (mimers), alto saxophone, cello, double bass and percussion (1975)
Ned Mark II—music theatre piece in two sections (1975–76)

Discography

Farben (1968) [7'28"]. Adelaide Singers (Patrick Thomas, conductor). 25 July 1969.
ABC recording RRCS/384

Crisis: Thoughts in a City (1968) [6'53"]. Strings and percussion of the West Australian Symphony Orchestra (John Hopkins, conductor). Feb. 1969.
ABC recording RRCS/134
Five Windows (1969) [17'03"]. Sydney Symphony Orchestra (John Hopkins, conductor). 30 Jan. 1970.
ABC recording RRCS/384
Water ... Footsteps ... Time ... (1970–71) [19'30"]. Melbourne Symphony Orchestra (John Hopkins, conductor). Universal. 14 Apr. 1971.
Festival disc SFC 800/27
Three (1971) [20'05"]. Barry Heywood, Ian Bloxam (percussion); Austral String Quartet: Donald Hazlewood, Ronald Ryder (violins), Ronald Cragg (viola), Gregory Elmaloglou (cello). Universal. 5 Dec. 1970.
ABC recording RRCS/1468

Ian Cugley
(*b.* 1945)

Melvyn Cann

Ian Robert Cugley was born in Melbourne in 1945. His family later moved to Sydney, where he completed his schooling. He graduated in music from the University of Sydney in 1966, and for a while taught music in high school. In 1967 he became Lecturer-in-charge of Music at the University of Tasmania.

Cugley first achieved prominence in 1967 with a performance of his *Prelude* for orchestra in the Australian Broadcasting Commission's Promenade Concert series in Sydney that year, since when two of his orchestral works, (*Pan, the Lake* and *Prelude* for orchestra), have been released on a commercial recording. Like other young Australian composers Cugley has had a good share of support through grant, commission and fellowship.

Undergraduate years gave Cugley a thorough background in European musical tradition. He developed a special interest in the early serialists (Schoenberg, Webern, and Berg) and in Pierre Boulez. His interest is not uncritical; and whereas aspects of instrumentation, motivic and rhythmic process, and melodic contour show a measure of the influence of these composers, Cugley rejects many of their fundamental structural devices. The reasons help to chart the course of Cugley's own development.

His general objection is that the devices are not aurally perspicuous.[1] In Cugley's view, for example, the transformations of a given twelve-note row, as systematically employed in a work typical of the serialists, cannot be perceived as related by the operations of retrogression, inversion, and transposition which determine them. He is not prepared, therefore, to admit such applications of these operations as meaningful elements of musical language.

Behind this view lie the beliefs that music is a language of the emotions; that meaningful transformations of musical material are those, and only those, which contribute to control of emotional response; and that emotional response can be controlled only through perspicuous transformations.

It is not to the point here to enter dispute over the philosophical issues raised by this theory; which, for all its intuitive appeal, is difficult to sustain. Rather, the point is to see how this general philosophy determines Cugley's style; and where that philosophy places him relative to other composers. To this end two aspects of aural perspicuity need attention.

Aural perspicuity is not to be confused with ease, or immediacy, of comprehension. One of Cugley's aims is to write music which operates at more than one level, yielding more to the listener as aural comprehension deepens. His criticism of the long-note style of Penderecki, as it has been taken up by Sculthorpe in his various Sun Musics, is that it produces, first and foremost, *sound* music; capable of great immediacy, but yielding little to further hearing. The solution is to devise structures which are perspicuous, but not immediately so. Particular devices used by Cugley to achieve this are: thematic, or motivic cross-reference; diminution and augmentation; tonality (not keys); rhythmic counterpoint; variation of harmonic and melodic tension.

Nor, in Cugley's view, is aural perspicuity to be regarded as a perceptual absolute; rather, it is something to be determined relative to a given musical culture. A composer wishing to maximize control of the emotional responses of a given audience will need, therefore, to draw upon the powers of aural discernment which that audience has. Cugley writes for an audience brought up in classical European tradition. This is shown by the techniques already mentioned; also, by his choice of more general forms: variation and sonata, recapitulation and coda.

What we have, then, is an outline of a thoroughly conservative compositional ideology; a fact which Cugley admits. He describes himself as a mainstream composer. It would be mistaken, however, to think that it follows that Cugley's work is not strikingly original; or that the average Euro-educated listener would immediately recognize the appeal to his existing sensibilities, and not classify Cugley as a radical. Classifications in the categories, conservative or radical, and original or unoriginal, are in fact quite independent, and Cugley's work confirms this. Since radicalism is frequently thought to serve originality, and conservatism the opposite, the point is worth noting.

We now have some conception of Cugley's objectives, and guiding philosophy. We need a closer examination of specific techniques, and an assessment of their success.

Transformations from harmony to melody, from melody to harmony, and all grades of subtle and systematic ambiguity between the two, pervade Cugley's work. In the *Prelude*, for example, the treatment of the rising augmented fourth and semitone in the first two bars is primarily harmonic (Fig. 110). However, the possibility of melodic evolution is already implicit: the notes of the chord are introduced one at a time. Evolution begins in the next bar, where the same material is found transposed up a major third (Fig. 111). The notes of this sequence are not held against one another, except for a brief clash between the D and E flat. At the end of the piece the motive returns in retrograde purely melodically on solo horn (Fig. 112): the emancipation of melody from harmony is complete.

Fig. 110 *Prelude* for orchestra, Bar 1

Fig. 111 *Prelude*, Bar 3

Fig. 112 *Prelude*, last bars

Nor is this transformational device arbitrary, and unrelated to general formal considerations. The initial harmonic treatment is taut, and serves well for the commencement of the piece. The purely melodic treatment is more relaxed (largely through the elimination of the semitone clash), and thus helps to create a cadence at the end.

This method of controlling overall form is found in other of Cugley's pieces. Perhaps the most striking example is in the *Three Pieces* for chamber orchestra. The principal material is melodic. In the third piece which is ternary in form, the first and third sections consist in a full statement of the basic melodic material on solo flute: the mood is quiet. The middle section is a more elaborate transformation of the same material, harmonically and rhythmically tense.

At the opening of the first piece, however, the melodic properties of the basic material are obscured (Fig. 113); and in such a way as to create a tension from which the whole work is generated. The C, D and E flat which in their melodic form are contemplative are given driving force by being held against one another, and by addition of the D flat in a secondary harmonic role. The loud dynamic helps.

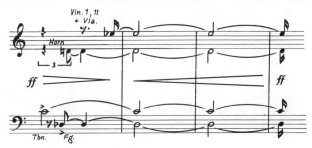

Fig. 113 *Three Pieces* for chamber orchestra, the opening of the first piece

The two solo flute passages from the same work (Figs 114 and 115) show other more subtle ways in which Cugley varies the harmonic properties of melodic material. For seven bars the notes in the two passages are the same: the durations, however, are different. The most obvious function of these differences is rhythmic. The rhythms of the second passage are gentler: by that means the ending is prepared. However, there is also an harmonic function. By using longer rests, and by compressing selected groups of notes together in time, the harmonic properties of these groups are varied. The groups, R: F, B flat and E, in the third bar, and S: A flat, G, F sharp and C, in the fifth, are examples. As a consequence of its rhythmic structure, R is emphasized as an harmonic field in Fig. 114, but lacks the cohesion to do so in Fig. 115.

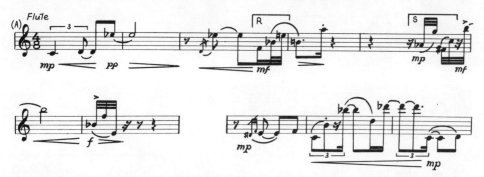

Fig. 114 The first of the solo flute passages in *Three Pieces*

Fig. 115 The second of the solo flute passages in *Three Pieces*

The transformation of S is different. In Fig. 114 S is treated as one harmonic unit; in Fig. 115 S is broken up into a three-note group S', with the C rhythmically detached so as to belong, not to S', but to the following B.

A further example of intertwining harmonic and melodic functions, beautiful for its simplicity, is in the very last bar. Consider the A flat and G (Fig. 115T). These could have been scored purely melodically, thus:

Fig. 116 Possible melodic scoring

Instead, Cugley introduces the G harmonically against the A flat, three quavers earlier. When the A flat disappears, the relationship between the two notes becomes melodic. This is not clear, however, until the last quaver. This is another example of the creation, and relaxation, of tension, by moving from harmony to melody; this time within the space of one note. More elaborate forms of the same cadence are at the end of the *Six Days of Creation*, and the *Five Variants*.

Influenced by the philosophy of Bergson, a number of composers (notably Peter Maxwell Davies, who is an influence on Cugley, and Karlheinz Stockhausen, who is not) have developed an interest in the phenomenology of time, Cugley shares this interest, and uses temporal perspective as a primary parameter in controlling emotional response. Two categories of perspective device are to be distinguished: those relating concurrent events, and those relating events at a temporal distance.

Of the first kind, note two examples from the *Prelude*. In the second bar (Fig. 117) different rates of forward movement in the 'celli and timpani create a dimension of temporal perspective: much similar things happen simultaneously at slightly different speeds, a device elaborated in subsequent bars.

Fig. 117 *Prelude* for orchestra, Bar 2

More interesting is the structural counterpoint in the first six bars. These constitute an anacrusis to the heavily scored chord in bar seven. The anacrusis is in three sections which, because of the scoring, may be regarded as three large beats. The figurations worked against these large beats increase in pace until the seventh bar, which is approached in an accelerating rhythmic frenzy. The sections (or beats) themselves, however, increase in duration: that is, sub-structure decelerates, whilst surface structures accelerate. This is bidirectional rhythmic counterpoint. Emotively, one of the most powerful moments of the *Prelude* is in a bar (41) where preparation of another frenzied climax is suddenly withdrawn, and a remote and static string chord interpolated before proceeding towards a climax which is ultimately denied. The effect would have been impossible but for the ambiguous sense of direction present since the opening bars.

Perspective devices of the second kind relate events at a temporal distance. In the *Prelude*, in each of bars 18, 22 and 23, there is a descending three-note figure consisting of two intervals of a semitone. The durations are approximately 1-1/3 beats, 1/2 beat, 4-1/2 beats. The shortest is so brief as to be almost purely ornamental, the third is ponderously melodic, and the first is ambiguous between the two (Fig. 118). The analogy with visual perspective is illuminating: it is like a sequence of camera shots of the same thing from different distances.

Fig. 118 *Prelude*, Bars 18–23

The present example is simple, effective, and easily illustrated. The same technique of repetition in different rhythmic proportions is applied, also to long sections of pieces.

These details do much less than justice to the intricacy and subtlety of Cugley's work. At every point it is striking how well the parameters of harmony, rhythm, melody and timbre are worked together in the service of overall design. Striking also is the success of the programme for controlling emotional response. Each piece has a highly individual, and memorable, emotional content; more articulate in later works like the *Aquarelles* and *The Six Days of Creation*, than in earlier works like the *Prelude* and *Pan, the Lake*.

The emotions are tragic: sometimes apocalyptic, never light-hearted. Even *The Six Days*, big with the wonder of Creation, is not exuberant. In Haydn's oratorio on the same theme, when God says, 'Let there be Light', there is a blaze of orchestral joy: mutes come off, minor becomes major, soft becomes loud. In Cugley the wonder of that moment is there, even the suggestion of C major; but introverted, very quiet, tightly strung. The *Aquarelles* are exquisite, wrought of love; but a love acquainted with grief. The more aggressively passionate pieces are somehow less successful: Wagnerian elements in the *Prelude* go largely unfulfilled. Cugley thinks of the orchestra as his métier: but his acutely sensitive perceptions seem better expressed in more intimate ensembles. Perhaps he will discover a way to use a large orchestra consonant with the emotional content he wishes to communicate; perhaps he will come to favour smaller ensembles; or perhaps these judgements are simply wrong. Regardless, it is a striking achievement, by force of an intellect guided by intense feeling, to have forged new works, highly individual in character, and compelling attention.

Note

1. The term is mine. In the account which follows, I have had to systematize elements of Cugley's thought gleaned principally from conversation, aided by some lecture notes which Cugley has prepared for teaching purposes. Were Cugley to write up his own thoughts, he would almost certainly choose other terminology, and doubtless reject some of the contentions I attribute to him as either misleading, simplistic, or both. However, I believe there is accuracy in my account sufficient for the purposes of a very general essay of this kind.

Publishers

J. Albert

Bibliography

Covell, Roger. *Australia's Music: Themes of a New Society*. Sun Books, Melbourne, 1967, pp. 233–4.
Murdoch, James. *Australia's Contemporary Composers*. Macmillan, Melbourne, 1972.

List of Works

Orchestral Music
Pan, the Lake for fl hn vc perc str (1965)
Prelude for orchestra (1967)
Three Pieces for chamber orchestra (1968)
Smaller pieces include *Little Suite* for brass (1964)
Fanfare for brass (1966)
Works for school orchestra
Fanfare (1968)
Five Variants for string orchestra (1969)

Instrumental Chamber Music
Three Fragments for fl vc and pf (1963)
Variations for fl ob and hn (1963)
Adagio for four hns (1964)
Sonata for fl va guit (fl va and harp) (1966–67)
Three Little Pieces for cl and pf (1967)
Chamber Symphony for eleven wind instruments (1971)
Sonata Movement for violin and pianoforte (1973)

Pianoforte
Aquarelles (1972)

Vocal Music
Zum for voice and chamber ensemble (1965)
The Six Days of Creation for soprano, contralto and instrumental ensemble (fl cl hn trb harp va vc)

Choral Music
Agnus Dei (1965)
Two Arabic Songs (1965)
Canticle of All Created Things (1966)
Canticle no. 2 for soli, chamber orchestra (1967)
Alma Redemptoris Mater (1967)

In Excelsis Gloria (1967)
Song of Reproaches (1967)
Psalm 42 (1967)
Sea Changes dramatic cantata

Discography

Prelude for orchestra (1967) [5′23″]. Sydney Symphony Orchestra (Joseph Post, conductor). Albert. 23 Mar. 1968.   *HMV disc OASD/7547*
Pan, the Lake (1965) [6′24″]. Sydney Symphony Orchestra (Joseph Post, conductor). Albert. 23 Mar. 1968.   *HMV disc OASD/7547*
Three Pieces for chamber orchestra (1968) [11′05″]. Tasmanian Orchestra (Patrick Thomas, conductor). Albert. 30 Aug. 1968   *ABC recording RRCS/124*
Fanfare (1968) [2′01″]. Tasmanian Orchestra (Patrick Thomas, conductor). MS. 2 May 1968.
ABC recording RRC/72

Australian Music:
A Widening Perspective

Margaret Seares

Previous chapters have examined the changing scene of Australian composition this century through the music of individual composers; the present one widens its focus to take a broader view as revealed in the works of the many composers not dealt with in earlier pages. The changed perspective allows for less detail than before, the individual profile receding in the interests of the overall view.

The tendency for Australia's composers of the early and middle years of the century to express themselves in a musical idiom largely redolent of that of the late nineteenth century is, as Roger Covell has pointed out, very much a result of the colonial and provincial attitudes current in Australian society of the time.

> It became one of the first tasks of able musicians to demonstrate that they could write fluent and grammatically acceptable music in established idioms. It was necessary that the idioms should be established in order that the demonstration should be convincing to their fellow countrymen.[1]

Some of the more talented composers living in Australia were assisted in this task by the considerable number of English composer-teachers who resided in Australia during these years, among the most prominent of whom were Fritz Hart (1874–1949) in Melbourne, and Edgar Bainton (1880–1956) in Sydney. Others felt the need of stimulus from an overseas environment and travelled to England where they enrolled in one of the teaching institutions in London and there absorbed to a greater or lesser extent the musical language of the British school of composers known as the 'English pastoralists'. Frank Hutchens (1892–1965), Lindley Evans (*b*. 1895), Roy Agnew (1893–1944), and Alexander Burnard (*b*. 1900) eventually returned to Australia where they are remembered today primarily as teachers and as composers of 'miniatures' for keyboard and for voice in something of what Covell has termed 'the overgrown pastoral style' of some of the lesser English composers.[2] Arthur Benjamin (1893–1960), who was born in Sydney, returned to Australia only briefly after his period overseas, for two years holding the position of Professor of Piano at the New South Wales State Conservatorium of Music. He then returned to London and became increasingly interested in operatic music, perhaps his most important work in this field being *A Tale of Two Cities* (1949–50) which won the Festival of Britain Opera Competition in 1951. Benjamin's music is that of an

Arthur Benjamin

Peggy Glanville-Hicks

William Lovelock

Edgar Bainton

elegant stylist, revealing a flair for orchestral writing and, in his operas, a strong sense of theatre. He never relinquished his links with his home country and played a major role in the organization of Australia House concerts in London, concerts which have done much to promote the names and music of a large number of Australian composers. A younger expatriate, Peggy Glanville-Hicks, who was born in Melbourne in 1912 and who is now an American citizen, has also achieved considerable success overseas in the field of theatre music, notably with her opera *Nausicaa* which was greeted with acclaim at the 1961 Athens Festival.

One composer who, although a comparatively recent arrival in this country, nevertheless sums up in his music and his ideals many of the attributes of this generation of composers is William Lovelock, who came to Australia in 1956 as Director of the State Conservatorium of Music in Brisbane, a post he held for three years. Born in London in 1899 and educated first at Trinity College of Music and later at the University of London, which admitted him to the Degree of Doctor of Music in 1932, he spent four years early in his career as private organist to the Viscountess Cowdray, a position which was virtually that of *Kapellmeister*.[3] This experience, together with his natural musical inclinations, undoubtedly moulded Lovelock's opinions that 'one of the most important functions of music is to provide entertainment rather than cold-blooded intellectual abstractions'.[4] This attitude is reflected strongly in all of his work, whether this be in the large amount of teaching material and school music which he has produced or in some of his large-scale compositions for orchestra. The Concerto for flute and orchestra (1961), for example, is a congenial work strongly reminiscent of the music of Vaughan Williams and shows a dexterity in the handling of the orchestra which is characteristic of Lovelock's music for this medium. Structurally the Concerto is in cyclic form, while in the treatment of the flute Lovelock attains an ideal balance between the lyrical and virtuosic potential of the instrument reminiscent of the concertante writing of the eighteenth century. Lovelock's rather obtuse comment that the Flute Concerto is not a 'think work'[5] may, it seems, also be readily applied to the Concerto for trumpet and orchestra (1968), the implication being that both works are designed primarily for entertainment, the latter concerto nonetheless requiring a high level of virtuosity from the soloist. The Symphony in C sharp minor (1966), on the other hand, presents a somewhat more formal and imposing manner and in conception is a continuation of the grand symphonic ideal of the late nineteenth century. As in the Flute Concerto a traditional tonal scheme and a cyclically recurring motive are the bases upon which the work is built. One feels, however, that in this work the equanimity between spirit and content of the two concerti is somewhat more precariously balanced: the tendency towards romantic gesture, the reliance upon tempi to direct the music's impulse, and the occasional interpolation of rather precious solo passages in the latter part of the work, all recall some of the less successful habits of nineteenth-century musical practice.

William Lovelock is a self-proclaimed and unrepentant romantic in musical outlook. His music has on occasion been met with accusations of being conservative, even reactionary, in content. But it is important to remember here that Lovelock is expressing in his music the attitudes of a considerable proportion of Australia's musical public. And until such time as this general attitude undergoes dramatic change, composers such as Lovelock may validly claim that in their music they are reflecting the musical values of a large majority of Australians.

Moneta Eagles

Mirrie Hill

Dulcie Holland

Miriam Hyde

George English

Felix Gethen

Donald Hollier

Eric Gross

For Lovelock the Englishman the problem of reconciling environment with heritage in music scarcely arises. But for other Australian composers of his generation the conflict between these two appears to have been of some concern. Mirrie Hill (*b*. 1892), the widow of Alfred Hill, shows in her *Arnhem Land Symphony* (1954) an attempt to reflect one of the unique aspects of the Australian environment in music. The Symphony utilizes Aboriginal melodic and rhythmic material but the result is nonetheless a work full of romantic gesture and is in many ways closer to the mainstream of European music than is some of the music of Mussorgsky or Borodin. The Symphony also reveals problems in reconciling an innate lyrical impulse with the generative, dramatic qualities of the medium, and suggests that Mirrie Hill's musical language is better suited to the small descriptive pieces with which her name is more readily associated.

The music of Dulcie Holland (*b*. 1913) shares this prevailing neo-romantic, lyrical spirit, which is not surprising when one remembers that her first studies were with Frank Hutchens and Alfred Hill, before her departure for London and the Royal College of Music. Perhaps the most important contribution which she has made to Australian music comes within the educational sphere. For many years now students of piano and voice throughout the country have been acquainted with her descriptive miniatures, while more recently she has become increasingly involved with music for the classroom.

Similarly the music of Miriam Hyde (*b*. 1913), one of the most prolific of her generation of composers, has been of considerable significance in the field of music education. Of her earlier works, perhaps the most important are the two piano concerti written in 1934 and 1935 and in which she appeared as soloist in performances given in England by the London Symphony and London Philharmonic orchestras. Both these works reflect her English training (she won an overseas scholarship to the Royal College of Music in 1935) and her strongly romantic tendencies. Roger Covell has suggested that Miriam Hyde is one of the composers working in Australia who have been thwarted in terms of achieving a more original mode of expression by the expectations of the society in which they have lived:

> Miss Hyde's musical equipment and the degree in which she has mastered particular sectors of her chosen craft are considerable; probably much more considerable than the skill of some of her younger detractors, who may have been liberated by time and changing circumstances from the necessity to satisfy Australian society that musical composition is possible within that society.[6]

The Sydney composer George English (*b*. 1912) has made his reputation in Australian music largely as a composer for film and radio, his most notable achievement in this field being his contribution to the radio documentary *Death of a Wombat* which won the Italia Prize in 1959. English's compositions of the fifties are largely traditional in approach and reveal the lyric strain and skilful handling of the orchestra which have contributed significantly to his success as a film-score writer. In more recent works English has espoused serial techniques as a means of structural organization, although the innate lyricism of his musical language would appear to preclude the fragmentary textures of the Viennese school.

Moneta Eagles (*b*. 1924) and Felix Gethen (*b*. 1916) are two other composers associated with music for the media, the former having been musical director of the Commonwealth Film Unit from 1957 to 1964, while the latter has been an important orchestral arranger for the Australian Broadcasting Commission as well as a prolific composer of orchestral music in a prevailingly late romantic vein.

It is not until the years after the Second World War that one can point to composers of some significance working in Australia who spent their formative years in countries outside the British Commonwealth and who, therefore, brought to this country an awareness of a different heritage and a different social environment. Dreyfus, Werder and Sitsky have been mentioned previously in this symposium. A fourth composer whose origins were European is Eric Gross, who was born in Vienna in 1926. Gross is in fact something of a link between the British-oriented and the more cosmopolitan groups of composers, for he migrated to England in 1938 and studied after the War at Trinity College in London and at the University of Aberdeen which has since awarded him the degrees of M.A. and D.Mus. Gross arrived in Australia in 1959 and in 1960 joined the staff of the University of Sydney's Department of Music where he now holds the position of Associate Professor. He has written for practically every musical medium but is perhaps best known for his choral music which has added a very distinctive note to the hitherto rather pale echoes of the English choral tradition which have abounded in Australia. His choral writing is characterized by a declamatory treatment of the text and by the parallel movement of rugged fourth chords, recalling the early organum style of medieval church music. It is interesting to compare in terms of harmony and texture the *Four Psalms* written in 1957 and his settings of Psalms 122 and 130 of 1972. The *Four Psalms* show considerable fluidity of line in all parts (they are written for unaccompanied choir) and while the metrical setting reflects the rhythms and accentuation of speech, there are times at which those rhythms are distorted by a melismatic flow of melodic line. The burgeoning of unison declamation into chordal declamation and then polyphonic elaboration is characteristic of the texture of the *Four Psalms* and suggests the influence of the choral music of Vaughan Williams, Holst and Walton. The two psalm settings of 1972 are typical of Gross's later choral style in that the triadic writing of the *Four Psalms* has given way to the organum-style harmonies mentioned previously and to a predominantly chordal texture with syllabic setting of the text. The traditional sense of linear tension in the early works is replaced by a contemplative atmosphere in which variety and anticipation stem from the organization of tempi and dynamics. In all his music, both choral and instrumental, Gross shows a certain preoccupation with regard to thematic integration of the material. Both in his *Sinfonietta* (1961) and in the Trio for flute, oboe and clarinet (1962), for example, the cyclic principle of recurrence and transformation of material is combined with the Bartókian technique of motivic generation from a small intervallic cell, both ideas being used in order to link the various sections or movements of the works into one organic whole. Harmonically and texturally the *Sinfonietta* in particular reflects the somewhat static character of Gross's choral music while both works display considerable subtlety and ingenuity in the handling of the rhythmic element. With its reliance to an extent upon the rhetorical statement of themes in the classical sense, and upon wholesale repetition of ideas, Gross's music does not reveal the highly organic impulse of the music of Bartók, in spite of his use of the principle of motivic generation, and his work appears to be more closely allied with that of the English and Russian nationalist composers of the twentieth century.

Peter Tahourdin (*b.* 1928) came to Australia from the United Kingdom in 1964 and in 1965 was appointed visiting composer at the University of Adelaide. Like

Eric Gross, Tahourdin had studied at Trinity College, London, after which he worked variously as a composer, teacher, lecturer, and broadcaster in the United Kingdom. During these years Tahourdin produced a considerable number of works for chamber ensemble and for orchestra, as well as one opera *Inside Information*. Representative of his music at this time are the Symphony no. 1 (1960) and the Sonata for clarinet and piano (1962), works which reveal a high level of craftsmanship and considerable inventiveness in the handling of material which is largely traditional in scope and idiom. In 1966 Tahourdin travelled to Canada where he enrolled at the University of Toronto as a graduate student. Here he studied, among other things, electronic music and contemporary techniques of composition. After being awarded the degree of M.Mus. in 1967 he returned to South Australia and joined the music staff at the University of Adelaide. The new directions of his musical thinking following his studies in Canada become readily apparent when one compares the First Symphony with Symphony no. 2 (1968–69). The latter work reveals a totally twentieth-century idiom, its linear texture, dissonant atonal harmonies, and angular melodic contours bringing to mind the music of early Hindemith and, at times, of Stravinsky in his neo-classic period. Structurally this symphony is based upon serial principles, but in its forward impulse it is strongly reminiscent of Tahourdin's earlier works and its general style owes little to the fragmentary techniques of the post-war Viennese school. In 1973 Tahourdin was appointed Lecturer in Composition at the University of Melbourne and in recent years has become more actively involved in the field of electronic music.

An Australian expatriate composer whose career has in many ways paralleled that of Tahourdin is David Lumsdaine (*b.* 1931). Lumsdaine left Australia in 1953 to take up residence in the United Kingdom after having studied at the New South Wales State Conservatorium. His years in England have been successful both in terms of composition, and from a professional point of view, Lumsdaine having been appointed Lecturer in the Music Faculty at the University of Durham in 1970. At Durham Lumsdaine has set up and taken on the directorship of the University Electronic Studio and in recent years his creative inclinations have been more and more towards the composition of electronic music.

Among the academics resident in Australia who, although working principally in fields other than composition have nevertheless produced works in various genres, are Nöel Nickson in Brisbane, John Gordon in Sydney, Trevor Jones and Harold Badger in Melbourne, the late Jack Peters in Adelaide, Donald Hollier in Canberra, Donald Kay in Hobart, and David Tunley and John Hind in Perth. Some of their works have attained considerable recognition, in particular Jones's *Essay* for string quartet (1954 rev. 1962), *Four Goliard Songs* (1955–57), and *Cantata Zoologica* (1963), Tunley's Concerto for clarinet and strings (1965), and Hollier's chamber opera *Orpheus and Eurydice* (1969). Kay is also recognized as an important composer of educational music. For most of these composers, however, the pressures of administrative and teaching duties, and of research projects in varying fields, have precluded a greater involvement in composition.

One can perhaps also include mention here of George Tibbits (*b.* 1933) who is almost unique in Australian music in that professionally he has no involvement in the musical field, being a Senior Lecturer in Urban Studies and Architectural History in the Department of Architecture and Building at the University of Melbourne. Something of an iconoclast in musical style, he has made some significant contributions to Australian music with works such as *I Thought You Were All Glittering with the Noblest of Carriage* (1969), *By the Rivering Waters of* (1969), and the String Quartet no. 1 (1968–72).

The music written in Australia during the sixties and seventies has reflected, as earlier chapters of this symposium will have indicated, the growing awareness of Australian society of its peculiar, almost schizoid, character as a nation of European extraction sharing the geographical environment of the ancient civilizations of Asia. Hence the music of composers such as Sculthorpe and Meale, for example, shows the influence of stimulus from both contemporary European music and the music of the Asian cultures. Another of their contemporaries, the Melbourne composer Helen Gifford (*b.* 1935), also shows in her music these dual stimuli. Since graduating from the Conservatorium of Music at Melbourne University in 1956 Miss Gifford has produced a steady stream of works in most of the principal musical genres. Two of the best-known of these are the instrumental works *Chimaera* (1967) and *Imperium* (1969). *Chimaera*, written for an orchestra which includes six percussionists, a harp, celeste, and harpsichord, reveals the hand of a skilled colourist. The work is characterized by a clarity of texture and vibrant yet refined colour reminiscent of the music of the Polish 'texturalists', and even of Messiaen and Ravel. The sense of static immobility, the use of *ostinato* fragments to build up a series of sonorous blocks of varying densities, the non-pulsile and non-dynamic treatment of material, all suggest a variety of influences from Stravinsky to the sound characteristics of much Asian music. *Imperium* reveals even more overtly Helen Gifford's response to the music of India in particular, a country which she explored during 1968. In *Imperium*, as in *Chimaera*, the shifting densities and colours create, not a sense of forward impulse, but a sense of immobility, of timelessness which is heightened by long sections during which the spasmodic utterances of the percussion instruments, or the shimmering clusters of the *divisi* strings, are the only sounds to combine with the silence. In 1970 Helen Gifford was approached by the Director of the Melbourne Theatre Company, John Sumner, with a commission to compose the incidental music for the company's production of Brecht's *The Caucasian Chalk Circle*. Since that time she has become increasingly involved in the composition of incidental music for other productions by the M.T.C. and other Melbourne companies, including the music for *Much Ado About Nothing* and *A Winter's Tale* (both in 1975). It may well be that her most significant contributions to Australian music in future years will be in the field of incidental music of this quality.

In spite of the ready availability in Australia of contemporary European and American music, either on recording or in score, and in spite of the various schemes which have brought overseas composers to this country for varying periods of residence, the need to be exposed directly to current overseas thinking on musical matters continues to manifest itself among Australian-born composers. Nearly all the leading composers of the generation born during or immediately after the Second World War have undertaken periods of study in Europe, America, or even Asia, either at leading institutions or privately with individual composers. Ross Edwards (*b.* 1943) is one of the most important of this younger group of composers, some of whom have already been mentioned earlier in this symposium. Edwards received his early musical training at the New South Wales State Conservatorium and at the Universities of Sydney and Adelaide where he studied with Sculthorpe, Meale, Peter Maxwell-Davies and Sandor Veress, the latter two of whom were

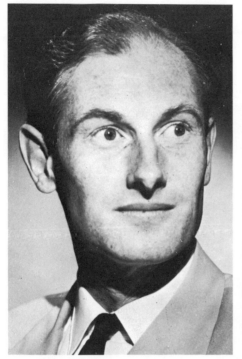

Peter Tahourdin

Helen Gifford

David Lumsdaine

Ross Edwards

Anne Boyd

Jennifer Fowler

David Ahern

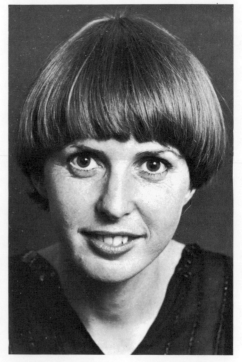

Alison Bauld

visiting composers in Adelaide. In 1970 he travelled to London to continue working with Maxwell-Davies and remained in Europe until 1973 when he was appointed to the teaching staff of the University of Sydney. Edwards has concentrated largely upon orchestral and chamber forms, his music ranging from advanced serial idioms to works of quasi-aleatoric nature and words embracing the principles of electronic music. His String Quartet no. 1 (1968–69) reveals a rigidly serial structure of considerable complexity which, while being cast unequivocally in a contemporary idiom, nevertheless is indebted to musical devices of the past. In Edwards' words:

> The first movement, which is in 'sonata-variation' form, moves through a series of related polarities, whose function closely resembles that of a tonal centre. Although the structure is thus based on homophonic form-building principles, the texture is essentially polyphonic, incorporating a number of contrapuntal devices of the early Renaissance.[7]

The String Quartet no. 2 is a work which avoids the structural complexities of the First Quartet and of the Wind Quintet no. 2 (1965), and it stands somewhat outside the mainstream of Edwards' musical development. It is perhaps for this reason that the work has been withdrawn by the composer. In 1970 Edwards began work on a series of short compositions for solo instruments, the first of which—*Monos I*—was written for the cellist Florian Kitt and the second—*Monos II*—for pianist Roger Woodward. Moving away from the strict serial processes of his earlier music *Monos II*, with its mellifluous flow, its sharply contrasted linear and vertical textures, and its carefully notated dynamic qualities, suggests an exploration of sonorities based upon a more intuitive approach to the music materials at hand. New directions are certainly suggested by Edwards' most recent chamber composition, *mboc* for string ensemble of three or more players.[8] It is an open form movement in which each player reads from a single score page containing ten melodic strands of fixed pitch and rhythm which may be played in any of four possible clefs and be thereby available to any instrument.

Structurally Edwards' music has undergone considerable change in the past decade as he has continued to examine and evaluate new modes of musical expression. Indeed this is, not unexpectedly, the case with the music of most of his contemporaries, the music of the Sydney composer David Ahern (*b.* 1947) in particular showing bold departures from the traditional forms and language of Western music.

Ahern has followed and adapted to his own ends the musical ideas and principles of the current European avant-garde as represented by Stockhausen in Germany and Cardew in London. Prior to 1968 Ahern studied composition privately with Richard Meale and Nigel Butterley. In 1966 his first orchestral work *After Mallarmé* made a considerable impact upon the Australian musical scene and has since been performed in Paris and in Sweden. The semi-static idiom of this work, which proceeds in a series of juxtaposed blocks of contrasted sonorities, and the highlighting of isolated sound and timbral events, both reflect the effective assimilation of the influences of Boulez, Penderecki and Stockhausen. *Ned Kelly Music*, written for the 1967 series of Sydney Prom Concerts, shows Ahern's continuing interest in the qualities of sound and the various ways in which one may act upon this material. Ahern has described this work as an examination of the problem of combining noise, sound, silence and speech into a unified whole.[9] Although the work was intended as a serious working-out of these ideas, it was generally received with amusement by the Proms audience and Ahern quickly came to be regarded as the *enfant terrible* of Australian music. In 1968, however, his convictions regarding the serious purpose of his music were vindicated when Stockhausen accepted him as an assistant in Cologne. During his two periods overseas Ahern also worked with Cardew in London, and from these two composers he gained a new understanding of the principles of acoustic and electronic improvisation, and since that time has, with his own performing group, Teletopa, endeavoured to introduce some of these radical new ideas into the mainstream of Australian music.

In a somewhat less extreme manner Martin Wesley-Smith (*b*. 1945) has also been working in Sydney to the same end.

> I'm interested in extending contemporary improvisation procedures ... and want to find ways of bringing contemporary music in a more meaningful way to a much larger audience than at present. This will entail ... going to the grass roots; working with children, not necessarily composing for them, rather composing with them, studying and learning from their own compositions and music-making.[10]

Wesley-Smith, at present Lecturer in Electronic Music at the State Conservatorium in Sydney is in the vanguard of younger Australian composers who have endeavoured to bridge the gap between 'serious' and 'educational' music and to bring to children some idea of the changing attitudes towards music and musical expression.

Anne Boyd (*b*. 1946) has shown particular interest in the introduction of some of the practices of Asian music into the classroom. Her first studies were as a flautist at the State Conservatorium in Sydney after which she enrolled at the University of Sydney and studied for an honours degree in music. During her years as a student she was actively involved as a performer and a composer, producing works for theatre, ballet and film as well as for various chamber combinations. Perhaps the most notable of her compositions from this period is the string quartet *Tu dai oan —The Fourth Generation*, a work based upon a Vietnamese folk-song and one which reflects both in its inspiration and in the handling of the musical material Anne Boyd's interest in the music of Asian cultures. In 1969 she was awarded one of the first Commonwealth Overseas Study Grants for composition and left Australia for England where she enrolled for her doctorate at the University of York. Her interest in the quality and characteristics of sound is more and more marked in the works which she composed at York, one of which, *The Metamorphoses of a Solitary Phoenix* (1971) for wind quintet, piano and percussion, was performed at Dartington in 1973. In 1972 Dr Boyd was appointed Lecturer in Music at the University of Sussex. Some indication of the directions in which her music is moving is given in the programme notes which Dr Boyd wrote for a performance of her piano work *Anklung* in 1974 in which she states:

> It would seem that my music is becoming more simple and refined; it is essentially melodic and monodic in character, being influenced by the ecstatic pure melody of the Japanese Shakuhachi (bamboo flute) and the soft and infinitely subtle tones of the ancient gamelan of the Javanese court ... My work for piano ... is concerned with the tuning of ourselves with others and with the natural world of which we are part.

Alison Bauld (*b*. 1944) and Jennifer Fowler (*b*. 1939) are two other younger composers who, like Anne Boyd, have seen their music meet with considerable success in Europe. Alison Bauld has, since her graduation from the National Institute of Dramatic Art in 1962 and from the University of Sydney in 1967, displayed a strong commitment to the theatre and to theatre music, her piece entitled *In a Dead*

Martin Wesley-Smith

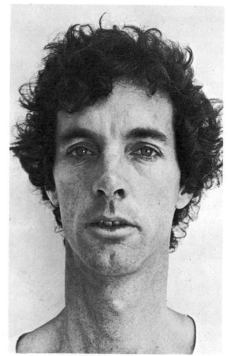

Ian Farr

George Tibbits

Ian Bonighton

Brown Land having been performed by visiting tenor Gerald English and actors from the National Institute of Dramatic Art in Sydney in 1975. Jennifer Fowler's composition *Ravelation* for string quartet won second prize in the Radcliffe Trust Award in 1971 (there was no first prize awarded) while the selection of *Chimes Fractured* (for wind, bagpipes, organ and percussion) for performance at the U.N.E.S.C.O. International Rostrum of Composers in Paris made her the first West Australian-born composer chosen to represent Australia at this event.

Ian Bonighton (1942–75) was another composer who had for some years been exploring chance elements and improvisatory techniques in his music until his tragic and untimely death in England. Ian Farr (*b.* 1941) in Sydney has produced a small number of interesting works in the fields of chamber music and song although he is better known in Australia as an outstanding performer of contemporary music, having been associated with public performances of many of the recently-composed works for piano by Australia's leading composers.

One can say but little at this stage of the newly emerging groups of composers working in the various States of Australia, some within the universities, others preferring to pursue independent studies. Many of these composers have benefited from the unprecedented level of government assistance to the creative arts which has been a feature of Australian artistic life during the past few years, and which is also a factor that has not figured in the development of most of the composers mentioned hitherto in this symposium. In 1970 a Young Composers' Training Scheme was instituted by the Advisory Board of the Commonwealth Assistance to Australian Composers scheme, and this training scheme, together with the National Young Composers' Seminar organized annually by the Department of Music of the University of Western Australia, has been instrumental in bringing young composers together from various parts of the country, thus enabling them to discuss ideas relating to current musical trends. Young composers who have been sponsored by the scheme since its inception are Elaine Doe, Vincent Plush, Martin Wesley-Smith and Kim Williams (1970); Peter Brideoake, Gregg Howard and John Poole-Johnson (1971); Christopher Bryce and John Nickson (1972); Stuart Davies-Slate, Chester Schultz and James Cotter (1973); Anthony Brennan, Max Hynam and Charles Seja (1974); and Cameron Allan, John Huie and Carl Vine in 1975.

One could not even begin to guess as to which of these composers will figure prominently in the Australian musical scene in fifteen or so years time. Indeed, the evolutionary nature of musical thought is such that many of the names mentioned hitherto in this chapter may well in years to come be completely forgotten while other composers who may have been mentioned either fleetingly or not at all may prove to be of major import in the development of Australian music. This chapter has not aimed at presenting either a definitive or comprehensive view of Australian music for this very reason. It will be for posterity to make judgements on the value of any one composer's music; and we can do little more than survey from the standpoint of the mid-1970s some of the materials from which these judgements will be made.

Notes

1. R. Covell, *Australia's Music: Themes of a New Society*, Sun Books, Melbourne, 1967, p. 146.
2. Covell, *op. cit.*, p. 143.
3. *Kapellmeister:* a term used to describe the director of music to a prince, or some such dignitary.
4. Editorial note in *Australian Journal of Music Education*, no. 8, April 1971, p. 47.
5. Notes by the composer on the recording of the Concerto for flute and orchestra released by *Australian Festival of Music* (Festival Recording, Vol. 9).
6. Covell, *op. cit.*, p. 147.
7. From the programme notes supplied by Edwards for the 1970 International Rostrum of Composers.
8. This work is generally regarded as Edwards' third quartet.
9. Quoted in J. Murdoch, *Australia's Contemporary Composers*, Macmillan, 1972, p. 4.
10. Murdoch, *op. cit.*, p. 203.

Discography

Roy Agnew

Album Leaf. Michael Barton (piano).
Brolga recording CTX/1122
Poème tragique [5'17"]. Gordon Watson (piano). Allan.
ABC recording RRC/70 (ABR)
Six Australian Forest Scenes (1913) [11'24"]. (i) 'Gnome Dance'—1'15"; (ii) 'When Evening Shadows Fall' —2'45"; (iii) 'Forest Nymphs at Play'—1'23"; (iv) 'Night in the Forest'—1'52"; (v) 'By a Quiet Stream' —2'00"; (vi) 'The Forest Grandeur'—2'09". Gordon Watson (piano). Nicholson.
ABC recording PRX/5432
Miscellaneous Piano Pieces [16'58"]. (i) 'Rhapsody'— 4'54", Augener; (ii) 'Capriccio'—2'42", Augener; (iii) 'Dance of the Wild Men'—2'11", Allan; (iv) 'Album Leaf'—1'15", Augener; (v) 'Rabbit Hill'— 1'18", O.U.P.; (vi) 'Elf Dance'—1'55", O.U.P.; (vii) 'The Windy Hill'—2'43", Augener. Gordon Watson (piano). *ABC recording PRX/5432*
Five Contrasts (arranged for string orchestra by John Antill) [10'45"]. Strings of the Sydney Symphony Orchestra (Joseph Post, conductor). MS. 13 Apr. 1955. *ABC recording PRX/3875*

David Ahern

After Mallarmé (1966) [8'25"]. South Australian Symphony Orchestra (Patrick Thomas, conductor). Universal Edition. March 1967.
ABC recording RRC/72
After Mallarmé (1966) [8'50"]. Sydney Symphony Orchestra (John Hopkins, conductor). Universal Edition. 7 Feb. 1969
World Record Club disc S/4930
Music for Nine (1967) [12'42"]. Betty Jaggard, Elizabeth Gajeska (violins); John Gould (viola); Leslie Strait (cello); William Tuck (flute); Aloha Hunter (clarinet); Ian Farr (piano); John Purdon, Richard Miller (percussion). Southern Music. 10 Dec. 1967.
ABC recording RRCS/126

Ned Kelly Music (1967) [5'57"]. Sydney Symphony Orchestra (John Hopkins, conductor). Southern Music. 13 Feb. 1968. *ABC recording RRC/401*
Journal (1968) [56'59"]. Sandra Gore, Patrick Bishop, Rona McLeod, James Bowles, Jeffrey Kevin, David Whitford (voices); George Thompson (didjeridu and double bass); David Ahern (violin and ring modulator). Narrated and directed by the composer. MS. Apr. 1969. *ABC recording RRCS/177*

Harold Badger

String Quartet no. 1 (1961) [16'50"]. Paul McDermott String Quartet. *W & G disc A/1635*

Edgar Bainton

Symphony no. 3 in C minor (1956) [37'52"]. Sydney Symphony Orchestra (Sir Bernard Heinze, conductor). 1957. *Brolga disc BZM/12*
Symphony no. 2 in D minor (1956) [25'38"]. Sydney Symphony Orchestra (Joseph Post, conductor). MS. 12 July 1968. *ABC recording RRC/401*
Symphony no. 2 in D minor (1956) [26'00"]. Sydney Symphony Orchestra (Dr Edgar Bainton, conductor). 13 Apr. 1955. *ABC recording PRX/3875*
Three Pieces (1919) [11'40"]. (i) 'Elegy'—4'47"; (ii) 'Intermezzo'—3'52"; (iii) 'Humoresque'—2'48". Sydney Symphony Orchestra (Joseph Post, conductor). 13 Dec. 1967. *ABC recording RRCS/128*
Pavane—2'36"; *Idyll*—3'20"; *Bacchanale*—4'25" [10' 33"]. Sydney Symphony Orchestra (Joseph Post, conductor). O.U.P. 20 Sept. 1968
ABC recording RRCS/128
String Quartet in A (1915) [26'03"]. Austral String Quartet; Alwyn Elliott, Ronald Ryder (violins); Ronald Cragg (viola); Gregory Elmaloglou (cello). *Festival disc FC/30802, Universal Record Club disc No. 586*
Into the Silent Land—3'24", Allan; *The Goddess's Glory*—2'10", Novello. Adelaide Singers (Patrick Thomas, conductor). *ABC recording PRX/5600*
In the Wilderness—3'10", O.U.P.; *The Winter is Passed*—0'53", Novello; *The Golden Skein*—1'54", Novello; *Pastorella*—1'25", Elkin; *Phyllis the Fair* —2'12", Elkin, Adelaide Singers (Patrick Thomas, conductor). 1967. *ABC recording RRC/66*
Bridal Song—2'01". Novello; *Lully, Lullay*—3'04"; Joseph Williams, Noreen Stokes (piano in *Bridal Song*), female voices of the Adelaide Singers (Patrick Thomas, conductor). Nov. 1967.
ABC recording RRC/67
And I Saw a New Heaven [4'20"]. James Thiele (organ), Adelaide Singers (Patrick Thomas, conductor). Novello. 6 Feb. 1968. *ABC recording RRCS/400*
And I Saw a New Heaven [4'02"]. David Merchant (organ), Adelaide Singers (Patrick Thomas, conductor). Novello. 10 Nov. 1967.
ABC recording RRC/65
A Red, Red Rose [1'34"]. Robert Gard (tenor). John Champ (piano). Chappell.
ABC recording 0/N40525 (ABR only)
White Hyacinth—3'56". O.U.P.; *Visions*—3'19". Allan. Muriel Cohen (piano).
ABC recording PRX/5616 /ABR only)

Arthur Benjamin

Overture to an Italian Comedy (1937). Royal Philharmonic Orchestra (Myer Fredman, conductor).
Lyrita disc SRCS/47

Romantic Fantasy (1935). Jascha Heifetz (violin), William Primrose (viola); RCA-Victor Symphony Orchestra (Solomon, conductor).
RCA-Victor disc LSC/2767

Cotillon Suite (1938) [11'07"]. Sydney Symphony Orchestra (Joseph Post, conductor). Boosey & Hawkes. 13 Dec. 1967   *ABC recording RRCS/128*

Cotillon Suite (1938). London Pops Orchestra (Frederick Fennell, conductor).   *Mercury disc 90440s*

Piano Concertino (1928). Lamar Crowson (piano); London Symphony Orchestra (Arthur Benjamin, conductor). Released in Australia by the World Record Club.   *Everest disc SDBR/3020*

Concerto quasi una fantasia (1949). Lamar Crowson (piano); London Symphony Orchestra (Arthur Benjamin, conductor). Released in Australia by the World Record Club.   *Everest disc SDBR/3020*

Harmonica Concerto (1953). Larry Adler (harmonica); London Symphony Orchestra (Barry Cameron, conductor).   *Columbia disc 33 OS 1023*

Harmonica Concerto (1953). Larry Adler (harmonica); Royal Philharmonic Orchestra (Morton Gould, conductor).   *RCA-Victor disc SB/6786*

He Is The Lonely Greatness [1'59"]. Adelaide Singers (Patrick Thomas, conductor).
ABC Recording RRCS/1470

Jamaican Rhumba (1938). Cleveland Pops Orchestra (Lane, conductor).   *Decca disc LXT/5304–33*

Jamaican Rhumba (1938). Hollywood Bowl Symphony Orchestra (Carmen Dragon, conductor).
Capitol disc SENC/9075

Jamaican Rhumba (1938). Philadelphia Orchestra (Eugene Ormandy, conductor).
CBS disc SBR/235 200

Jamaican Rhumba (1938). Sydney Symphony Orchestra (Joseph Post, conductor). Boosey & Hawkes. 13 Dec. 1967.   *ABC recording RRCS/128*

Jamaican Rhumba (1938). Larry Adler (harmonica); Pro Arte Orchestra (Eric Robertson, conductor).
Pye disc PLP/1013

Jamaican Rhumba (1938) [1'03"]. Gordon Watson (piano). Boosey & Hawkes.
ABC recording PRX/5433

Spring (1942). Glasgow Orpheus Choir.
Pye disc PCS/3044

Spring (1942) [2'25"]. Adelaide Singers (Patrick Thomas, conductor). Boosey & Hawkes. 27 Oct. 1967.   *ABC recording RRC/66*

The Mystery [1'15"]. Adelaide Singers (Patrick Thomas, conductor). O.U.P. 8 Dec. 1967.
ABC recording RRC/66

Nightingale Lane (1937) [2'38"]. Noreen Stokes (piano); Adelaide Singers (Patrick Thomas, conductor). Boosey & Hawkes. Nov. 1967.
ABC recording RRC/67

Linstead Market [1'15"]. John Cameron (baritone), Olga Krasnik (piano). Boosey & Hawkes, 1956.
ABC recording PR/2644 (ABR only)

Valses caprices (1949). Gervase de Peyer (clarinet), Colin Preedy (piano).
L'oiseau lyre disc SOL/60028

Sonatina (1925) [17'00"]. Carmel Hackendorf (violin). Lance Dossor (piano). O.U.P.
ABC recording PRX/3903

Etudes improvisées; Pastorale, Arioso and Finale (1936); *Scherzino* (1936); *Siciliana* (1936). Lamar Crowson (piano).   *Lyrita disc RCS/20*

Pastorale, Arioso and Finale (1936) [15'12"]. Lance Dossor (piano).   *ABC recording PRX/3903*

Three New Piano Fantasias [6'15"]. Max Olding (piano). Mar. 1960.
ABC recording PR/3162 (ABR only)

Siciliana (1936) [3'03"]. Lance Dossor (piano). Boosey & Hawkes.   *ABC recording RRC/70* (ABR only)

Six Fantasies (1935) [8'14"]. (i) 'A Cloudlet'—1'48"; 'A Song with a Sad Ending'—1'00"; (iii) 'Soldiers in the Distance'—1'00"; (iv) 'Waltz'—1'46"; (v) 'Silent and Soft and Slow'—1'43"; (vi) 'A Gay Study'—0'57". Gordon Watson (piano). Winthrop Rogers.   *ABC recording PRX/5431*

Three Little Pieces [3'53"]. (i) 'The Tired Dancer'—1'37"; (ii) 'White Note Tune'—1'01"; (iii) 'Buffoon's march—1'15". Gordon Watson (piano). Boosey & Hawkes.   *ABC recording PRX/5433*

Six Odds and Ends (1924) [9'07"]. (i) Etude prelude—1'44"; (ii) 'A Negro Sings a Glad Song'—0'45"; (iii) 'A Quiet Garden'—2'30"; (iv) 'Legend'—2'05"; (v) 'A Negro Sings a Sad Song'—1'04"; (vi) 'The Hobgoblin'—0'59". Gordon Watson (piano). Stainer & Bell.   *ABC recording PRX/5431*

Ian Bonighton

Three Pieces for orchestra (1968) [12'20"]. Melbourne Symphony Orchestra (Keith Humble, conductor). MS. Nov. 1969.   *ABC recording RRCS/387*

Anne Boyd

String quartet no. 1 (1968) [10'10"]. Oriel String Quartet: Graham Wood, Ashley Arbuckle (violins), John Dean (viola), Brian Meddermen (cello). MS. Feb. 1969.   *ABC recording RRCS/126*

Alexander Burnard

Puck [1'27"]. Gordon Watson (piano). MS.
ABC disc RRC/70 (ABR only)

The Answer 3'20". Rosalind Keene (soprano), Henri Penn (piano). MS. *ABC disc 0/N40525* (ABR only)

Various songs (12'30"]. (i) 'The River'—2'34"; (ii) 'Night Piece'—2'40"; (iii) 'Berceuse'—2'21"; (iv) 'There's Snow on the Mountains'—1'28"; (v) 'Magnolia'—1'28"; (vi) 'Carol'—1'59". William Coombes (baritone), Henri Penn (piano). MS.
ABC disc PRX/5615 (ABR only)

Moneta Eagles

Sonatina (1954) [9'12"]. Max Olding (piano). Allan.
ABC recording PR/3162 (ABR only)

The Singing of the Stars (1953) [2'12"]. Adelaide Singers (Patrick Thomas, conductor). MS.
ABC recording RRC/66

Spring on the Plains (1961) [2'37"]. Adelaide Singers

(Patrick Thomas, conductor). MS.
ABC recording PRX/5600
I Will Lift Up Mine Eyes [4′30″]. David Merchant
(organ), Adelaide Singers (Patrick Thomas, conductor). MS. 1967. *ABC recording RRC/65*

Ross Edwards
String Quartet no. 1 (1968) [15′07″]. Austral String
Quartet: Donald Hazlewood, Ronald Ryder (vio-
lins), Ronald Cragg (viola), Gregory Elmaloglou
(cello). Albert. 3 May 1970.
ABC recording RRCS/388
String Quartet no. 2 (1970) [15′53″]. Austral String
Quartet: Donald Hazlewood, Ronald Ryder (vio-
lins), Ronald Cragg (viola), Gregory Elmaloglou
(cello). Albert. 3 May 1970.
ABC recording RRCS/388
mboc (1972) [9′23″]. Austral String Quartet: Donald
Hazlewood, Ronald Ryder (violins), Ronald Cragg
(viola), Gregory Elmaloglou (cello).
ABC recording RRCS/1465
Sextet (1966) [5′25″]. Owen Fisenden (flute), Jack
Harrison (clarinet), Neil Pierson (horn), John Dean
(viola), Brian Meddemen (cello), Wendy Nash
(piano). Albert. Feb. 1969.
ABC recording RRCS/129
Wind Quintet no. 2 (1965) [6′55″]. Adelaide Wind
Quintet: David Cubbin (flute), Jiri Tancibudek
(oboe), Gabor Reeves (clarinet), Stanley Fry (horn),
Thomas Wightman (bassoon). MS.
ABC recording RRC/31
Little Orchestra Piece (1968) [1′38″]. Tasmanian Or-
chestra (Patrick Thomas, conductor). MS. 2 May
1968. *ABC recording RRC/72*
Etude (1970) [5′10″]. Sydney Symphony Orchestra
(Charles Mackerras, conductor). Albert. 23 Apr.
1971. *ABC tape*
Monos II (1971). Roger Woodward (piano). Albert.
1972. *HMV disc OASD/7567*

George English
Chiaroscuro (1966) [14′46″]. Donald Hazlewood (vio-
lin), Ronald Cragg (viola), Gregory Elmaloglou
(cello). Southern Music. 5 Dec. 1967.
ABC recording RRCS/29
Death of a Wombat (1959) [27′13″]. Alistair Duncan
(narrator); Sydney Symphony Orchestra (Nicolai
Malko, conductor). Southern Music. 1961.
RCA Red Seal disc LI/6233
Quintet for wind (1969) [17′48″]. New Sydney Wind
Quintet: Neville Amadio (flute), Guy Henderson
(oboe), Donald Westlake (clarinet), Clarence Mellor
(horn), John Cran (bassoon). Chappell. 1971.
RCA Red Seal disc SL/16374
Cypress Tree [2′25″]. Stewart Harvey (baritone), Henri
Penn (piano).
ABC recording PRX/5598 (ABR only)
Myuna Moon [4′36″]. Light Concert Orchestra (Kurt
Herweg, conductor). *HMV disc OCLP/7132*
Ski Trails [3′05″]. ABC Sydney Dance Band (Jim
Gussey, conductor). *ABC recording*
Yulunga [2′27″]. Light Concert Ensemble (Kurt Her-
weg, conductor). *ABC recording PRX/5281*

Lindley Evans
Vignette. Michael Barton (piano).
Brolga disc CTX-1122
Idyll (1945) [9′23″]. Wendy Pomroy, Stephen Dornan
(piano); West Australian Symphony Orchestra
(Thomas Mayer, conductor). MS. 4 Oct. 1969.
ABC recording RRCS/381

Ian Farr
Sonata for cello and piano (1970) [9′57″]. Gregory
Elmaloglou (cello), Nigel Butterley (piano). Albert.
20 Dec. 1970. *Festival disc SFC 800/22*

Jennifer Fowler
Sculpture in Four Dimensions (1967) [4′59″]. West
Australian Symphony Orchestra (John Hopkins,
conductor). MS. 5 Mar. 1970.
ABC recording RRCS/385
Fanfare (1968) [2′22″]. Brass and strings of Tasmanian
Orchestra (Patrick Thomas, conductor). MS. 2 May
1968. *ABC recording RRC/72*
Chimes Fractured (1971) [7′39″]. Sydney Symphony
Orchestra (John Hopkins, conductor). MS. Mar.
1972. *Festival disc SFC 800/27*

Helen Gifford
Chimaera (1967) [9′30″]. South Australian Symphony
Orchestra (Patrick Thomas, conductor). Allan. 29
July 1969. *ABC recording RRCS/386*
Canzone (1968) [1′53″]. Tasmanian Orchestra (Patrick
Thomas, conductor). MS. 2 May 1968.
ABC recording RRC/72
Phantasma for strings (1963) [8′35″]. Strings of the
West Australian Symphony Orchestra (Patrick
Thomas, conductor). MS. 22 Feb. 1968.
ABC recording RRCS/124
Imperium (1969) [9′35″]. Melbourne Symphony Or-
chestra (Keith Humble, conductor). Albert. Nov.
1969. *ABC recording RRCS/387*

Peggy Glanville-Hicks
The Transposed Heads (1953) [approx. 90′00″]. Opera
in six scenes; text by Thomas Mann; Nossaman,
Harlan, Pickett. Louisville Opera Company; Louis-
ville Orchestra (Bombard, conductor). 1955.
Louisville disc LOU 546-6(M)
Excerpts from *Nausicaa* (1961). Opera in three
acts; text by Robert Graves. Nausicaa—Teresa
Stratas (soprano), Aethon—John Modenos (bari-
tone), Phemis—Edward Rhul (tenor), Clytoneus—
George Tsantikos (tenor), Queen Arete—Sophia
Steffan. Athens Symphony Orchestra and Chorus
(Carlos Surinach, conductor; John Butler, director
and choreographer). *CRI–175*
Etruscan Concerto (1956). Carlo Bussotti (piano);
MGM Orchestra (Carlos Surinach, conductor).
MGM/3557
Concerto Romantico (1956). Walter Trampler (viola);
MGM Orchestra (Carlos Surinach, conductor).
MGM/3559
Letters from Morocco (1952). Loren Driscoll (tenor);
MGM Orchestra (Carlos Surinach, conductor).
MGM E/3549

Sinfonia Pacifica (1953). MGM Orchestra (Carlos Surinach, conductor).   *MGM E/3336*
Gymnopédies 1, 2, 3 (1953). RIAS Orchestra (Jonel Perlea, conductor).   *Reminaton disc 199/188*
Gymnopédies 1, 2, 3 (1953). MGM Orchestra (Carlos Surinach, conductor).   *MGM E/3336*
Sonata for piano and percussion (1952). Carlo Bussotti (piano), New York Percussion Group.
Columbia disc ML/4900
Harp Sonata (1951). Nicanor Zabaleta (harp).
Everest (Counterpoint) disc 8523(M)

Eric Gross
Sinfonietta (1961) [15'15"]. South Australian Symphony Orchestra (Henry Krips, conductor). MS.
ABC recording PRX/5586
Trio, Op. 10 (1962) [9'42"]. David Cubbin (flute), Jiri Tancibudek (oboe), Gabor Reeves (clarinet). Allan. 1971.   *HMV disc OASD/7565*
Song cycle: *Labyrinth of Love* (1958) [7'03"]. (i) 'How Many Times'—2'44"; (ii) 'The Leaf'—2'08"; (iii) 'The Song'—2'11". Lance Lloyd (tenor), Eric Gross (piano). MS. *ABC recording PR/3445* (ABR only)
Ding Dong Bell—0'58"; *A Ditty*—1'24". Female voices of the Adelaide Singers (Patrick Thomas, conductor). Leeds, Nov. 1967. *ABC recording RRC/67*
Psalm XIII (1958)—3'13"; *Psalm CXXI* ('I Will Lift up Mine Eyes') (1958)—2'25". Adelaide Singers (Patrick Thomas, conductor). Leeds.
ABC recording RRC/71
Psalm XLVII ('O Clap Your Hands') (1958) [3'17"]. Adelaide Singers (Patrick Thomas, conductor). Leeds.   *ABC recording PRX/5600*

Mirrie Hill
Symphony in A ('Arnhem Land') (1954) [31'62"]. Sydney Symphony Orchestra (Henry Krips, conductor). MS. 17 May 1968.
ABC recording RRCS/145
Let Your Song be Delicate [3'55"]. Rosalind Keene (soprano), Henri Penn (piano). MS.
ABC recording 0/N40525 (ABR only)

Dulcie Holland
Symphony for Pleasure (1968) [22'45"]. South Australian Symphony Orchestra (Henry Krips, conductor). MS. 22 Feb. 1972.   *ABC tape*
Secret Pool [5'08"]. Light Concert Ensemble (Kurt Herweg, conductor). MS. *ABC disc PRX/5281*
Ballad (1954). Clive Amadio (clarinet), Olga Krasnik (piano).   *Columbia disc 33 OS/7560*
This Land is Mine (arranged by Robert Hughes) [2'23"]. Stewart Harvey (baritone), Sydney Symphony Orchestra (Joseph Post, conductor). MS. 1959.   *ABC recording PRX/4558*
At The Edge of the Sea (1934) [2'44"]. Heather McMillan (soprano), Henri Penn (piano). Paling.
ABC recording 0/N40525 (ABR only)
Various Piano Pieces: (i) 'The End of Summer'—3'07"; (ii) 'The Scattering Leaves—1'46"; (iii) 'The Lake'—2'53"; (iv) 'Christmas Greetings'—2'29". Muriel Cohen (piano). MS.
ABC recording PRX/5616 (ABR only)

Donald Hollier
Musick's Empire (1965) [24'55"]. Raymond Myers (baritone), Sydney Symphony Orchestra (Dobb Franks, conductor). MS. 7 July 1970.
Festival disc SFC 800/24
Variations on a Theme of Larry Sitsky (1969) [17'10"]. Carl Pini (violin), Beryl Potter (piano). MS. 19 Dec. 1970.   *Festival disc SFC 800/22*
Four Songs of John Dryden (1966) [17'56"]. Raymond Myers (baritone), Donald Hollier (piano). MS. 10 July 1970.   *ABC tape*
Magnificat (1968) [3'40"]. Adelaide Singers (Leonard Burtenshaw, conductor). MS. 4 June 1968.
ABC disc RRC/68

Frank Hutchens
Airmail Palestine (1946) [8'50"]. Kevin Kitto (baritone), South Australian Symphony Orchestra (Clive Douglas, conductor). MS. 1957.
ABC recording PRX/4137
Airmail Palestine (1946) [8'34"]. Stewart Harvey (baritone), Sydney Symphony Orchestra (Joseph Post, conductor). MS. 1958. *ABC recording PRX/4558*
Phantasy Concerto (1944) [16'50"]. Wendy Pomroy, Stephen Dornan (pianos), West Australian Symphony Orchestra (Thomas Mayer, conductor) MS. 4 Oct. 1969.   *ABC recording RRCS/381*
Quintet for piano and strings (1930) [15'20"]. Austral String Quartet: Joyce Hutchinson (piano), Donald Hazlewood, Ronald Ryder (violins), Ronald Cragg (viola), Gregory Elmaloglou (cello). MS. 26 Sept. 1971.   *Festival disc SFC 800/25*

Miriam Hyde
Kelso Overture (1959) [5'00"]. Queensland Symphony Orchestra (Rudolf Pekarek, conductor). MS. 1961.
ABC recording 2XS-2378
Happy Occasion Overture (1957) [4'05"]. Victorian Symphony Orchestra (Clive Douglas, conductor). MS. 1959.   *ABC recording PRX/4783*
Happy Occasion Overture (1957) [3'58"]. Victorian Symphony Orchestra (Clive Douglas, conductor).
ABC recording PR/3040
Lyric (1935) [5'38"]. Strings of the Queensland Symphony Orchestra (Rudolf Pekarek, conductor). MS. 1958.   *ABC recording PRX/4158*
Heroic Elegy (1934) [8'41"]. Queensland Symphony Orchestra (Rudolf Pekarek, conductor). MS. 1957.
ABC recording PRX/4158
Piano Concerto no. 2 in C sharp minor (1935) [24'21"]. Miriam Hyde (piano), Sydney Symphony Orchestra (Joseph Post, conductor). 1957.
ABC recording PRX/4158
Sonata in G minor (1958) [11'40"]. Patrick Thomas (flute), Larry Sitsky (piano). 1962.
ABC recording PRX/5334 (ABR only)

Trevor Jones
Essay for string quartet (1954; revised 1962) [12'14"]. Oriel String Quartet. MS. *ABC recording RRC/31*

Donald Kay
Dance Movement (1968) [2'52"]. Tasmanian Orchestra (Patrick Thomas, conductor). MS. 2 May 1968.
ABC disc RRC/72

William Lovelock
Symphony in C sharp minor (1966) [21'45"]. Sydney Symphony Orchestra (Joseph Post, conductor). MS.
ABC recording PRX/6514
Sinfonietta (1952) [15'52"]. Melbourne Symphony Orchestra (Patrick Thomas, conductor). MS. 19 Mar. 1969. *ABC recording RRCS/380*
Divertimento for strings (1965) [17'21"]. Strings of the Sydney Symphony Orchestra (Sir Bernard Heinze, conductor). MS. 21 Oct. 1967.
ABC recording 'RRCS/137
Flute Concerto (1961) [15'22"]. Vernon Hill (flute); Melbourne Symphony Orchestra (Leonard Dommett, conductor). MS. 29 Mar. 1972.
Festival disc SFC 800/26
Trumpet Concerto (1968) [17'02"]. John Robertson (trumpet); Sydney Symphony Orchestra (Joseph Post, conductor). Southern Music. 20 Sept. 1968.
RCA disc SL/16371
Gaudium Vitae [15'40"]. Cathy Weber (soprano), Thomas Edmonds (tenor); Adelaide Singers, South Australian Symphony Orchestra (Patrick Thomas, conductor). *ABC recording RRCS/379*

Noël Nickson
Sonata for violin and viola [14'35"]. Sybil Copeland (violin), John Glickman (viola). MS. 3 Aug. 1967.
ABC recording RRC/67 (ABR only)

J.V. Peters
Serenata fugata [11'59"]. Adelaide Wind Quintet: David Cubbin (flute), Jiri Tancibudek (oboe), Gabor Reeves (clarinet), Stanley Fry (horn), Thomas Wightman (bassoon). MS.
ABC recording PRX/5616 (ABR only)
Music, When Soft Voices Die—1'25"; *Spring, the Sweet Spring*—1'25". Adelaide Singers (Patrick Thomas, conductor). Elkin. *ABC recording PRX/5600*

Peter Tahourdin
Symphony no. 1 (1960) [34'37"]. Sydney Symphony Orchestra (Henry Krips, conductor). MS. 17 May 1968. *ABC recording RRCS/32*
Symphony no. 2 (1969) [28'15"]. South Australian Symphony Orchestra (Henry Krips, conductor). APRA. 17 September 1970.
Festival disc SFC 800/23
Sinfonietta no. 2 (1959) [14'25"]. West Australian Symphony Orchestra (Verdon Williams, conductor). Hinrichsen. February 1969.
ABC recording RRCS/132
Sonata for clarinet and piano (1962) [17'41"]. Gabor Reeves (clarinet), Clemens Leske (piano). MS.
ABC recording RRC/30
Seven Gnomic Verses (1968) [2'50"]. Adelaide Singers (Leonard Burtenshaw, conductor). MS. 4 June 1968.
ABC recording RRC/68

George Tibbits
Neuronis Nephronicus and His Lowly Queen (1968) [13'00"]. Melbourne Symphony Orchestra (Leonard Dommett, conductor). MS. Nov. 1968.
ABC recording RRCS/386

I Thought You Were All Glittering with the Noblest of Carriage (1969) [9'28"]. South Australian Symphony Orchestra (Patrick Thomas, conductor). MS. November 1971. *Festival disc SFC 800/27*
Five Songs (1969) [7'52"]. (i) 'Are You Looking at Me, Dead Man'; (ii) 'From Now on I'll Link You to the Full Moon'; (iii) 'The World Is Fair'; (iv) 'I Have Come to Tell You Death Waits'; (v) Your Uncle, the Great Harry'. Lauris Elms (contralto), Marie van Hove (piano). MS. 25 Nov. 1971.
ABC tape
String Quartet no. 1 (1968–72) [19'26"]. Austral String Quartet: Donald Hazlewood, Ronald Ryder (violins), Ronald Cragg (viola), Gregory Elmaloglou (cello). *ABC recording AC1001*

David Tunley
Concerto for clarinet and strings (1966) [20'05"]. Jack Harrison (clarinet); Strings of the West Australian Symphony Orchestra (Henry Krips, conductor). MS. 15 Feb. 1968. *ABC recording RRCS/125*
A Wedding Masque from 'The Tempest' (1961: revised 1970) [15'00"]. Margot Robertson, Lesley Perrin, Marie Warrington (sopranos), University of Western Australia Singers, Owen Fisenden (flute), Strings of the West Australian Symphony Orchestra (Georg Tintner, conductor). MS. Feb. 1972.
ABC tape

Martin Wesley-Smith
Interval Piece (1970) [10'40"]. South Australian Symphony Orchestra (Patrick Thomas, conductor). Universal Edition. Mar. 1972.
Festival disc SFC 800/27
Media Music (1972), tape on Electronic Music from York. *V.E.S. 2–4*

General Bibliography

Covell, Roger. *Australia's Music: Themes of a New Society*. Sun Books, Melbourne, 1967.
'Music in Australia', *Current Affairs Bulletin*, xxxviii, 8 (September 1963).
Gleason, James. *Australian Music and Musicians*. Rigby, Adelaide, 1968.
McCredie, Andrew. *Musical Composition in Australia*. Advisory Board, Commonwealth Assistance to Australian Composers, Canberra, 1969.
Murdoch, James. *Australia's Contemporary Composers*. Macmillan, Melbourne, 1972.
Peart, Donald. 'Some Recent Developments in Australian Composition', *Composer*, xix, 1966.
'The Australian Avant-Garde', *Proceedings of the Royal Musical Association*, 1966/67.
Tunley, David. 'A Decade of Musical Composition in Australia 1960–1970', *Studies in Music*, v, University of Western Australia, 1971.

Index